RESOURCE ALLOCATION IN THE PUBLIC SECTOR

Values, priorities and markets in the management of public services

C. M. *Fisher*

London and New York

First published 1998
by Routledge
11 New Fetter Lane, London EC4P 4EE

Simultaneously published in the USA and Canada
by Routledge
29 West 35th Street, New York, NY 10001

© 1998 C. M. Fisher

Typeset in Goudy by
Florencetype Ltd, Stoodleigh, Devon
Printed and bound in Great Britain by
MPG Books Ltd, Bodmin, Cornwall

British Library Cataloguing in Publication Data
A catalogue record for this book is available
from the British Library

Library of Congress Cataloguing in Publication Data
Fisher, C. M. (Colin M.), 1951–
Resource allocation in the public sector :
values, priorities and markets in the management
of public services / C.M. Fisher.
p.   cm.
Includes bibliographical references and index.
1. Public administration. 2. Markets. 3. Resource allocation.
I. Title.
JF1351.F57 1998
352.3©941 – dc21   97–45127
CIP

ISBN 0–415–17873–8 (hbk)
ISBN 0–415–17874–6 (pbk)

RESOURCE ALLOCATION IN
THE PUBLIC SECTOR

This volume analyses the ways in which public services are allocated and delivered. It examines the competing values that underlie the public service ethic, as well as the role of markets and quasi-markets, in public service provision.

The 'rules of thumb', or heuristics, that people use when making resource allocation decisions are explored in great detail. The author identifies a number of different heuristics, such as deservingness, individual need, ecology, fairness and utility and describes the conflict in culture and rhetoric between these. Equal importance is given to the nature of markets and the mechanisms used to marketise public services such as vouchers and quasi-markets. In a detailed overview, the author analyses the enormous changes in the public sector over the last decade and predicts the future development of public services.

C. M. Fisher is Principal Lecturer in HRM at Nottingham Business School.

CONTENTS

FIGURES

TABLES

ACKNOWLEDGEMENTS

The publisher and the author would like to thank the following for permission to reproduce copyright material:

Blackwell Publishers for figure 4.6 from Winstanley, D., Sorabji, D. and Dawson, S. (1995) 'When the pieces don't fit: a stakeholder power matrix to analyse public sector restructuring', *Public Money and Management*, 15, 2; the Controller of Her Majesty's Stationery Office for figure 3.2 from the Audit Commission for Local Authorities in England and Wales (1985) *Managing Social Services for the Elderly More Effectively*; Gower Publishing for the appendix, *Cave Rescue*, from Woodcock, M. (1989) *50 Activities for Teambuilding*; NTL Institute for figure 4.4 from Kouzes, J. M. and Mico, P. R. (1979) 'Domain theory: an introduction to organisational behavior in human service organisations', *Journal of Applied Behavioral Science*, 15, 4; Wiltshire County Council, Social Services Department and Wiltshire Health Authority for figure 4.1.

Every effort has been made to trace all the copyright holders but if any have been overlooked the publisher will be pleased to make the necessary arrangement at the first opportunity.

Thanks to the AV staff at Nottingham Business School for preparing the figures.

1

THE PROBLEMATICS OF PUBLIC SECTOR RESOURCE ALLOCATION

One important thing people working in the public services have to do is decide how scarce resources should be allocated between competing demands. They decide who should receive which services and how they should be provided. Resource allocation is at the heart of the matter of public services and it has long been a difficult and contentious issue. It can be found in the annual process of public expenditure management in Whitehall, it can be seen in the decisions of GPs when deciding whether to refer patients to hospitals, in the decisions of the regulators of utility companies about the controls they wish to place on the companies they oversee, in contract negotiations between care managers in social services and the providers of care and in the decision of a library assistant in the public library who chooses to spend ten minutes shelving returned books rather than updating membership records on the computer.

Public service problems and priorities

The arguments about resource allocation and priority setting have become more complex with the expansion in the types of structures used to deliver public services. Before the 1980s the organisations that delivered public services were relatively uniform; there were local and health authorities, the nationalised industries and central government departments. The main source of diversity and complexity concerning resource allocation was not organisational but professional, emerging from the different values and criteria that the various groups within these organisations argued should be used to make resource allocation decisions.

Since the mid-1980s the range of organisational forms used for delivering public services has increased. To give a few examples, there are now:

- healthcare trusts;
- direct grant schools;
- fundholding medical general practices;
- higher education corporations;
- private companies providing public services on a contractual basis;

1

- the Training and Enterprise Councils (TEC) which are private companies but which are 90 per cent funded by the state (Committee on Standards in Public Life 1995b);
- central government agencies such as the driving standards agency which conducts the driving tests;
- privatised utility companies.

In many ways this diversity parallels the plethora of public boards and public authorities that characterised the structure of the public services in Victorian times (Jackson 1969: 36–7).

In the period which saw the burgeoning of structural diversity the ideological range of the debate about public services diminished. It can seem to an observer as if the values of the market have become the new consensus. The increase in the number of organisational forms has been paralleled by an apparent reduction in the number of arguments, principles and philosophies that compete in the public and organisational debates about the nature and allocation of public services. In secondary education, to give a particular illustration of this reversal, the traditional position was one which gave headteachers very little discretion in how they organised and managed their schools. Most changes a head might make in these areas needed the permission of the local education authority, but the traditional system also gave teachers great freedom to define their curriculum and to choose the teaching methods they would use. This pattern of structural and managerial uniformity combined with diversity of curriculum and teaching methods has been reversed. There is now structural diversity and managerial discretion, on the one hand, and the standardisation of curriculum and teaching methods, on the other.

In practice, however, the ideological differences about the allocation of public services have not gone away. The public debate may seem to have been won by the supporters of markets and competition but the proponents of public services are still working in the new organisations. The people who held sway in the old-style public sector organisations are often still there and are much involved in the delivery of services. The staff in housing associations with whom I have worked, for example, often work in a very entrepreneurial way and have the skills to cost and negotiate a contract, but they also reveal, not deep below the surface, values about public service that were acquired in housing and social services departments in the 1970s and 1980s.

Even in services where there has been a substantial move towards the use of market mechanisms, many decisions still have to be made on the old bureaucratic basis. Social service care may be provided through a market mechanism (Department of Social Security 1989a and b), but the purchaser (or commissioner) still has to decide who shall receive which services. The providers, who have to assure their survival by providing the services the commissioners want to buy, may still harbour dark thoughts concerning proper and professional values about the delivery of social services. The world of the public services has acquired extra levels of complexity. Onto the professional and philosophical arguments about resource allocation has been piled the mass of argument about the institutional and structural form of public service delivery.

It is inevitable, given the level of complexity just discussed, that there are many arguments about how public services should be allocated and about the values and mechanisms considered appropriate to the task. Some hint of the extent of these disputes can be gauged from the following glimpses of argument about resource allocation that I have collected from the media, from conferences and other sources over ten years.

- 'We spend our housing budget on repair and improvement grants rather than building council houses because that way you can touch politically a large number of voters with a small amount of money.'
  A housing department official in the early 1980s.

- 'The purpose of the NHS is to allow highly specialised professional staff to develop their specialised professional skills.'
  A management consultant at a NHS training conference.

- 'Questions of need should not be confused by prejudice against violence.'
  A cleric in a synod debate in the late 1980s talking about aid to Third World liberation movements.

- 'In reality, utility often wins out over individual rights. The French do not cut down the trees lining their roads even though a number of innocent people die in road accidents because of them.'
  James Griffin quoted in Waldron (1985).

- 'The publicly owned and managed Newcastle metro system used to be an integrated one in which buses arrived to meet, and exchange passengers with, the metro trains. Since bus deregulation the buses and the metro have been in competition and not in collaboration.'
  A report on Radio Four's *Today* programme on 30 April 1996. The Passenger Transport Executive, responsible for the Newcastle area, no longer wished to provide a public subsidy for the metro. The private sector companies claimed that they could run the metro more efficiently and profitably than the public sector ever could.

- 'The handling of the SWEB Gas affair by OFGAS [the industry regulator] was a glaring illustration of the low priority given to the protection of the interests of consumers' (Gibbs 1996).
  A quote from the chair of Devon County Council's public protection committee. From April 1996 gas consumers in the south west of England can buy their gas from competing suppliers. One of the new

3

suppliers, a subsidiary of South Western Electricity, was accused of sharp practices in the way it sold its services.

- 'This is a clear case of the left hand not knowing what the left is doing.'
  Labour MP Derek Fatchett on the alleged bureaucratic incompetence involved in the building of the new £79.7m NHS headquarters, Quarry House, in Leeds. The building has a swimming pool, sauna and squash courts. It was reported that it was too small to accommodate all the staff, some of whom were squashed into emergency offices in the roof space, and others were working in rented accommodation in Leeds. (Brown 1996; Comptroller and Auditor General 1996).

- 'Where the question is whether the life of a ten year-old child might be saved, by however slim a chance, the responsible authority must, in my judgement, do more than toll the bell of tight resources.'
  Mr Justice Laws in his High Court judgment (subsequently overturned by the Appeal Court) on the case of 'child B' who was denied treatment for leukaemia by Cambridge and Huntingdonshire Health Commission. The commission denied their refusal was based on cost grounds. They claimed it was a clinical decision not to put the patient through much suffering when there was only a 10 per cent chance of success (Victor and Penman 1995). A full account of the case is given in Klein *et al.* (1996: 77–81).

- 'It is disgraceful that the proceeds of that investment [by the European Union] can be used to bolster the profits of a private train operating company . . . This money was intended to improve our railways – not to buy tickets for the get-rich-quick gravy train.'
  Clare Short, the Opposition Labour spokesperson on transport. The east coast main railway line between London and Edinburgh had been modernised using, in part, a grant from the European Commission. The running of the line was franchised to a private company, Sea Containers, in 1996 (Hetherington 1996).

- 'The government believes that the principal responsibility for making that provision [for social and nursing care for the elderly] rests with the individual . . . We shall continue to provide a safety net . . . we shall reward the thrifty for their responsibility.'
  The Secretary of State for Health on proposals to protect the assets of those elderly people who need social care and who have taken out insurance against the risk (Thomas 1996).

These examples are neither exhaustive nor representative, but they do suggest the breadth of views that may exist on the question of public service resource allocation. They represent some of the problematics of resource allocation. Problematic is normally an adjective and it makes a clumsy noun which, in this form, means an area of difficulty in a field of study. It is used for two reasons. First, it rhymes well with the key words in the titles of the other chapters. Second, and more importantly, it expresses the notion that the ideas people use about resource allocation are the subject of great scrutiny and argument. Such terms as need, equity, cost effectiveness, markets and competition are not straightforward and it is largely the purpose of this book to review and debate the range of definitions and arguments that surround them. The aim is not simply to dissect the problematics and lay them out for inspection. It is also to identify how people cope with the difficulties caused by the problematics in the day-to-day business of allocating and delivering public services.

One problematic that needs to be considered is the nature of public services. A broad definition will be taken in this book. The economists' definition of public goods is too restrictive. It focuses only on those services, such as public health measures, from the enjoyment of which people cannot be excluded but for which they cannot be required to pay, except indirectly through taxation. It therefore excludes many services, such as public housing, which has long been a public service. Neither can public services be defined as those that are provided by a public body. Many are provided by private companies or voluntary organisations and by mechanisms of allocation which involve hierarchies, free markets, quasi-markets and combinations of all three. Public services are those considered by the state to be necessary to the well being of its citizens to a sufficient degree to justify the state providing the service, or paying for the service, or using the tax system to subsidise services (e.g. tax relief on mortgages on homes) or regulating the service. There will always be debate of course about services on the margin of the category. Some, and mortgage tax relief is a case in point, will be increasingly seen as outdated and an unnecessary public provision whereas others, public access to the Internet and the information superhighway, for example, will come to be seen as something which it is proper to provide, in certain circumstances, as a public service. The definition of public services is a relative and not an absolute one, the services included within the classification will vary with the circumstances and economic wealth of a country.

The idea that links all varieties of public service is that they provide an infrastructure (Seedhouse (1994) uses the term platform) on which people can build autonomous and worthwhile lives. Stretton and Orchard (1994: 71–9) provide illustrations of four categories of services necessary for this purpose. The first category contains those services needed to develop, inform and protect individuals. It includes a multitude of services such as sewerage, air traffic control, policing, monitoring pollution levels, health education, and so on. In the second category are the services which support and encourage the private sector of the economy. These services help create the wealth which funds, amongst other things, people's growth and achievements. This category includes public funding of applied research, transport systems, company and consumer law, support by foreign office diplomats of exporters and innumerable other services. The third category of public services includes those that provide and encourage a cultural infrastructure. It includes services ranging from public service broadcasting to running street festivals. Such services can deepen an individual's experiences but may also contribute to the development of wider and more encompassing social and cultural norms. The final category of public services concerns the redistribution of wealth. This has become one of the most contentious areas because of worries that the provision of financial benefits to the poor diminishes their incentive to find and remain in work. Nevertheless, it remains true that those with no job, with poor housing and little training have less opportunity than others to achieve full and satisfying lives and therefore deserve the support of public services. The infrastructure theory of public services does not enable categorical decisions to be made about what services, in any particular place and time, provide an adequate platform. It does, however, provide a framework within which the debates can be conducted.

If the idea of an infrastructure, which supports the autonomy and achievement of individuals within an economy and society, is crucial to the justification of public services, then the role of resource allocation in the management of public services is highlighted. The issues raised by this theory question which services are a legitimate part of any infrastructure. They concern who should have priority in receiving services and how it is ensured that the right people obtain the right services. These are difficult questions to answer because judging the success or failure of infrastructures is difficult. A private company can easily calculate if a division is making profits but there are no easy ways to decide whether, say, an embassy is achieving policy objectives, even assuming that the objectives are known (Tullock 1996: 64).

A summary of the chapters

It will be helpful to give a brief account of the contents of the chapters. This first chapter will clarify the subject matter of the book and lay down some concepts and definitions (such as the idea of values) as a foundation for the rest of the book. The main theme of the book is identified in chapter 2 which is about the heuristics of resource allocation in the public services. The starting point for this discussion is the question: how do public sector managers and officials make resource allocation decisions? The initial conclusion is that they do not apply formal and scientific decision analysis techniques. Instead, it is argued, public officials acquire or develop values, beliefs or schemata about the things which should be taken into account when making allocation decisions. These values are used heuristically, that is to say they perform the task of making complex issues more simple. A heuristic is a cognitive rule of thumb which helps a person decide which information is relevant and which is not.

It also provides a rough and ready decision rule. The official has to categorise the issue (Billig 1996: chapter 6) which means deciding which heuristic is appropriate to the question facing them; is it a matter, for example, of rewarding moral worth or is it a matter of cost effectiveness? Once this categorisation has been made, the value or heuristic provides a strong platform for making an inductive leap towards a solution.

I am by occupation a management trainer and my initial identification of the different heuristics used by public sector managers was made by reflecting on the way that such people tackled resource allocation decisions when doing management development simulations and exercises. A management development exercise called *monksbane and feverfew* was developed to help people think about their own values and their relevance and appropriateness. The results gained from using this exercise with public sector managers are discussed in chapter 2. The exercise is included in an addendum to chapter 2 to give the reader an opportunity to test out their own heuristic preferences.

Chapter 3 is a detailed analysis of the heuristics identified in chapter 2, which can briefly be defined as:

1   *deservingness*: a criterion based on moral worth, or the lack of it;
2   *individual need*: the belief that public services should be allocated according to objective assessments of clients' needs;
3   *fairness*: the belief that all people should have equal access to standardised services;
4   *utility*: the belief that resources should be allocated in a way that maximises a utility function or the good obtained;
5   *ecology*: the belief that decisions should take into account the aspirations and anxieties of critical stakeholder groups;
6   *personal gain and competence*: the belief that public resources should be used to benefit the decision maker in some way; this might include using proper and justifiable decision methods;

Each of these is discussed in turn in chapter 3. Definitions and interpretations for each of the heuristics are proposed and analysed. The chapter discusses the 'apologetics of bureaux' because it is focused on public sector organisations (PSOs) and because the heuristics, or values, that public officials use can be seen as their implicit justification for their power over public services.

Up to this point in the book most of the discussion concerns the ways in which public officials and managers think about resource allocation and priority setting. But, as has already been pointed out, there was during the 1980s a major shift towards the use of market mechanisms for delivering public services. Chapter 4 represents the transition, in the structure of the book, between a concern with public organisations and a concern with markets. The chapter is about the arguments that occur over how public services should be allocated and delivered. This chapter is entitled 'The rhetoric of resource allocation' because rhetoric is the study of argument and debate. These arguments are not just organisational and public affairs. After some introductory matter the chapter begins by considering the debates that individuals have with themselves about the proper basis of resource allocation. An attitude questionnaire, designed to identify respondents' stated preferences for the resource allocation heuristics identified in chapter 2, known as RAPS (Resource Allocation Preferences Survey) is used to explore middle managers' heuristic preferences in general terms and in the context of difficult and emotionally charged decisions. There is no pretence that such a blunt research instrument can capture the complexity and rhetorical colourings of people's thought processes over values but it is used to reflect some contradictory aspects of heuristic thinking.

In the second part of chapter 4 the emphasis is on the arguments public managers use on the appropriateness of the various heuristics. A framework is developed which is used to identify the similarities and the differences between the heuristics. The suggestion is then made that different domains within PSOs have preferences for different heuristics and that these contrasts explain some of the cultural diversity that can be found within public organisations. The discussion then moves on to look at the arguments about the relative merits of bureaux and markets for the delivery of public services. This leads to a detailed look at the arguments over the working of markets in the case of the privatised utilities.

The mechanisms used to create markets for the provision of public services are the subject of chapter 5. The supporters of markets argue that human reasoning is not adequate to the task of planning the provision of public services and that the job is better left to market mechanisms which can meet the expressed demands of consumers. A list is made in this chapter of the mechanisms and devices that have been used to create market mechanisms for public services. Included in this list are:

- the creation of corporate bodies, with an independent legal existence, that have to live with the possibility that they could become bankrupt;
- competitive tendering, whereby public providers of public services have to test whether the service could not be better provided by another, probably private sector, supplier;
- systems for regulation and inspection. There is a wide range of such mechanisms including inspection bodies, such as OFSTED, regulatory bodies, such as OFER, and codes, such as NHS clinical costing procedures;
- competitive bidding for public funding, such as the ways in which local authorities have to make bids to the Department of the Environment and the European Commission to win funding for inner city renovation projects;
- internal markets and contractual relations, whereby relations between public bodies, which ordinarily would have been co-ordinated by hierarchical control, are governed by contract;

- voucher systems, which enable the users of public services to become purchasers and customers;
- quasi-markets in which the purchasers of public services have a choice between different suppliers;
- proxy purchasing, in which a particular class of people are given the authority to purchase public services on behalf of their clients or stakeholders;
- mechanisms for bringing private capital into the construction of public service infrastructure. This includes the private finance initiative (PFI) and the BOT (build-operate-transfer) approach.

This is a formidable list of techniques; and in chapter 5 the use and combinations of these devices will be discussed. The different recipes for creating markets, which can be developed from this list of ingredients, parallel the use of the heuristics in arguments about resource allocation as discussed in chapter 2. But the resource allocation heuristics will also be used more directly in this chapter because it will be found that each of the marketisation mechanisms carries with it a characteristic criticism drawn from the list of six heuristics.

The purpose of chapter 6 is to give an overview of the book's argument. It has seemed at times during the last fifteen years or so that the speed and diversity of change in the field of public services have been such as to defy all attempts to impose thoughtful order on it, except that is in the crudest terms of a debate between wicked bureaucrats and noble market entrepreneurs. This chapter is an attempt to create a theoretical framework which encapsulates the processes that have been witnessed. The attempt is made by using the dialectic as a tool, not in its scientific materialistic form, but in its logical, epistemological form. A model will be proposed in which the idea of, and consciousness of, public services develop through a number of stages. At each stage the formal idea of what public services are and how they should be allocated and delivered is contradicted by an aspect of messy practicality. This internal tension provides the logical driving force which moves the dialectic onto its next stage. Such a chapter must look fearsomely academic and, to lighten it, the tensions within the dialectic are illustrated by stories about public services which have appeared in the media.

The concluding chapter is a short but important one. In this chapter some academic caution is jettisoned and conclusions are drawn which will have implications for policy makers, public sector managers and for private sector managers involved with the delivery of public services.

There are many titles published in the areas covered by this book. But this is the first one to place resource allocation decisions at the centre of the debate and to study the public services from this perspective. Most books fall into one of three categories. Some are written from the perspective of a particular public service, e.g. books on rationing in the NHS (Klein *et al.* 1996) or the social care market (Wistow *et al.* 1996). Others are written from the perspective of a particular academic subject or theory, e.g. Stretton and Orchard (1994) who set out to criticise public choice theory. Finally, there are books which deal with a particular management technique, e.g. TQM in the public sector (Joss and Kogan 1995). There is a shortage of works that take an overview of resource allocation. Those that do so are largely textbooks which have an obligation to cover a broader field adequately (Flynn 1993). The purpose of this book is rather to present an argument about the nature of resource allocation than to describe the field comprehensively. The argument is centred on the activity of resource allocation and priority setting; it is about how people do it and what mechanisms they use in the attempt.

Approaches to the definition of values

The concept of heuristics is an important one in this book. It is used to explain how public officials make resource allocation decisions, if they are working in traditional public services, and how they set about introducing market mechanisms into the systems used for delivering public services if they are working within the context of the new public management (Ferlie et al. 1996). It is also argued that the heuristics used for resource allocation or market building are values. The definition and nature of heuristics will be discussed in detail in chapter 2. In this introductory chapter it is important to consider the definition of the broader concept of values from which heuristics are developed.

A good starting point for considering values is Rokeach's (1973) definition because his intention was to reinstate values as a significant aspect of social analysis after the long hegemony of the behaviourists who argued that behaviour was controlled by conditioning, and that values and other airy notions were not necessary for an understanding of human actions. He defined values as follows.

> A value is an enduring belief that a specific mode of conduct or end state of existence is personally or socially preferable to an opposite or converse mode of conduct or end mode of existence. A value system is an enduring organisation of beliefs concerning preferable modes of conduct or end states of existence along a continuum of relative importance.
>
> (Rokeach 1973: 5)

There are many implications packed into this definition. The first is that values are defined only by reference to their opposites. In the case of a value about modes of conduct, for example, a person might think it better to be willing to forgive others than to be unforgiving; and in the case of end state values, a person might think a prosperous life better than a poor and uncomfortable one. Rokeach's twofold division of values into 'end state' and 'modes of conduct' categories also raised the question, which he discussed, of the relationship between them and whether they can be defined as ends and means. Values and value systems were seen by Rokeach as guides to action. They help individuals decide their actions, ideologies, attitudes towards others, presentations of self to others, judgements, evaluations and so on. In Rokeach's approach, values were seen as being few in number but enduring. In consequence, values were viewed as internal and personal rather than externally applied social norms because, if people had lots of values that changed regularly in response to fashion, it would be difficult for them to place much significance on them. He did not argue, however, that values are absolute because this would rule out any possibility that values or value systems might change. He argued that a person's values are relative to their context. If a person is involved in a situation connected with dishonesty at work then one or two values from their value system will dominate their thoughts, whilst they are concerned with that issue, to the exclusion of their other values. Finally, Rokeach assumed, and this assumption was built into the instrument he used for measuring values, that despite the relative nature of values, a person is capable of putting their values into a rank order of preference.

Since the 1970s people have taken various aspects of Rokeach's discussion of values and developed them in ways which have led to changes in the perception of values. Some have taken the idea that values are only defined by their opposites and pushed through the logic of that insight to a point where they can claim that values do not have fixed and specific meanings. Others have taken the idea that values are relative to context and extended the analysis in such a way that values are seen as arising from, and being heavily influenced by, whatever debates or arguments a person may be involved in at any given time. Others (Watson 1994a: 138), taking their cue from Weber, have argued that the complexity of the relationship between ends and means, which Rokeach identifies as the difference between terminal and instrumental values, is much more important, at least in organisational settings, than was at first thought. The key argument in this strand of thought is that people in organisations give importance to instrumental concerns in ways that undermine the achievement of terminal values. Finally, Rokeach did not give much weight to social factors, he saw values as essentially personal. He was of course writing before the idea of organisational culture became fashionable and there are no references in his index to organisational culture. The cultural view, in contrast, sees values as a necessary link between individuals and groups.

These changes in the perception and definition of values in the field of organisational studies can be presented historically. When I was first interested in these matters values were seen as a question of scientific study and, as in Rokeach's study, survey techniques could be used to measure them. With the publication of Peters and Waterman's book *In Search of Excellence* (1982), values were seen through the prism of organisational culture. During the 1990s, with the rhetorical turn in the social sciences, values came to be seen as things which are developed and metamorphose in the process of argument and debate. As a consequence of these developments values are dealt with in different ways in different parts of the book. This variation needs to be described and justi-fied and, in doing this, the various conceptions of values that are used in this book will be explained.

The idea of fragmentation is central to the attempt to explain the different academic stances which can be taken in the study of values. Fragmentation is the idea that things in the social world are disordered and disconnected. A fragmented view of values would see them as diverse, various and expressed through conflict between different views and opinions. There would be no expectation of a resolution of these arguments. One particular aspect of frag-mentation often referred to in the literature, and based on an insight by Kant, is that the arenas of science, morality and art have become disassociated. This distinction implies, for instance, that the methods of scientific understanding are not helpful to the politician grappling with ethical dilemmas. There are no wholes in a fragmented social and ethical world, only discordant parts which clash against each other. In contrast, a holistic view of values would see them as immutable, existing irrespective of time and space. At the least, holders of this view, would believe in an inexorable progress towards the formulation of absolute truth and the creation of a world shaped according to its dictates.

The importance of fragmentation as a fact (Harvey 1989: 10, 117), as mani-fested in the fleeting, the transient and the contingent nature of social and ethical life, is accepted by writers from the whole range of stances. The differ-ences between writers come into play when the relationship between fragmented reality and the desire for a unified society and morality is considered. Let us review three major positions on the relationship between the fragmented and the eternally whole; and let us refer to them as the modernist, the neo-traditional and the postmodern stances. These positions can be seen as points on a continuum. At one extreme is the modernist position of those who believe that fragmentation is a transitory phase and that, with enough rational thought, the pieces can be put back together and absolute values defined. At the other extreme of the continuum is the hard postmodern stance in which nothing in the social and intellectual world is tangible or fixed. By way of illustration, Derrida, the inventor of deconstruction, fought hard, but probably unsuccess-fully, to prevent his neologism of *différance*, which indicates the impossibility of assigning fixed meanings to words, becoming a fixed and definite idea (Baldick 1990: 58). Once *différance* was defined, by lecturers producing teaching slides which gave bullet pointed lists of its characteristics, then its myriad meanings were destroyed. This consequence would be unacceptable to postmoderns who accept fragmentation and its consequences (Harvey 1989: 116–17). The postmodernist stance emphasises the arguments over the meanings of values and the rhetorical methods people use in exploring the multiple meanings of statements. The neo-traditionalist position exists in between the extremes of modernism and postmodernism. This approach emphasises the function of culture as a device (sometimes defined as a mechanism and sometimes viewed heraldically or symbolically) for mediating the tensions between the fragmentation of values and the need of societies and organisations for a common purpose and mutual understanding.

The continuum of stances on the question of the appropriate response to fragmentation has more than these three positions on it. Each will be subdivided into two parts and all six stances will shortly be discussed in detail. The nature and definition of values are seen differently from each of the vantage points. The places in this book where traces of the different stances are to be found will also be indicated.

The modernist stance

Those who take this position believe a number of things. They believe that values are tangible, and can be unambiguously stated and defined. Values can also be subjected to formal and rational debate; there is an acceptance of deductive reasoning which allows truths to be logically developed from first principles. It follows from this style of thought that it must be possible to produce over-arching systems of philosophy and analysis that carry a universal validity. At the minimum level of expectation a modernist would believe that values can be defined and clarified (Kirchenbaum 1977; Smith 1977) as a preliminary to rational discussion about an organisation's or group's mission and core values. The work of Rokeach (1973) exemplifies this approach to the study of values because he believed that values can be observed and classified much as a botanist produces a taxonomy of plants. Figure 1.1 gives Rokeach's taxonomy of beliefs and values. The scientific tool used for studying values is the survey questionnaire. Rokeach made a distinction between attitudes and values. Attitudes were defined as the several beliefs an individual may have about a particular issue such as equal opportunities at work or the role of trade unions (Rokeach 1973: 17–18). Beliefs can be measured using attitude questionnaires, and Oppenheim's book (1966) specified the techniques – Likert scales, semantic differentials and Thurlstone scales, among others – that are available to the researcher. Values, in contrast, are general and transcend particular issues and situations. As values are simpler than attitudes, they can be measured using simpler tools and Rokeach's instrument was a straightforward one in which the respondent was presented with a list of values and asked to put them in order of rank.

The results of such research can, according to some, become the bedrock upon which, through the process of value clarification, a clear system of unified values can be developed. Many health authorities are beginning to use citizens' juries as arenas for conducting such debates. But the modernist stance is not entirely driven by measurement and the maximisation of agreed aims and ends. There is a strand of modernist thought which can be labelled critical and emancipatory (Legge 1995: 288). The instrumental rationality applied by managers assumes that cost effectiveness is the main value to be considered in

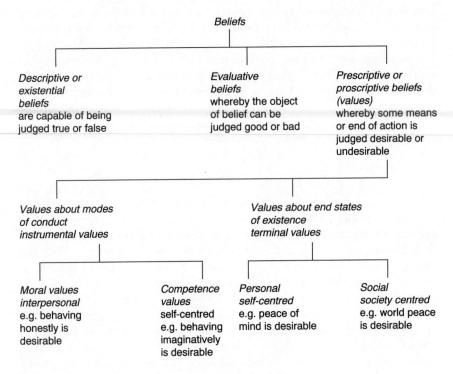

Figure 1.1 Rokeach's classification of beliefs and values

Source: Developed from material in Rokeach (1973).

public management. Critical modernism, however, allows a debate about ends and raises the question of whether performativity and maximising utility are a valid purpose for people to seek. But such challenges do not question the belief that it is possible to define rationally constructed value systems. Writers such as Habermas, according to Bernstein, argue that:

> We can accept this differentiation [between science, morality and art] and still seek ways to integrate and harmonise our everyday lives . . . he [Habermas] addresses himself to what many of us still believe, or want to believe; that it is possible to confront honestly the challenges, critiques, the unmasking of illusions; to work through these, and still responsibly reconstruct an informed comprehensive perspective on modernity and its pathologies.
>
> (Bernstein 1985: 24–5)

This describes the Enlightenment project which, even in its most modern manifestations, bears the fruit of Vico's seed. Vico, in the seventeenth century, identified three stages in the evolution of human sensibilities: the age of Gods, in which everything was seen as, or attributed to the actions of, gods; the age of heroes in which warriors established right through military might, and the age of men in which rationality dominated. This evolutionary sense still exists in the thought of writers such as Habermas who see modern cultures as an improvement on traditional cultures in terms of their 'cognitive adequacy' (Giddens 1985: 100–1).

There is a discussion of the modernist and instrumental view of values, and a critical response to it, in chapter 2. This chapter also contains the clearest application of this approach to the study of values. Chapter 2 presents a clear taxonomy of values (concerning the allocation of scarce resources) and a management development inventory which has its origins in the technique of questionnaires for attitude measurement. There is another instrument in chapter 4 which, although it is closer to being a Likert scale questionnaire, does reveal some of the difficulties of seeing values as fixed ideas that people store away in the same way that computers store data in read only memories.

The neo-traditionalist stance

The neo-traditionalists see values in the context of organisational and social cultures, indeed, cultures are defined by the values that characterise them. They argue that the fragmentation of values can be overcome and that organisations and societies can have unified values. But such an end cannot be achieved by rational analysis and classification of values because, from this perspective, values are not seen as objects but as shared myths. Myths can act as the glue which holds an organisation or society in unity because of their simplicity (which needs no sophisticated exegesis) and because of their ability to finesse dilemmas. Sometimes the glue is weak and sometimes strong. But there is agreement among neo-traditionalists that values, presented as vision and myth and not as cold rationality, are the keys to overcoming fragmentation. In Peters and Waterman's (1982) famous formulation, the key to organisational effectiveness lies in the warm triangle of staff, skills and style and not the cold triangle of strategy, systems and structure.

But the neo-traditional academics who study culture fall into two camps described by Smircich (1983). She identified five streams of research into organisational culture, two of these assumed culture to be a critical variable and three saw it, not as a variable at all, but as a root metaphor for conceptualising organisations.

Culture as a variable

Researchers who take this approach stress that organisations are culture-creating mechanisms and that cultures can change as their organisational context changes. This thought leads to the notion that culture may be a critical lever or variable with which managers can lead or direct their organisations. As Smircich puts it:

> Overall the research agenda arising from the view that culture is an organisational variable is how to shape and mould the internal culture in particular ways and how to change culture, consistent with managerial purpose.
>
> (Smircich 1983: 346)

Values, from this view, can be deliberately used as a means of overcoming fragmentation. Managers can claim that, by increasing the congruence between the values held by disparate organisational groups and subcultures, they will improve organisational effectiveness.

The discussion in chapter 5 is about the mechanisms for placing erstwhile public organisations on a market footing. The proponents of these changes often assume that the shift to a market basis will change the bureaucratic culture of public service organisations into an entrepreneurial one. The final part of chapter 7, in which I attempt to come out from the protective carapace of academic analysis and draw some conclusions that might be helpful to policy makers and public sector managers, is where I come nearest to the 'culture as variable' stance.

Culture as a root metaphor

This stance is a further step along the continuum towards the view that fragmentation has to be accepted rather than overcome. Researchers who take this position, when studying organisations, aim to understand culture, not to change it. They seek to describe or critique cultures from a symbolic, psychodynamic or cognitive perspective. One consequence of this approach is that, not only values, but all social phenomena are seen as not having the hard objective reality that the modernists ascribe to them. Again, to quote Smircich:

> The mode of thought that underlies culture as a metaphor gives the social world much less concrete status. The social world is not assumed to have an objective, independent existence that imposes itself on human beings. Instead the social or organisational world exists only as a pattern of symbolic relationships and meanings sustained through the continued processes of human interaction.
>
> (Smircich 1983: 353)

Since the work of Heclo and Wildavsky (1981) on the British Treasury there has been a recognition of the importance of the culture and values of those responsible for resource allocation. Thain and Wright (1988) reinforced the importance of culture to the understanding of the policy process but pointed out that in central government the cultural norms and the rules of the game (such as the move to cash limited budgeting) had changed since Heclo and Wildavsky made their study.

Cultures change, but there is no certainty, from this viewpoint, that cultures can be managed. If an organisation does develop a unified culture and set of values it will be the result of a complex and emergent process and not a consequence of deliberate managerial will and action. Unity may exist but it is difficult to call it into being. All that academic work can achieve is an understanding of how cultures change themselves and how they cope with fragmentation. The emphases of this stance are on the study of rhetoric within an organisation, on the ways in which myths are developed and disseminated and on the development of values through argument and debate.

'Culture as a root metaphor' is a stance that is quite often taken in this book. There is an attempt in chapter 3, in which the values and heuristics of resource allocation are discussed in detail, to understand the values that are found in public service and to understand how these values are created, nurtured and modified in organisations. The 'culture as metaphor' stance also reflects my position on manager development, which I see as being about increasing managers' awareness of the values they use in their work and helping them review and develop them.

Postmodernism

This stance is at the far end of the continuum. At this vantage point fragmentation is accepted as part of the human condition. In Lyotard's famous phrase there is 'incredulity towards metanarratives' which means that the large ideological schemes, such as capitalism and communism, that used to dominate people's lives no longer have credibility. In the postmodern view there is nothing 'real' out there, what we think of as objectively real emerges through discourses which are themselves embedded in power and knowledge relationships where some have more influence on what emerges from the discourse than others. But what emerges is in any case uncertain because the language we use is uncertain and carries no single, clear messages (Legge 1996: 306). The problem is how to respond to the fragmentation. Two broad answers to this question can be defined. The soft postmodernists (the term is from Watson 1994b) accept ambiguity but argue that this should not prevent people leading purposeful lives. The hard postmodernists take a more baleful stance and argue that nothing can be done except explore the indeterminacy of human communication.

Soft postmodernism

The line taken by soft postmodernists is that the inability to ground our values in some grand overarching theory such as Christianity, Marxism, Islam or capitalism does not prevent people making sensible and practical arrangements for

17

living a civil and well-mannered life. As Rorty expresses this view, reflecting the arguments of the pragmatic Scottish philosopher Hume:

> No such metanarrative is needed. What is needed is a sort of intel-lectual analogue of civic virtue – tolerance, irony and a willingness to let spheres of culture flourish without worrying too much about their 'common ground', their unification, the 'intrinsic ideas' they suggest or what picture of man they presuppose.
>
> (Rorty 1985: 168)

He argued that the lack of a metanarrative can be overcome by dealing with the concrete and practical concerns of a community and by finding ways of harmonising, but not abolishing, the conflicts of values within the community. In terms of Rokeach's classification of values (figure 1.1), Rorty's analysis suggests that uncertainty about end-state values can be compensated for by focusing on social norms and instrumental values.

But living in an ungrounded system may call upon people's resources of humour, tolerance and irony. Humour and tolerance are needed because value conflict will be endemic in such a situation and irony because people's purposes may require them to act in ways that seem naïve in the absence of metanar-ratives that justify the simple behaviours. Let me explain this latter claim by two examples. Eco (1985: 67) in his reflections on his best-selling novel *The Name Of the Rose* uses the example of the postmodern lover. The lover wishes to say to his partner 'I love you.' But he cannot do so because everyone is aware that the proliferation of romantic novels has devalued that particular metanarrative. He would feel too naïve and unsophisticated if he said that simple sentence even though it is the emotion he wishes to express. Being a soft postmodernist he does not give up and stalk away undeclared. Instead he says 'As Barbara Cartland would say, "I love you".' He has thereby expressed his purpose but in a way which reveals his knowledge that such sentiments can no longer be justified by reference to transcendental values. A shorter example can be taken from John Wyver's article on television and postmod-ernism, by quoting a statement he makes apropos mass culture.

> indeed, if it didn't sound hopelessly sentimental, I'd say that my only support for the idea is some kind of faith (but that's another word banished from the postmodern vocabulary) in the individual (and that's certainly another).
>
> (Wyver 1989: 161)

It may be sentimental to say it, but he says it nonetheless, and without loss to his sophisticated lack of sentimentality. Irony, by which an apparently straightforward statement is undermined by its context, is essential to the soft postmodern stance.

The soft postmodernist stance, to borrow a concept from Bakhtin, sees the question of values (and much else) as dialogic (Baldick 1990: 56). People's utterances are dialogic because they respond to an interlocutor's previous statements and/or try to draw a particular response from a particular listener. Eco's imaginary lover and Wyver were not making authoritative pronouncements of their views, they were phrasing their thoughts in ways that owed much to the particularities of their listeners and the discussions they were involved in. It is the emphasis on the dialogic aspect of statements that gives importance to other characteristics of the postmodern style in both academic debate and, by way of contrast, architectural style (Porphyrios 1989). These features typically include playfulness and ironic quotation; managers might pepper their conversation with terms from the latest managerial fad (*paradigm* is current as I write) whilst signalling the phrase's presence within distancing quote marks by waggling their fingers like a Nick Park plasticine Wallace figure. An architect might similarly decorate a building with motifs and themes taken from a dozen different architectural styles and periods. Facades are also important in this mode of discourse, whether it is the facade that an architect assembles to disguise the fact that their building is a standardised, prefabricated industrial shed or the managerial report a manager assembles to justify a decision they know intuitively to be right. From a soft postmodern view, in summary, it is recognised that there is confusion and conflict over the ends of a good organisation or society and that the meanings people ascribe to values change and develop as they debate and discuss issues with others. Nevertheless, the soft postmodernist believes that with good humour and irony it is possible to make organisations and societies more bearable.

Soft postmodernism is the stance I have aimed at in chapter 4 in which there is an attempt to describe the dialogic nature of debates, about resource allocation within the public sector, about the relative advantages and disadvantages of markets and bureaux and about the tensions created when public services are delivered through a market mechanism. However, no conclusion, about whether markets produce better societies than the application of the resource heuristics by bureaucrats, is arrived at. Instead, the discussions explore whether organisations adopt proper standards of behaviour. On the one hand, can traders in markets be made to behave better? (can all the companies that use the gas pipeline network, for example, be persuaded to help in keeping the flows of gas into and out of the network in balance? q.v. p. 162). On the other hand, can resource allocation decisions, within public organisations, be made more fairly, effectively and equitably? Chapter 4 therefore typifies the soft postmodernist concern with instrumental rather than terminal values. Soft postmodernism is also the pervading style of the polemic in the final chapter. The theme of the argument is that the failure of the big metanarrative of public policy and administration (which is a belief in the combination of the expert judgement of professionals and the power of analytical planning) should not lead us to a total acceptance of the arbitrary devices of markets and personal preferences for allocating and delivering public services. Instead, it is argued, there is a need to provide some steerage against the buffeting of prejudice and of ecological and market pressure even if our basis for doing so rests on civility and tolerance rather than rigorous theory.

Hard postmodernism

From this position there is no hope that the fragmented pieces can be put back together again. There is no certainty that the words we use to express our values have any fixed meaning. Statements of value have to be treated as texts and deconstructed. As already mentioned, *différance* is Derrida's device for exploring the limitless instability of language. One aspect of *différance* is that no word has a positive meaning attributed to it, it only has meaning to the extent that it is different to other words. Another aspect is deferral because the meaning of one word is always explained by reference to another and the search for meaning can involve a complex chain of cross references as one chases a word through a vast thesaurus. Let us take an innocuous statement about public management.

> The first steps to achieving accountability for performance must be to clarify objectives and develop a recognised approach to measuring and reporting performance.
>
> (Dallas 1996: 13)

This is enough to cause a deconstructionist to salivate. Most of the words in the sentence do not have an unambiguous or uncontested meaning. Accountability, for example, can only be defined by relating it to other words such as hierarchy, responsiveness, transparency, and so on. Different people may well view accountability from different discourses, political accountability, audit and accounting, consumer rights and investigative journalism. If we had the time to explore this sentence in detail and to plot its webs of signification, we would find that the sentence could mean almost anything.

The search for meaning may not be endless; but the end will probably be a terminal confusion rather than a clear understanding. The function of deconstruction is to reach a final impasse or aporia. Aporia is well defined by an illustrative quotation from 1657 given in the *Oxford English Dictionary*.

> Aporia is a figure whereby the speaker showeth that he doubteth either where to begin for the multitude of matters or what to do or say in some strange and ambiguous thing.

Deconstruction is not intended to overcome fragmentation but simply to map the instabilities, paradoxes and aporetic states that define it.

The difference between soft and hard postmodernism reflects the distinction between the beautiful and the sublime (Rorty 1985). The soft postmodernists want to develop beautiful social harmonies to cope with the fragmentation of values. The hard postmodernists want to experience the vertiginous thrill of gazing upon the disempowering vastness and obscurity of our social and moral world. The soft postmodernists will wish to cultivate their own neat and pretty garden, whereas the hard postmodernists will prefer the soaring qualities of a sublime landscape such as Hawkstone Park (Schama 1995: 542–4; The Rough Guide 1996: 391). Rhetorical seductiveness and intellectual elegance alone remain as touchstones for the hard postmoderns. As Rorty argues:

> More generally, one should see the intellectual as having a special, idiosyncratic need for the ineffable, the sublime, a need to go beyond the limits, a need to use words which are not part of anybody's language game, any social institution. But one should not see the intellectual as serving a social purpose when he fulfils this need.
>
> (Rorty 1985: 174)

The political passivity of postmodernism particularly annoys Harvey.

> The rhetoric of postmodernism is dangerous for it avoids confronting the realities of political economy and the circumstances of global power . . . meta-theory cannot be dispensed with.
>
> (Harvey 1989: 116)

But, as Derrida (1989) says, to deconstruct the Enlightenment project is not the same thing as criticising it. Just because someone may choose to pick holes in the language used by other people when they attempt to analyse the realities of global power does not mean the task is unworthy.

The hard postmodern view of value is the opposite of that taken by Rokeach. From this perspective, values are unspecified and carry no fixed meaning. Consequently, they can scarcely be guides to action or ideological preference. But it is interesting to note that the seeds of the postmodern critique of values can be seen in Rokeach's own discussion of values; particularly his belief that a value does not have meaning in itself but only in relation to its opposite (Rokeach 1973: 10).

The part of this book which comes closest to hard postmodernism is chapter 6 which deals with the dialectics of resource allocation. In this chapter a series of oppositions are created between, for example, fairness and quasi-markets. The tensions between these pairs of concepts are explored in a dialectical if, not quite, a deconstructionist manner. The use of a Hegelian dialectic ought to make the chapter very un-postmodern because the dialectic was invented as a teleological device which, by working through many contradictions and tensions, leads to the realisation of ultimate values. But in the version used in this book the dialectic folds back in on itself and leads to no ultimate fulfilment; and in this sense it is the identification of a state of aporia.

Justification of the use of many stances

This book, in different parts, takes various stances in relation to the understanding of values. The justification for this is pragmatic. Each stance adds a new aspect to our understanding of the issue of resource allocation. As William of Baskerville says in Eco's postmodern novel *The Name of the Rose*, anachronistically paraphrasing a modern Austrian philosopher:

> The only truths that are useful are instruments to be thrown away . . .
> The order that your mind imagines is like a net or a ladder built to attain something. But afterwards you must throw the ladder away, because you discover that, even if it is useful, it was meaningless.
>
> (Eco 1983: 492)

The ways in which contributions from the various stances can be differentiated but also integrated can be seen in chapter 2 which deals with the identification of the resource allocation heuristics. At one stage in the chapter a 'culture as metaphor' stance is taken. It is assumed that groups have shared values, or at the least a shared set of values which they can argue about, and observation of groups playing a management development game is used to identify what these values might be. This neo-traditional stance enables the identification of shared themes and ideas by relegating concerns about individuals' interpretations or commitment to those values to a lesser level. Later on in the chapter a modernist stance is taken when the values identified are incorporated into an exercise cum inventory designed to gauge people's reactions to the different values. An assumption is made in this mode of thought that values are a property of the people filling in the inventory that can be measured and ranked. The benefit from such a reductionist perspective is that the prevalence of the different values can be mapped on a much larger scale. But the end of the chapter is more soft postmodernist because resource allocation and decision making are viewed heuristically. This involves seeing values as part of the rhetorical resources available for people to pick and choose from, perhaps in an arbitrary way, when they are trying to come to a view on a decision. Such a stance adds to the understanding of the complexity of decision making processes but also reduces the ability to draw sharp conclusions about which decision would be best. In the study of management, there are trade-offs to be made between the applicability and the sophistication of knowledge and understanding. How the trade-off is made will differ according to the stances of the people to be convinced and the purpose of the argument; whether, in brief, it is to understand the world or to change it.

On heaps: the nature of the book

Academic books can be written in two ways: they are either holes or heaps. When a hole is dug all the earth has to be removed and, in the case of specialised holes such as archaeologists' trenches, the spoil is carefully sieved and the revealed strata minutely surveyed. Similarly, when a book of the hole type is written the author sifts and sorts all the material drawn from his or her academic excavations. The literature dug up is finely delineated and the past history of the field of study is revealed. This type of book has a great density of reference and citation to other authorities on the subject as the writers trace through the arguments and counter-arguments that define the academic development of their topic.

Heaps, however, are made by walking all over the field, picking up objects that look interesting or exotic and throwing them onto a pile. The author of a book of the heap type therefore is constantly on the lookout for elegant arguments and exotic and eclectic examples and illustrations. Nennius, the author of a ninth-century *History of the Britons*, which is one of the few sources of the history of the Dark Ages, scoured monastery libraries for old manuscripts. He wrote unapologetically as the first sentence of his collection, 'Coacervarvi omne quod inveni' (Myres 1986: 16) which loosely translates as 'I have made a heap of everything I have found.' I have studied my chosen subject in a similar manner. Much rummaging through the newspapers, academic and professional journals, and through my own experiences, was necessary in the search for interesting nuggets. Nennius at least had the excuse that, if he had not made his heap, our knowledge of British history in the Dark Ages would have been slighter than it is. Heap making is less excusable in the late twentieth century when we are in danger of suffocating under the mountains of information and data available to us. I justify the use of a heap making method by claiming that heaps are intrinsically more fascinating than holes because they have a denser concentration of meaning and a wider range of content.

The writer of a heap book is a collector, an antiquarian. A collection is defined by the similarities between its elements. Often the content of the collection is based on little more than the idiosyncratic interests of the collector. If you visit Sir John Soane's museum in London you will see crammed into a town house a heap of Canaletto and Hogarth pictures, cameos, medals, Etruscan vases, gargoyles, architectural capitals, a skeleton and an ancient Egyptian sarcophagus. The linking theme of the collection is simply that all the objects interested John Soane. Heap books, which also show a diversity of content, can be identified by their eclectic indexes. The subject index to Watson's (1994a) book on management contains the following items under 'H': Hawthorne experiments; heaven; hedgehogs; Hill, Benny; human nature; humour and hymn sheets. The book you are now reading includes references, *inter alia*, to potholing, the Hegelian dialectic, the regulation of public utilities, Dante's *Inferno*, school dinners, critical illness insurance, the history of the British Raj in India, public sector policy making and the case of the heart patient who smoked.

Heaps can be fascinating but they are meaningless without a strong linking theme which brings together all the disparate parts. Unfortunately heap makers often get bored when they arrive at this part of collection building. John Aubrey was an antiquarian collector who, in pursuit of his obsession, made a vast heap of biographies of his contemporaries in the seventeenth century. But on his own admission the heap was disorganised and chaotic because he 'wanted the patience to go through (the) Knotty Studies' (Lawson Dick 1972: 18) necessary to put the heap into order. The classical teachers of rhetoric stressed the importance of putting materials and collections into order.

> So in speaking however abundant the matter may be, it will merely form a confused heap unless arrangement is employed to reduce it to order and give it connexion and firmness of structure.
>
> (Quintilian 1986: 3)

If care is not taken, however, the order that is imposed on a heap may be based on similarity rather than on logical connection. Early renaissance thinkers, by way of illustration of the danger, believed that the bulbs of the orchis plant were a remedy for medical complaints of the testes because they looked like a pair of testicles (Eco *et al.* 1992: 51). The hermetic idea of signatures and correspondences, which proposes that a similarity, of shape for example, between two things must mean that there is a deeper and functional relationship between them, is a very powerful one. It follows, from a hermetic style of argument, that if market principles are right for the economy at large (the macrocosm), then they must also be right for the public sector; and relations, say, between a doctor and patient (the microcosm) should be based on the same economic principles as the relationship between large multinational companies. But other approaches to the doctor–patient relationship emphasise differences rather than similarities. Commentators, such as Smith and Morrissy (1994), who see the relationship between patients and doctors as a fiduciary one, in which economic considerations should play no part, objected when market devices such as indicative drugs budgets were introduced into general practice.

Heap makers often assume that, because all the items in their collection share at least one thing in common, there must be some greater significance to the similarities. The bigger the heap becomes, the greater is the proof it provides of hermetic links. The assumption of correspondences can be detected in the large heap of organisations that have been privatised since the late 1980s, (including British Steel, Amersham International, British Airways, the water companies, the Royal Ordnance factories, international airports and British Rail). They may have been similar in that they all had paying customers but this disguises the many differences between them that needed to be taken into account when deciding whether and how they ought to have been privatised.

There are many other examples of argumentation by hermetic signature, or similarity, in the field of public sector management. The morphological resemblance between a school canteen and a greasy spoon café, for example, does not necessarily mean that they should be run on the same lines. It is possible to argue that the similarity between them is insignificant and misses the main issue which is that school canteens are designed to meet school children's *needs* for nutritionally balanced meals (q.v. p. 241) whilst greasy spoon cafés are there to meet a *demand* for comforting stodge. I came across another example of this type of thinking when attending a seminar on quality in the provision of care for people with learning difficulties. The technique being discussed was PASS, programme analysis of service systems (Wolfensburger and Glynn 1975). The presenters were explaining a particular method, based on the use of photographs, for alerting care staff to the quality implications of their habitual working methods. They showed a picture of a room and invited the audience to say what it was used for. All agreed that it was a nursery for under fives. It was of course a day room for adults with learning difficulties, but the decoration of the room reflected the staff's unconscious view that their clients behaved as, and should be treated as, kids. In particular there were several posters on the wall showing chimps being naughty, throwing toilet rolls down the toilet pan and suchlike. The staff had put the posters up to 'make the place more cheerful'. The trainers' photographs were used to jolt staff into an awareness of the inappropriateness of their assumptions and behaviours for the task of creating a good environment for the clients. In other words, they were pointing out that an apparent metaphorical or morphological similarity between the behaviour of the clients, on one hand, and children and chimpanzees, on the other, was not a sound basis for planning the clients' care.

Unless care is taken, the throwing together of materials in a heap can lead to uneconomic and misleading connections and conclusions being drawn. The danger is increased because, in writing this book, I have wandered across many academic fields in which I am not an expert. This book has been put together as a heap and the reader is warned to look out for errors that may have arisen from drawing conclusions from items which, coincidentally, happen to be found contiguously in the pile. But I hope that the reader will find in this heap enough interesting things to include in their own collection of heuristics, examples and insights concerning public services.

2

THE HEURISTICS OF RESOURCE ALLOCATION

How people determine priorities

A. J. P. Taylor, the prolific historian of the twentieth century, once remarked that when he came upon a subject of which he knew and understood little he would write a book about it. This book on resource allocation had a similar origin. In 1980 I started a job as a management trainer and I became responsible for running courses for managers in local authorities and health authorities. As a result of listening to public sector managers' problems it struck me that the issues they worried about were either concerned with managing people or with difficult resource allocation choices. There was no problem finding training material to help them with managing people but this was not the case with resource allocation. If I looked in the text books and the manuals of training material there was little which could help managers improve their skills in resource allocation. I was of course making the naïve assumption that it was a matter of skill. But this gap in the range of available training material started me thinking about how trainers might be able to help public sector managers with resource allocation. The first question to be answered was – how do managers make resource allocation decisions? I hoped that the answer might lead to the development of training material.

The concept of heuristics, taken from the psychological literature, proved helpful in understanding resource allocation decision making. Heuristics are mental rules of thumb, or tricks of the trade, which people learn from various sources, which function by reducing the complexity of the decision to be made. They are cognitive swords used to cut Gordian knots, but the image must be right. They are not fine rapiers with stiletto tips, they are two-handed broad swords used for slashing through the thickets of decision making. Heuristics function as part of a person's way of looking at the world. They are a set of values, which are used to edit competing demands upon attention rather than tools for fine forensic dissection of policy dilemmas.

The idea of heuristics will play an important part in this chapter. In the first part, the context will be set by sketching the main arguments about the role of values in public decision making. The next section will provide an analysis of the heuristics and values managers use to approach a management

26

development exercise about setting priorities. From this discussion the common values used in resource allocation will be identified. In the penultimate section a training exercise, monksbane and feverfew, which was devised to train managers to deal with these resource allocation values in decision making will be discussed. The implications of the role of values and heuristics in resource allocation will be systematised, by comparing heuristic thinking with that prescribed by rational decision making theories, in the final section.

Values and resource allocation

The literature on the place of values in public sector decision making will be reviewed before identifying the particular values used, and the ways in which they are used, in resource allocation decisions. There are three main areas to be considered. The first concerns whether managers and officials ought to be involved in value-based decision making. In practice this argument has been a territorial one about the boundaries between the role of managers and officials, on the one hand, and politicians and board members, on the other. The classical distinction between the two groups is that the latter are responsible for policy (which involves thinking about values) whilst the former are focused on administration or operations. This apparently tidy distinction has, as will be seen, been subject to much disagreement. It is difficult in practice to see managers and officials as ethereal creatures who can switch off their value preferences when doing their jobs. This presumption identifies the other two areas which need review. They are the alternative answers that writers have given to the question of how public officials and managers should apply values in their work. The first alternative is a formal one which involves treating values objectively as defined and discrete inputs to a policy analysis procedure. The alternative is an informal use of values which allows public managers to be involved in the rough and tumble of policy debate and to argue on the basis of their personal values and preferences. The idea of informality will be applied to individuals' value systems which will not be seen as immutable and unchanging. As Watson suggests:

> The combination of values held, and the various strengths with which each is held, is a matter of the way each person is shaping their identity at that time.
>
> (Watson 1994a: 74)

Should public sector managers and officials be involved in value-based decision making?

The question of whether public managers and officials should be involved in questions of value preferences will be considered first. The traditional view is that public sector managers should be objective and focus on technical, not value-based, approaches to decision making. A consequence of this view is the belief that questions of values, if they cannot be avoided, should be the concern of politicians rather than of officials. It was this view that the Bains Report (Department of the Environment 1972) on management in the new local authorities, which were then being formed, began to challenge gently by suggesting that local government officials did have a role to play in the formulation of policy. Officials' task, it was argued, was not simply to implement policy. During the 1980s there was much debate on this issue, especially in the local government context. Elected members of the ruling parties in many local authorities began to consider that, if officials were to be allowed views and values, they, as elected politicians with a mandate, were entitled to insist that officials' values should be required to coincide with theirs. Some councillors began to expect ideological support from their chief officers rather than the bland impartiality which had previously been the town hall officials' stock in trade (Laffin and Young 1985). Other commentators argued, in contrast, that elected members should give way to the officers in policy making. Houlihan (1983) argued that, at least in some functions such as housing, the increasingly technocratic nature of policy making (e.g. the use of housing investment programmes, HIPs) caused policy making to become officer dominated. The policy task was becoming so technical that the politicians were frightened of putting their tuppenny-ha'penny values into the mighty discourses of the technical experts. A similar shift in power, from members to officers, was also experienced in health authorities in the 1980s when the authority members' common experience of confusion allowed officers to dominate policy making (Klein 1982; Ranade 1985). Although there were arguments between politicians and officials over their respective roles in policy making, the politicisation of officials and the complexity of policy made it unexceptionable for officials and managers to be involved in debates about values and policies.

Often, in recent years, disputes over the roles of politicians and managers have concerned the tendency of politicians to usurp the operational role of the managers and have not challenged the right of managers to make a contribution to policy. In 1993, to give an illustration, the prison service was set up as an agency under the Next Steps initiative, and a formal distinction was made between policy, which was the responsibility of the Home Secretary, and operational management which was the responsibility of the agency's chief executive. This neat division came under pressure when the governor of Parkhurst prison was dismissed following a prison breakout. The Home Secretary, Michael Howard, informed the House of Commons that he had not instructed Derek Lewis, the chief executive of the prison service, to dismiss the governor because it was an operational matter under the jurisdiction of the chief executive. Lewis, however, said that he had been instructed by the Home Secretary to sack the governor (Wintour 1995). The question of who was telling the truth in this issue became a long-running political saga. It gained impetus when Michael Howard was nominated as a candidate for the leadership of the Conservative Party and his truthfulness was challenged in the House of Commons by Anne Widdecombe.

The involvement of politicians in the, allegedly, neutral task of administration suggests that values manifest in the detail as much as in the policy and the mission statement. If this is true then it is not possible to argue that managers and officials ought not to be involved in questions of value. If value considerations reside in all aspects of operational activity, then a ban on managers dealing with value-based decisions would leave them with no work to do. Public managers and officials are seen as having a legitimate role in arguments about values and in developing policy, even though the politicians or appointed board members have the final say. This acceptance has arisen from practical necessity because public and media arguments about policy and values are often started by the implementation rather than by the promulgation of policy.

The formal approach to the use of values

Although acceptance of managers' role in issues of value and policy had spread by the 1990s, there still were people who were uncomfortable when value conflicts impinged upon the public management task. Their position was that managers and officials could be involved with values but that they should be very particular about how they were involved. This is the formal position on the role of values in the work of public officials. It is one which presupposes that values are a part of managers' work but that they are not a problem because of the manner in which they are identified and used. From this perspective officials who want to know what values are to be taken into account in a policy analysis either ask the board members and the politicians or they commission an attitude survey or focus group research. The use of these channels means that officials do not need to become involved in the disputes about which values should be applicable to any particular policy question. Once clear consensus values have been determined, they can be used as variables and parameters in the technical evaluation of policy options. In short, the formal and rationalist position is that values can be included as part of a calculation which will show which of the available policy options is best. The rationalist view on how public officials should deal with values implies a highly analytic approach to decision making (illustrated in figure 2.1) which sidelines and proceduralises the role of values.

People who take the formal view seek to develop management systems and techniques which would replace organisational politics with clear information and analysis. This trend can be illustrated from the writings of those who argue that if only we had, in the NHS for example, better information (on clinical effectiveness, public views on medical priorities, costs and hospital activity rates) and better information technology to process the data, then questions of medical priorities could be settled technically, optimally, without recourse

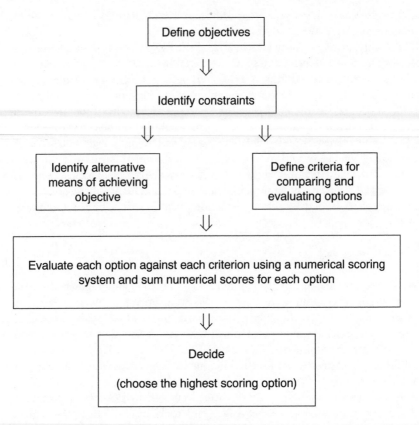

Figure 2.1 The rational model of decision making

Source: Based on figure 19.1 in Filley *et al.* (1976: 430).

to messy arguments about competing values in which the loudest arguer gets the most resources.

The most famous of the attempts to rationalise healthcare priorities was the Oregon experiment. This was an a study which tried to put medical treatments into order of rank, so that the health authority could decide where to draw the line between what it would and would not fund. Community meetings were called to elicit the priorities given to various categories of diseases and the various benefits that could be gained from medical intervention (Klein *et al.* 1996: 110–11). The hope behind these methods was that the findings could be used to enable a more calculative approach to the determination of health priorities and budgets. In Boyd (1979) there is discussion about how a computer model could be constructed to take all the resource allocation decisions required in the health service. Meadows (1986), a few years later, developed a system-atic process for resource allocation and budgeting in the NHS. The computer software for implementing the scheme suggests that the needs for medical services can be built up from data on population and morbidity and that decision rules can be built in to bring the costs of meeting needs into line with the financial allocations made available. Meadows' scheme does not claim to remove the need for debates about values, but it does suggest that better information and algorithms can make these processes easier.

A further illustration of calculation in value decisions can be seen in Walker and Smith's (1995) review of build-operate-transfer (BOT) schemes which are mechanisms for securing private finance for public infrastructure projects such as power stations and road bridges (q.v. p. 201). They recommend (Walker and Smith 1995: 199–201) the technique of multi-attribute utility analysis (MAUA, although later in this chapter the technique is referred to as MAUT when *analysis* is replaced by *testing*) to evaluate BOT proposals. The analysts, when using this method, identify the criteria against which the proposals will be judged and give each a priority score on a scale of 1 to 20. These figures are then transformed into *rationalised priority ratings* (RPR) by calculating the rating of each criterion as a percentage of the total ratings. The proposals are then analysed in turn by comparing them against each of the evaluation criteria. A proposal that performs well against a criterion will score highly on a scale of 10 to 110 whilst a low performing proposal will score poorly. Once all these assessments are made, utilities are calculated by multiplying proposals' scores for effectiveness on each criterion by the RPR. The products of all these calculations are summed, giving an overall utility score for each proposal. The scores can then be used to put the proposals in order of rank. All other things being equal, and the analysts being content with the method, the highest ranking proposal ought to be the best. MAUA gives arithmetical flesh to the logical bones of formal decision making as defined in figure 2.1. In MAUA evaluations arguments between competing values and preferences become transmuted into sensitivity analyses in which the calculations are adjusted to see the impact that changes in the RPRs and the proposal scores would have on the bottom-line rankings of the different proposals.

In the 1990s argument about the role of analysis in health policy making took a new form when it was suggested by politicians and health managers that if resources were allocated to clinical activities according to the research findings of evidence-based medicine, then the unedifying sight of public wrangles over health rationing could be avoided. A study of the methods of evidence-based medicine can be found in Gray (1997). The strengthening of evidence-based medicine was one of the Department of Health's (1995) priorities for 1995/6. The row in the media which was triggered when the Berkshire Health Commission decided, because of the pressures on their budget, that sex change and certain plastic surgery procedures would no longer be available on the NHS (Pilkington 1995), provides an example of the sort of spat the supporters of evidence-based medicine would like to see replaced by considered analysis. There is a great deal of support for such a view. Dillner

(1995) pointed out that lives have been lost and money wasted because clinical habit has caused certain procedures to be practised long past the point at which they were known by medical researchers to be ineffective, or worse, dangerous. But she also pointed out the problems which make the ideal of science-based medicine difficult to follow. She calculated that doctors would have to read seventeen research papers a day to keep up with the pace of medical research. Doctors do not have time to take on board the implications of all clinical trials. This difficulty is heightened when there are contradictory results to be reconciled. There is also a form of inertia in all professional practice which makes the dissemination of new knowledge a slow process. For example, it was known for fifteen years before it became common in clinical practice that the drug streptokinase would dissolve blood clots and could reduce the risk of dying after a heart attack. Another difficulty militating against acceptance of evidence-based medicine is doctors' predilection for the learning they gain from their own clinical practice over that which can be found in the reports of clinical trials. This preference is similar to the conclusion drawn by the old man who noted that all the medicines that made him feel better bore the legend 'BP' on the label. He told all his friends to ask their doctor for the medicine with BP in it when they felt unwell. BP is the abbreviation for British Pharmacopoeia and merely confirms that the medicine has been produced to a standard. Instrumental or technical rationality has to overcome the barriers of lack of knowledge and the preference for concrete over abstract learning if it is to be the method professionals and managers use in their decision making.

It has long been a complaint of academics who study public administration that values are seen by public officials only as a source of irritation and that, as such, officials try to avoid them. Hart and Scott argued in 1973 that public officials in the USA achieved this desire by making ethical assumptions about the universality of the principle of optimisation and cost benefit. This foundation allowed them to treat their task as if it were a purely technical one and to view debates about ends and values as not germane to their job. Hart and Scott suggested that public officials had become bored by questions of value and that the neglect of 'metaphysical speculation' in the training of public officials would have disastrous public consequences.

It could be argued that the 'normative sterility', which Hart and Scott suggested followed from the adoption of the paradigm of the natural sciences by public administration, led to the problems of public distrust of government experienced in America in recent years. The 1960s and 1970s were a period in the history of the USA when scientific approaches to policy making were the accepted norm. The Department of Defense of the federal government, under Robert McNamara, introduced PPBS (programming, planning, budgeting systems) in 1962 and in 1965 President Johnson ordered all agencies to install PPB systems. Many saw these systems as an attempt to 'quantify and computerise the imponderable' (Anthony and Herzlinger 1975: 55–6, 189). These attempts led to the publication of a spoof government report called the 'Report from Iron Mountain on the possibility and desirability of peace'. One of the conclusions of the report was that:

> Government decision makers tend to choose peace over war whenever a real option exists, because it usually appears to be the 'safer' choice. Under most immediate circumstances they would be right. But in terms of long-range social stability, the opposite is true. At our present state of knowledge and reasonable inference, it is the war system that must be identified with stability.
>
> (Lewin 1968: 122)

The tendency of policy makers to respond intuitively to events rather than to systematically analyse them had prevented governments from recognising that social stability and technological and economic growth came more easily in war than in times of peace. The report further argued that the stabilising function of war was in jeopardy because no serious quantified studies were being made, even though, as stated in a footnote, appropriate techniques were available:

> e.g. the highly publicised 'Delphi' technique and other more sophisticated procedures. A new system, especially suitable for institutional analysis, was developed during the course of this study in order to hypothecate mensurable 'peace games', a manual for this system is being prepared.
>
> (ibid.: 140)

This satire, which was aimed at the scientific planning techniques used in the Department of Defense and in the work of think tanks such as the Rand Corporation, expressed the worry, which was much discussed at the time, that these methods could drive out human judgement and the consideration of ethical issues from the evaluation of policy. The problem was not exclusively American. MacCreadie (1976) who tested out the applicability of Rawls' theory of justice on British policy issues concluded that, in the context of UK public administration, the treatment of questions of value was 'very woolly'.

The informal approach to the use of values

The incompatibility between the rigours of rational theory and the sloppiness of human thinking probably explains why the rationalist view has been challenged on the empirical grounds that managers do not make decisions on a purely technical basis. Researchers, such as Ferlie and Judge (1981), tried to find out whether public sector managers, in this case in social services, followed the calm precepts of the rational model of decision making. They concluded that, at least in times when hard decisions have to be made, they do not.

Thain and Wright made a similar claim about the Treasury and its management of public expenditure.

> in times of growth a *modus vivendi* between different types of expectation about rationality is possible in the budgetary process. But in a period of restraint there is potential for increasing conflict about how to allocate resources, and the consequences of those allocations and the growing incompatibilities among different forms of rationality.
>
> (Thain and Wright 1988: 14)

Heclo and Wildavsky (1981), in their study of the Treasury in the early 1970s saw the Treasury and a small group of departmental officials in the expenditure community as a village of like-minded individuals who rationally planned public services and expenditure through the PESC mechanism. This approach to public expenditure management focused on volume planning of services for a number of years into the future. A consequence of this enumeration of service levels was that programme plans were protected from inflation. Services were budgeted for at constant prices and, if inflation rose more than anticipated, the Treasury would increase the service departments' budgets to enable them to deliver the planned volume of services. In the hard times of 1982 volume planning was replaced by cash budgeting. This change, together with different government priorities led, in Thain and Wright's view, to a loss of mutuality in the expenditure community and an increase in conflict and mutual suspicion. The implication of an increase in conflict is that the emphasis in public officials' jobs will shift from implementing a rationality to arguing and lobbying for a particular rationality; to maximise the chances that their preferred rationality will gain acceptance.

Some commentators argued that formal rationality is not only rejected by officials and managers in times of financial restraint but that decisions are mostly made on the basis of intuition, nous and feeling. This view of decision making can be illustrated by the garbage can theory of March *et al.* (1972). Into the metaphorical dustbin, according to this account, go problems, solutions, people involved in decision making and opportunities or occasions for decision making. The combinations of these ingredients that are drawn from the dustbin when decisions emerge depend on many random factors. The problem that is chosen for discussion at a meeting, and the solution picked, will be affected by, amongst other things, the status of the group discussing it, who turns up for the meeting and who happens to miss it because they have the flu. Often, March *et al.* argued, decisions are not made by conscious resolution at all but by oversight or by flight. From this perspective values are not part of a formal analysis of policy options but are part of the dustbin's contents. March and his co-authors concluded that the theory should not be viewed negatively, as describing an unpleasant fact of organisational life. They claimed that the uncoupling of problems and solutions (by which is meant that solutions are generic entities which can exist independently from particular problems, as when new people join an organisation bringing pet packages and techniques with them), and the degree of unpredictability with which they can be combined, add originality and creativity to corporate thinking which can, on occasion, be valuable.

Other authors developed this theme and argued that the technical procedures and frameworks of management science are only used as a way of imposing a *post facto* structure and neatness onto a previously formless decision process. As Weick has argued:

> Rationality is viewed as (1) a set of prescriptions that change as issues change, (2) as a facade created to attract resources and legitimacy, and (3) as a post-action process used retrospectively to invent reasons for action.
>
> (Weick quoted in Reed 1992: 224)

Impugning the practicality of the rational model is not a new pastime. In the context of public administration one of the most compelling attacks was published by Lindblom in 1959. He later revisited the issue in 1979 and concluded that his analysis still held good. In these articles he argued that planning is an incremental process of muddling through. This implies that the test of a good policy is not whether it was derived from a proper and formal analysis but whether it was sufficiently acceptable to make it implementable. It does not matter therefore if the way in which policy is created involves inconsistency, reaction to events and a preference for policy baubles rather than for the understated purity of the platinum of policy analysis.

Mintzberg's (1987, 1994) arguments about the nature of strategic planning support a postmodern view of technical rationality. He argues that strategy is not made by working systematically through a series of steps, such as defining and evaluating options, but by a process of design in which strategy emerges from the interactions between people's perceptions of the problems facing an organisation and their intuitive attempts to deal with them. As formal rationality proceeds by analytically decomposing problems into their parts, he argues, it is inimical to the strategists' need to create new possibilities for action. His main argument is that strategic planning is a formal process based on procedures for decomposing issues into manipulable elements. 'Formalisation is achieved through decomposition, in which a process is reduced to a procedure, a series of steps, each of which is specified' (Mintzberg 1994: 298). An example of the procedural stages involved in rational decision making can be seen in Pinkus and Dixson's (1981: 273–305) review of operational science applications in local government. The general conclusion Mintzberg draws from his criticism of formal thinking is expressed as the grand fallacy: 'because analysis is not synthesis, strategic planning is not strategy formation' (Mintzberg 1994: 321). In other words, procedures cannot generate ideas or proposals for action. Mintzberg's argument can be adapted to apply to the limitations of formal methods in relation to values. Formal methods cannot manipulate values because values are ineluctable and therefore immune to forensic analysis.

Mintzberg's questioning of the ability of formalised systems to create strategy extends to the suggestion that, in practice, attempts to plan strategically on the back of technical systems have always failed, and he points to the history of Programme, Planning and Budgeting Systems (PPBS) in the public sector in the 1970s as an example (ibid.: 298). One of the assumptions underlying PPBS was that it is possible to distinguish ends and means in policy analysis through the mechanism of the programme structure (which is the first P in PPBS, q.v. p. 106). But it became apparent that such distinctions were unreal; as were the distinctions made between policy and expenditure in the Treasury in the 1970s (Heclo and Wildavsky 1981). These arguments suggest that the managerial job in the public sector cannot be seen as a purely technical one, in which values have no role, because values and intuition are central to the processes of management.

The criticisms of the rational model do not imply that it has no role to play. The objection is only that it denies a role for values and intuition in the policy and decision making processes. This is not to suggest that the rational model should be disposed of lock, stock and barrel. Mintzberg, for example, conceded a control role to technical rationality. But Leach (1982) ascribed a largely rhetorical role to it. He argued that the rational framework provides a contrary argument to policies derived from incrementalist processes. In other words, even if the full application of rational analysis is beyond most people, and they prefer to muddle through, the rationalist tradition does provide a platform from which policies can be criticised and improved by being subjected to debate. The rational model is also important because it provides the accepted language of policy debate in the public sector. Even if, for example, everyone knows that the origin of a policy position is the opportunistic championing of a once neglected idea that has only survived in the forgotten depths of an organisation, this knowledge does not prevent people justifying it through the language of technical rationality. As Leach suggests, the rational model:

> is valuable not as an accurate description of how policy is made in practice, but rather as a mode of thought which can be used to 'open up' critical discussions about processes of policy making. In particular it is most usefully seen as a countervailing force to the well-documented tendencies within organisations and departments to perpetuate existing policies and resist innovation and change. The language and tenets of the rational model are widely accepted within public organisations as an appropriate way to talk about policy making and policy justification. Although policy may be made and justified in ways which owe very little to the rational model, battles can be fought using the generally accepted terminology of rationality.
>
> (Leach 1982: 7)

In a nice ironic inversion, the use of the rational model lies not in its analytical techniques and processes, but in its rhetorical role as a source of language and argumentation for policy debates.

Summary

The role of values in official decision making will remain a question for debate. But some conclusions can be drawn from the arguments that have been reviewed. In the debate about whether officials and managers should be involved in questions of value there is a general agreement that this is not improper as long as politicians retain ultimate authority. When the focus is moved to an empirical level, the conclusions are that:

- most managers do not use the formalised methods of the rational model of decision making when dealing with values;
- that the rational model is used as a rhetorical device with which decisions can be justified;
- and that objective and value-free analysis cannot create strategy and policy initiatives.

These conclusions clear the decks for an investigation into the ways in which officials and politicians think and argue about values when setting priorities and allocating resources.

Understanding resource allocation and priority setting decisions

My views on the use of values in resource allocation and priorities have their origin in the experience of observing managers undertaking exercises and simulations on management development programmes. Reflective observation of managers' practice is a valid research method. Silverman (1993: 38), for example, describes how he used tape recorders to collect data in a study of medical consultations in a hospital. Because he knew that the basic research material he needed was being recorded, he was free to use his eyes and his ears to make more informal observations which would eventually be useful when he came to analyse the contents of the tape.

Reflective approaches to learning are highly applicable to the problems of researching the role of values in resource allocation. People are commonly aporetic and inarticulate when asked to talk about, or complete a questionnaire on, their values. This raises doubts about the truthfulness of people's replies to attitude questionnaires. Reflective observation can avoid the problems of asking people their thoughts about their values by studying their words when they are discussing issues with important value implications. McClean and Marshall (1991), writing on the problems of interpreting organisational cultures, have given examples of how reflective thought experiments, exercises to help people reflect on their own experience of an organisation's culture, can provide useful insights in highly subjective research fields.

At one level reflective observation can be a form of isolated Joycean epiphany (Levin 1960: 37–9) in which a chance regard can trigger understanding where before there had been only confusion. But it can be incorporated into a wider theory of learning. Eisner (1979), for example, attempted to do this in relation to his interest in classroom research. He offered the idea of connoisseurship as a method of capturing research material lost by more objective techniques. If you conducted an observational study of a classroom and converted the material into data in frequency charts, showing the relative use of different types of behaviours by teachers and pupils, then all the information about the atmosphere of the classroom, the tone of voice people spoke in, the expressions on their faces, and so on would be lost. Connoisseurship, according to Eisner, is the ability to trace qualities, patterns and relationships in what is being observed; and its success depends upon the development of the observer's mental frameworks and schemata for discernment.

Impressionistic research material needs to be used with caution. Evidence acquired in this way is obviously open, qualitative, novelistic and dependent upon judgement. Because of these qualities Eisner proposed that conclusions drawn from reflective observation should be tested against relevant theory and literature. In other words, published literature and research can be used to brake an observer's tendency to over-interpret or misinterpret what they thought they saw and experienced. The observations used later in the chapter are observations of people involved in a management development simulation. This increases the duty of care in the use of the material for not only is there a problem concerning the validity of the observation process, there is also the danger of drawing conclusions from observing a simulation rather than observing actual practice. In the analysis, shortly to be reported, connoisseurship is used to produce an initial rough sketch of an argument. These preliminary conclusions will then be checked out using more traditional, questionnaire-based, research tools (monksbane and feverfew and RAPS) and will also be tested, in chapter 3, against the research findings in the published literature. Reflective observation will provide a depth of understanding of the values of resource allocation; the questionnaire results and the comparison with the literature will be used to check the robustness of the conclusions. As Mintzberg (1979) argued, formal and quantitative research techniques, such as tick box questionnaires, can identify important issues, but qualitative techniques are necessary to explain how and why they are important.

Connoisseurship therefore will be used as the starting point to identify the values that people use in resource allocation and to understand how they use them. My initial observations on these issues arose from using a well-known management development exercise called Cave Rescue (Woodcock, 1979, 1989: 81). Another version of this exercise can be found in Francis and Young (1979).

Both are variations on a classic management game theme, of which The Kidney Machine is another popular version (Jones and Pfeiffer 1974). In these exercises groups have to decide how to allocate scarce resources between a number of people who are described in thumbnail sketches that are deliberately brief and partisan. Cave Rescue concerns six volunteers in a psychological experiment which requires them to be in a pothole. The cave is flooding and the research committee in charge of the experiment have called for a rescue team. When the team arrives they will only be able to rescue one person at a time because of the narrowness of the cave's entrance. The committee has to decide the order in which the volunteers will be saved from the cave when the rescue party arrives. The purpose of these exercises is to help people reflect on the way in which they allocate scarce resources, in this case the chance of rescue, and so they provide a good opportunity to research the values that are articulated in such debates.

Observation of groups of public sector middle managers playing this management game has suggested that a limited range of criteria are used to make the decision. Initially some people think in terms of moral obligation or deservingness. Someone might suggest for instance a criterion of 'women first', although this is frequently objected to by the women in the group. Others might latch onto some of the negative characteristics (as they interpret it) that all the volunteers have, and suggest that because 'Edward is a Freemason from Barnsley' or because, 'Paul has been convicted of indecent exposure' that they ought not to be ranked highly in the escape list. Some participants express these moral criteria with gusto. Others suggest them tentatively because they are working in a newly formed group and do not wish to endanger themselves or the group by revealing the nature of their prejudices (Tuckman 1965). Many people consider themselves professionals and they often feel that judgemental criteria are not appropriate to their status. Nevertheless, throughout the exercise, participants continue to make judgements which are based upon their notion of morally acceptable behaviour. 'Without being crude,' as one participant explained it, 'we have to choose between a flasher and a drunk.' This first type of criterion used by groups working on this allocation problem therefore is a moral one which discriminates between the worthy and the unworthy. As a practical tool for making the decision it has the drawback that participants have ill-matched conceptions of worthiness.

After this first phase most groups try to find a more objective method for making the decision. This can involve ranking the volunteers according to their need. This is difficult to do because at one level the needs of all the volunteers are the same, to be rescued and to continue living. However, need can be construed as a right to the opportunity to have a normal life; so that age becomes the test of need. The young have the greatest need because they have their life before them whereas the old 'may have had a good innings', or at least have had the opportunity for a good innings. This criterion creates difficulties if applied in policy analysis. As Daniels (1981: 170) has noted, 'the young will always suffer greater impairment of opportunity if their healthcare needs are not met'. This consequence is quite acceptable to many participants, who make age the criteria for rescue and the young are saved first. But for others this surcharge on age is unacceptable and they try to apply the criterion of opportunity to a normal life relative to age in order to prevent the old always being disadvantaged. Need can also be defined in other ways. Sometimes, for example, a belief in God is assumed by the participants to diminish the need for life in this world. The differing abilities of the volunteers to withstand the trauma of being left in the cave is also occasionally taken as a measure of need for rescue. Those who are believed capable of coping are considered to be less needy and are left to the end. But, however need is defined, it is always used to rank the volunteers according to some intrinsic aspect of them as individuals.

Frequently the participants' concern is not with individual needs but with maximising a wider and external objective. This objective is commonly construed as the saving of the greatest number of lives. In this case groups try to identify the people most likely to panic as the cave floods and so hamper the rescue effort. They decide to rescue these volunteers first to give the rescuers a better chance of saving more people. For some groups, though, this objective is too intermediate and fails to consider the final consequences, or impact, of their decisions. For these groups the objective they wish to maximise is contribution to society. They attempt to rank the cave volunteers according to the good they will contribute to society if rescued. This approach raises a number of difficulties for the group. First, there is again the problem of age because it is easier to assess the potential contribution of someone with an established life than that of a youngster with very little track record. Whereas need favours the young, maximisation of contribution can favour those in mid-life. When groups work on this criterion, however, they soon recognise the difficulty of making probability assessments about people's likely contribution. If they decide to rescue the man with a cheap cure for rabies first their decision could be nullified if he were to be run over by a double decker bus the day after being rescued.

But, to add to the difficulty of this exercise, each of the volunteers in the cave has a contribution to make; or at least each symbolises a particular valued goal. Helen represents family and motherhood, Tozo represents art and culture; Jobe, religion; Owen, outdoor pursuits and courage; Edward, industry; and finally the last volunteer, Paul, signifies science. Not only, therefore, does the group have to assess the likely contribution of each individual to their own areas but they also have to rank the areas in importance. They have to discuss their terminal values, or values about end states, and come to some agreement on their relative importance. Whether groups wish to maximise the greatest number of lives or generate the greatest contribution to society, their concern is not with the potholers as individuals but with the greatest good of the society beyond the cave.

Many groups involved in such discussions become bogged down and they begin to doubt that they can arrive at a consensus decision. At this stage many groups will have set up a complicated multi-attribute utility testing matrix in which they try to score the volunteers against the criteria of potential contribution to society. When they try to complete this table they begin to see that they have too little information about the volunteers to be able to draw any conclusions about their deservingness, need or contribution to society. This brings many people to the conclusion that the only fair method of making the decision is to use some arbitrary means such as drawing lots. In this way all the volunteers would be given an equal chance of being rescued. The arbitrary approach is adopted not just as a simple means of making the decision but also, more positively, as the proper way of reaching a decision. Random technique is seen as the only way of being fair to all the volunteers since all the other criteria available are tainted by ignorance and bias. The application of chance precludes the possibility of discrimination.

Occasionally groups see the decision they have to make as a potential threat to them as a group. They see that their decision could be criticised and challenged by other bodies. The media, for example, might disapprove of their decision and they could become the target of a vitriolic press campaign. They might wonder how the tabloid press would react if all the women were placed at the bottom of the rescue list. Groups applying this perception try to identify the constituencies which support each of the volunteers in the cave and give high priority to rescuing those with the most powerful support. One of the volunteers, for example, is the daughter of a foreign industrialist and the fear of causing a diplomatic incident could lead to her being among the first rescued. Although many middle management groups identify this as a possible criterion for selection, few finally use it in their decision. But it does represent an additional criterion for allocation.

Finally, in making their decision, groups obviously have views about the fitness as well as about the external validity of the criteria to be used. Fitness is contingent upon their personal competence values which are defined as their beliefs about how a job should be done properly. Competence involves a wish to avoid the shame they would feel if they used inadequate methods. People often interrupt the group's discussion, for instance, to declare that it is far too subjective and that more objective methods should be adopted. As one participant framed the sentiment, 'We have got to look at this logically. I don't think your own personal thoughts should come into it; shouldn't be judgmental.' The desire for objectivity is often expressed by the group using a rating mechanism in which the volunteers are numerically assessed against a number of criteria such as age, number of children, and so on. This simulacrum of objectivity seems to be a powerful sop to personal competence values. Similarly, there is often a debate about whether the need to arrive at a decision is more important than the quality of the decision. Many individuals object to using arbitrary methods because to do so would mean abdicating their responsibility to use all their abilities in arriving at a decision. A theologian who had played this exercise, for example, argued very fiercely with me about the morality of using arbitrary methods. Following the teachings of Thomas Aquinas he argued that as God had given us the gift of reason, then we were obliged to use that reason as best we can when making decisions such as those in the exercise. Not to do so, he felt, was a lessening of our spiritual worth. Seedhouse (1994: 120) also argues against the use of lotteries in the allocation of public services. Personal satisfaction with the method of making the decision is therefore another factor in the process of playing Cave Rescue.

Beyond the issue of satisfaction with process, an element of personal gain can also be isolated. The exercise, although only a simulation and an unlikely one at that, does create a degree of angst. And so it can be important to minimise the amount of anguished debate and to spread the responsibility for the final decision amongst all the participants. This is most easily achieved by taking a vote and going along with the majority decision. Voting creates a joint responsibility, and a diminished sense of personal liability, for the participants. As voting can be disguised as a rational means of summating preferences (which it isn't) as well as a conflict-reducing technique, it appeals to the sense of competency as well. In considering personal criteria for making resource allocation decisions therefore, we have to be aware of both competency values, using appropriate methods, and personal gain, in this case the emotional gain of a reduced sense of responsibility.

A large number of epiphanies gained from working within the public sector and with public sector managers have contributed to my views on the role of values in resource allocation. But it has been convenient to summarise these through a discussion of one particular management development exercise. The conclusion is that people use at least six different types of criteria in resource allocation. They are:

1 *Deservingness*: moral worthiness.
2 *Individual need*: assessments of individuals' needs in relation to the concept of a 'normal life'.
3 *Utility*: maximising contribution, maximising a function.
4 *Fairness*: equal opportunity and the application of arbitrary methods.
5 *Ecology*: minimising threats to the group.
6 *Personal satisfaction and gain*.

It is worth pointing out that each of these criteria can be described as a value. Edwards *et al.* (1981) developed a public sector Professional Values Scale questionnaire, based on Rokeach's definition of instrumental values (cf. figure 1.1). One of the items in their list of professional values was equity, which they defined as a belief in a just distribution of resources. The values of resource allocation listed above are, with the exception of the final one, interpretations of the notion of equity. That is to say they are all values concerned with the mechanism and outcome of resource distribution; they are not statements about ideal forms of society. Values (1) to (5) in the list are moral or interpersonal values but (6) is a competence or personal value. The other instrumental values listed in Edwards' scale, including items such as compromise, empathy, leadership, practicality and so on, constitute a checklist from which people can create their own conceptions of professional competency. Each of the six values of resource allocation represents a moral precept to be used in allocating resources.

The definition of the resource allocation criteria as values can be confirmed by looking for other factors which separate beliefs, which are about how the world works, from values which state how it should work. Eden *et al.* (1979) believed values are ineluctable; people cannot say why their value is better, 'it just is'. People also have a strong commitment to the values they hold. In fact, according to Young (1977), it is this cathexis (or sense of attachment) which forms the link between normative and existential beliefs, on the one hand and intentionality and action, on the other, within an individual's assumptive world. In plainer words, if people did not have a strong commitment to their values there would be no motivation to act in the world. Third, values are enduring and are not easily changed. All these characteristics of values can be observed in the way that people use the resource allocation values in exercises such as Cave Rescue. People will argue strongly for the use of a criterion in the exercise, but they are hard put to it to explain why, and they find it difficult to accept other criteria or methods.

Heuristics values and decision making

A case has been made that values are important in resource allocation and priority setting. It will now be argued that values are used heuristically. The term heuristic has a number of elements in its definition including: serving, or leading to, finding out, and depending upon assumptions based upon past experience. According to some definitions it also implies the use of trial and error. The function of a heuristic is to structure or simplify an issue in such a way that it becomes easier for a person to make a decision or choice. Very often this cognitive function will be performed unconsciously. For example, in the case of the recency effect in judging probabilities (Hogarth 1980), newly acquired information carries greater weight with the decision maker than information received earlier, without the thinker being aware of it, even though in formal terms it is equally pertinent to the decision.

There are a number of questions about the alleged heuristic use of values which need to be discussed. The first is whether heuristics are a common cognitive device and therefore likely to be found at work in resource allocation; the second is whether values can operate as heuristics; and the third is whether there is any evidence that heuristics are in play when resource decisions are made.

Visual perception provides an illustration of the heuristic nature of cognitive processes. The amount of experimental work done on visual perception is vast and any conclusions drawn here will seem banal and crude to anyone well versed in the subject. But it is relatively safe to conclude that seeing things is made possible by the existence of cognitive schemata which develop as people learn to see (Abercrombie 1960; Sekuler and Blake 1994). The brain seeks to relate incoming nervous impulses from the eyes to the schemata and if there is a fit then we 'see' a thing. If the data doesn't fit, then we fail to see it as is often the case with the 'Hidden Man' visual perception test (Abercrombie 1960: 25). In this test a picture appears to be a random mix of patches of dark and light but if the observer is told what to look for they can often see the face of a man. When people are told what they are looking at they frequently see it. If the visual data we receive are contradictory, as in the case of the 'distorted room' visual illusion, then the brain forces the data to coincide with the schemata (Abercrombie 1960: 50). This is achieved by editing out data which do not conform. Objectively, the distorted room is irregular yet we see it as normal. The impact of many paradoxical visual illusions is created by the effects of editing, interpretation and expectation in the processes of perception. The interpretation of these paradoxes implies that the brain gives a higher priority to fitting data to a schemata, and so making sense of it, than it gives to taking all the data into account and reformulating the schemata. This is an essential mechanism if the brain is not to be overloaded with incoming sensory data (Gregory 1987: 343).

The discussion of visual perception suggests that vision works heuristically in that filters are used to simplify incoming sense perceptions. It is worth using this insight to point up a particular characteristic of heuristic processes. In contrast to the rational model, which suggests that all the available data need to be collated and evaluated, a heuristic process emphasises an initial culling of the material using expectancy as a criterion. I am not a psychologist or a physiologist and must not push my limited knowledge of visual perception too far, but the findings reported suggest that heuristics may be a common cognitive device.

Arguments from the nature of visual perception to other cognitive processes have been made before. Kuhn (1970) in his study of science and scientific revolutions suggested that there is more than a sharing of words in the analogy between literal 'seeing' and the metaphorical use of 'seeing' as a synonym for understanding. He argues that communities of scientists who practise normal or mature science share common understandings. These are derived from shared exemplars which show how the world is to be classified and understood. These exemplars, together with other elements in a common disciplinary matrix, identify the scientific problems to be solved, how they are to be investigated and the likely outcomes. Described in this way the exemplars seem similar in character to heuristics because both have the function of rules of thumb and tricks of the trade. The foreknowledge of the likely outcomes (of scientific experiments, for example) caused by the use of a common disciplinary matrix is worth emphasising because it indicates another characteristic of heuristic thinking. If expectancy, or conformance to an existing framework, is used to edit the available data, then it would not be surprising if the conclusion drawn from the selected evidence supported the expectation. In consequence therefore, what scientists learn through these heuristics is an understanding of how past problem solving approaches can be adapted to solve the problems of normal science. Kuhn's analysis suggests that normal science is successful and cumulative because it is heuristic and edits complex reality into a relatively simple construct that can be approached on a problem solving basis.

When scientists work within such heuristic paradigms, anomalies develop between the accepted conventions and the occasional divergent experimental results, which cannot be explained from within the paradigm. When the tensions between these two become too great, scientific revolutions occur, and a new paradigm takes the place of the old. The replacement of Newtonian physics by the physics of relativity and quantum theory is one recent historical example. The new paradigm requires a different way of 'seeing' the world. Many scientists, fully imbued with the old paradigm, cannot make the transition. Kuhn argued that a change in paradigms is analogous to the gestalt perceptual shift observed in experiments on visual perception. The scientist who suddenly understands light as a particle rather than as a wave is experiencing something like the perceptual shift of the experimental volunteer in the anomalous cards experiment. In this experiment (Kuhn 1970: 63) the volunteers are exposed to a series of playing cards, some of which are odd (e.g. a black four of hearts). Initially the volunteers identified the cards as standard. But, as the length of exposure to the cards was increased, the volunteers at first became confused and hesitant but finally came to recognise new perceptual categories (black hearts) and to make correct identifications. However, there were some subjects who never learnt the new way of seeing. Kuhn proposed that the practice of normal science is a wider extension of these visual processes in which perceptual categories are learnt and used to understand the world. He admitted that the process of scientific discovery cannot be proved to be the same as the operation of categories of visual perception because of the lack of external standards for researching the paradigms of science. But Kuhn's discussion does suggest that heuristics may play a part in cognitive processes beyond visual perception.

The importance of heuristics is supported by researchers working in other areas. Heuristics have been identified in the making of judgements. Judgement is defined in this context as the assessment of the probabilities of outcomes or future events and Kahnemann et al. (1982) summarise much of the work in this field. Hogarth (1980) provides a more accessible and less technical introduction to the study of judgement. A number of heuristic devices have been found to operate in judgement which, in certain circumstances, can be the cause of bias or distortion. In illustration, it has been found that when people are faced with a range of data relevant to a problem, some of which appears to be direct and some of which is background, there is a tendency to ignore the latter. Look at the following problem.

A taxi was involved in a hit and run accident at night. Two taxi companies, the green and the blue operate in the city. You are given the following data
a) 85 per cent of the taxis in the city are green and 15 per cent blue
b) a witness identified the cab as blue. The court tested the reliability of the witness under the same circumstances that existed on the night of the accident and concluded that the witness correctly identified each of the two colours 80 per cent of the time and failed 20 per cent of the time.
What is the probability that the cab involved in the accident was blue rather than green?

(Tversky and Kahneman 1982: 156–7)

The correct answer, derived from Bale's theorem (which takes both items of data into account), is 0.41. Most people, when asked to answer this question however, ignore the data in (a) because it is considered too general and distant from the event, and produce an answer around 80 per cent which is based on the information given in section (b) alone. Other heuristics involved in judgement include the gambler's dilemma (or third time lucky) and anchoring and adjustment where the answer given is heavily influenced by an initial number given in the question (Kahneman *et al.* 1982: chapter 1).

In judgement, as well as in visual perception, heuristics operate to help the individual make sense of the world. Heuristics are ways of simplifying and reducing the complexity of the world so that solutions can be achieved. In the case of judgement, heuristics are preferred ways of tackling problems which enable people to extract from a mass of data that which will be useful in solving the problem. By simplifying they also increase the possibility of error and it is this which has allowed the cognitive researchers to devise experiments to identify the presence of heuristics.

The role of schemata and heuristics in human thinking must not, as Billig (1996: 152–85) warns, be overstated. He has argued that if the essence of thought is categorisation (by which he means the processing of information according to pre-existing heuristics or schemata), then thinking would be doomed to be either bureaucratic or bigoted. Someone who is enslaved by their own mental schemata are, like the souls in Dante's hell, obliged to live out the truth of their sins. In the sixth bowge of the *Inferno* Dante found the hypocrites, who were condemned to wear heavy cloaks that were gilded and lined with lead, and who were thereby constrained by their own showy facade. In a similar manner those, in modern times, who constantly carp against the frivolity of much public spending eventually cease to be able to discriminate between the good and the bad and they are condemned to suffer public embarrassment without ever understanding why.

Such an end was reached in Scarborough in 1997 in the 'luvvies and lavvies' row when some local councillors felt that the local authority's subsidy to the

new Stephen Joseph Theatre should not be increased because such expenditure would leave insufficient money to run the resort's public conveniences
(Wainwright 1997). When the issue came to council the subsidy was agreed
despite the noisy clamouring of the objecting councillors. The councillors who
featured in the media defending their town's public conveniences wondered
why people saw their stand as comic.

In cases where strong schematics lead to a bureaucratic rather than a bigoted
cast of mind, the penalty is a loss of creativity. In many public organisations
this can be seen in a failure to see public services through the eyes of the
client or customer. An example is when general practices will only give patients
a month's supply of medication on a repeat prescription because it would take
too long to re-set their computer's database to provided two months' supply
on each prescription. It will be argued, in this chapter and the next, that these
fates can be avoided because people can be involved in a constant debate, with
themselves and with others, about the appropriateness of their schemata and
heuristics. The constraints that, it might be thought, schemata and heuristics
impose are lessened by the availability of alternatives and by the arguments
people have with themselves about which heuristics or schematics apply to
particular circumstances.

People use heuristics to decide which evidence is relevant to cope with a
situation, and values can assume this heuristic, filtering, role. The next step is
to try to show that people use values in this way when making resource allocation decisions. It would seem, *prima facie*, very likely. Thompson (1967)
identified two variables in decision making: beliefs about outcomes (judgement)
and preference between outcomes (values). If, as we have seen, heuristics operate
to cope with the complexity of the former, it is likely they are also used to
cope with the difficulties of the latter. In addition, the effort that writers, such
as Fischer (1983), have had to put into 'understanding ... what it means to
be rational in the process of dealing with values and norms', when such things
are incommensurable, suggests that everyday ethical discourse must be facil-
itated by devices and heuristics which promote movement without necessarily
achieving philosophical rigour.

The resource allocation criteria are values, but are they used heuristically?
How can this question be answered? A few clues can be teased out by the use
of critical reflection on the Cave Rescue exercise already discussed. It is significant that in group discussions during Cave Rescue the initial talk is most
often about the appropriateness of different values rather than about collating
data about the volunteers. In the chronology of the debate, value questions
precede consideration of the data. It is tempting to see this as a microcosm of
the priority of values in individual decision making. Another observation, drawn
from consideration of the sequence of debates when groups play Cave Rescue,
is that people do approach the game on a trial and error basis. They try out
different approaches, they move back to earlier ideas when later ones seem
unsatisfactory, they do try to convince the group 'to try an idea out to see if

it gets us anywhere'. To this extent at least, groups can be said to use a heuristic approach when tackling the task.

The characters in the Cave Rescue exercise each pose a moral dilemma. Each of them has positive and negative aspects included in their thumbnail sketches. It is relevant to the heuristic use of values to see how people deal with the polarisation inherent in the descriptions of the volunteers they are given. Some material about each of the characters has to be edited out in order to allow other information to become salient and useful in making the necessary ranking decisions. A tentative suggestion is that the information edited out is chosen according to the resource allocation value being used. If this is the case, then it represents a heuristic use of values. Those who used a deservingness criteria tended to edit out all the positive features and to concentrate on the negative ones, such as Paul's record of sexual crime, Edward's Freemasonry (most public sector groups saw this as a negative characteristic) and so on. Those who used a utility (maximising contribution) criterion tended to edit out the negative and to accentuate the positive.

The process of editing just described can be explained by the theory of cognitive dissonance (Festinger 1957). This is the psychological theory that people become uncomfortable if they have incompatible ideas in their mind; and that when someone has competing thoughts they will reject notions from consideration until all the remaining ideas fit snugly together. Many people, for example, had difficulty with the volunteer Jobe, one of the characters in Cave Rescue, who was described as both a minister of religion and an active communist. They often averred that he could not be both, and they played down one aspect of his character. If cognitive dissonance explains why editing has occurred, the value heuristics might explain why a particular element in the cognitive polarity was suppressed. Let me take volunteer Paul as an example. Paul has been convicted of indecent assault. But he also has, in his working notes, details of a cheap cure for rabies. People who used the deservingness criteria assumed that the cure could be understood from the working notes (and that in any case he was bound to have a research assistant who understood and could continue the work) and there was, consequently, no barrier to using his anti-social behaviour in deciding his order of rescue. Other people, using the utility approach, assumed that it was impossible to make sense of the working notes. This allowed them, when making their decision, to ignore Paul's problem and concentrate on his potential contribution to society. People edited out, or rationalised into insignificance, that information which inhibited the application of their preferred values.

From my observation of people doing Cave Rescue there is also a suggestion that, not only are the resource allocation values used to identify the relevant information but also that the type of information presented to the groups can trigger the application of different values. As will be argued later, middle managers with whom I have used Cave Rescue tended not to give highest priority to the utility criteria, but they used it extensively in this exercise.

Most groups at some stage spent time assessing and rating each volunteer's contribution to society. This emphasis may have been a response to the fact that the data they are given in the exercise lends itself to this kind of analysis. A possible hypothesis is that, when there is a clash between the need to do a good job with the data available (competency value) and the importance of applying the right criteria (moral value), then competency might win. People will choose a criterion according to whether there is sufficient information to do a competent job, even if it is not a criterion they would normally favour.

In this section the ways people tackle resource allocation decisions have been identified. It is concluded that values are critical to the process; that a determinate number of resource allocation values can be identified which are used heuristically in the process of resource allocation.

Monksbane and feverfew

A management development exercise

My original interest in public sector resource allocation was how, as a manager developer, you might train people for the task. I felt there was a need for some kind of exercise or simulation that could be used to sensitise managers to the value issues implicit in priority setting. The monksbane and feverfew exercise was developed as a tool for management and organisational development, rather than as a research instrument. The exercise was designed to identify which of the resource allocation heuristics a person responds to. It is a little like the psychologists' tests for discovering the heuristics of judgement. Like them it is intended to identify how information is used in decision making. In the fields of the psychology of visual perception and probability judgement, objective tests have been developed to identify the presence and function of heuristics. Researchers have used test situations, for which there are objectively correct answers, and presented questions to respondents in such a way that, if heuristics are being used, the respondents will probably give an incorrect answer (Kahneman *et al.* 1982). Monksbane and feverfew differs from these tests in that there is no objectively correct answer against which respondents' answers can be compared. In the monksbane exercise responses are assessed by the extent of the reaction to predetermined cues.

As monksbane was produced for a training purpose I am diffident about the degree of confidence that can be placed in its results. The validity requirements of a training exercise are less rigorous than those of a research tool as an exercise is used mainly as a stimulus to discussion. In training courses analysis of the course members' responses to the instrument is the start of the process of learning. However, the exercise has generated results which are worth discussion. A copy of the instrument is given in an addendum to this chapter.

The construction of monksbane and feverfew

First the construction of the exercise will be explained. Monksbane and feverfew is concerned with allocating a budget of £70, 000 between two disease-screening and treatment programmes. In practice, in contrast to the situation in the exercise, managers in the health service are not required to make budget allocations between diseases but they do have to set priorities between patient groups, for example deciding whether ENT patients should receive priority over gynaecology patients (Gray 1997: 173). The respondents are given information about the two diseases sequentially and, after reading each piece of information, they are asked to make an allocation of the budget between the two diseases. The instrument consequently matches the typical way in which people receive information in organisations. Rarely do they have all the information they would like when they have to make a decision.

The information in each section is designed to provide a cue to a different value heuristic. From the respondents' decisions their degree of responsiveness to each of the value heuristics can be assessed. The scoring system classifies responses to each cue as high, medium or low. These ratings are derived partly from the internal logic of the data and partly from the analysis of the results from the first seventy-five completed questionnaires. The heuristics embedded in each section are discussed next.

Section 1

This section, which is based on a utilitarian perspective, gives information about the consequences of different allocation decisions. The information given allows respondents to calculate the allocation of budgets which will maximise the number of lives saved. The marginal number of lives saved as a result of spending an additional £10k on each disease is shown in table 2.1.

From this data, which can be approximated from the graph in section 1, it can be concluded that the allocation which maximises the number of lives

Table 2.1 Marginal benefits (additional lives saved) as a result of extra expenditure on monksbane and feverfew

Level of expenditure in £'000s	Additional lives saved Monksbane	Lives saved by a marginal expenditure of £10k Feverfew
10	2	26
20	2	18
30	2	12
40	2	7
50	3	7
60	2	5
70	4	5

saved is monksbane £0 and feverfew £70k. This is because, at all levels of expenditure, the marginal return of additional expenditure on feverfew is always higher than that of expenditure on monksbane. A decision to spend nothing on monksbane therefore is classified as a high response to utility. A decision to spend £10k on monksbane is classified as a medium response. Some people decide on £10k because, although they are aware that zero is the optimum answer, they either do not approve of totally neglecting a need or feel it is important to keep a 'seed corn' investment in monksbane in case it becomes necessary to extend the programme in the future. In either case this suggests that concerns other than the purely utilitarian are affecting their decisions. An expenditure on monksbane of £20k is also classed as medium. Anything above £20k is classed as low. The utility heuristic implies an ability to cope with numerical and graphical information. Not all the respondents are able to inter-pret the graph and they tend to claim that the data provided in section 1 are not the type of information they require to make the decision. In a real sense their preferences for other heuristics means they cannot 'see' the use or signi-ficance of the data given.

Section 2

This section provides information intended to trigger an individual need response amongst those who have a preference for this heuristic. Although the information given relates to populations, it is easily interpreted in an individual sense. It suggests that the needs of monksbane sufferers are greater than those of people afflicted with feverfew because the former have a greater chance of dying from the disease. It also states that medicine can do more to treat monks-bane than it can feverfew. People who are identified by screening as having monksbane have a 100 per cent chance of being cured. This fact appeals to the concern of those applying the individual need criterion to do all that can be done for people. A concern with professional technology and standards is an integral part of the individual need heuristic. Interestingly, just as some people reject the information in section 1, those who are committed to a utility heuristic cannot understand the importance or significance of the data in section 2. The scoring of responses is based on the distribution of actual scores. The more that is spent on monksbane, the higher the rating of the response to individual need.

Sections 3a and 3b

These sections invite a negative deservingness response by telling the respond-ents that those suffering from the disease (either feverfew or monksbane depending upon whether they have been directed to section 3a or 3b) have brought the disease upon themselves by their behaviour and way of life, and are, in addition, aggressive and troublesome people. Respondents who value the deservingness heuristic respond to this information by reducing the budgetary allocation for the disease. The responses to this question by the sample of respondents showed a tri-modal distribution. One group did not alter the budgetary allocation at all. They felt that moral judgements about the patients ought not to affect their decision. One group reduced their allocation by a third or less relative to their allocation in section 2 and the final group reduced it by more than a third. These groupings have been used to determine the classification of responses. Those who reduce their expenditure are classed as medium or high, dependent upon the extent of the cut, in their response to the deservingness cue.

Section 4

This section invites an ecological response. It tells the respondents that there are powerful constituencies, both internal and external, who are pushing for an increase in the budget for monksbane. The section is drafted to imply that the pressure is not simply self-seeking but reflects a general feeling in the community that more needs to be done for monksbane sufferers. If a respondent increases the budget, in relation to their previous decision, it is taken to mean that they accept the ecology heuristic. The actual responses from the sample are interesting. Some people represent the demands of the constituencies as political blackmail and believe it is wrong to react to such threats. Some go as far as to punish the constituencies by actually reducing the budget for monksbane. Many people simply refuse to respond and keep the budget at the same level. These two groups are categorised as low in their reaction to ecology. This response was often rationalised in the debriefing on the exercise by saying that the Monksbane Research Committee was doing a good job in raising more funds (although this may not be spent on screening or treatment) and that there was no need for the budget to be increased. Those who increased the budget tended either to raise it by £5k, which is the smallest adjustment allowed by the rules of the questionnaire, or by £10k or more. The former response is classified as medium because it represents a reaction to the ecology cue, but only by the smallest amount possible, whilst the latter is classified as a high response.

Sections 5 and 6

These two sections relate to the fairness heuristic. The statistical table in section five tells the respondent that if they distribute the budget, £60k to monksbane and £10k to feverfew then the sufferers from each disease will have an equal chance of being treated. This allocation of course would not mean that people with the two diseases would have an equal opportunity of being cured. But then the fairness heuristic is more interested in input than output. Respondents who decided to spend £50k or more on monksbane are classified as highly responsive to fairness. Those who increased their expenditure on monksbane in section 5, but not by so much as to bring it up to £50k, are classified as a medium response. There is of course a technical problem in the design of the exercise at this point. It is the problem of how to categorise the respondents who have increased their expenditure to £50k before they arrived at section 5. In response to this problem it is stated in section 5 that the current spending on monksbane is £30k. By asking the respondent to assume this, it is hoped that the anchoring and adjustment heuristic will cause the respondent to reconsider their expenditure on monksbane in the light of the cue for fairness given in the section. Section 6 offers another fairness cue by allowing respondents to opt for a queue as a means of allocating expend-iture. If people say yes to this option it is interpreted as a medium response to fairness. It implies people wish to be fair (a queue can be defined as a mech-anism for achieving fairness) without wishing to go to the extent of deliberately planning for fairness. However, given a random distribution of the sufferers of the two diseases within the community, the consequence of a queue would be to cause, on average, £60k of expenditure on monksbane and £10k on feverfew. The scoring mechanisms for sections 5 and 6 have been combined in the questionnaire.

Section 7

This section, which provides cues designed to trigger a personal gain heuristic, was added to the instrument after the first round of research had been done, as a result of feedback from respondents. Initially this section had been left out because the possible range of triggers for personal gain, such as professional interest, financial gain, political advantage, family benefits, and so on was too wide. But, within the context of the instrument, there was one trigger which narratively demanded inclusion: loyalty to family or friends. In this section respondents are told that someone close to them is suffering from the disease which they have given the least resource priority to. They are then invited to reconsider their budget allocation decision in the light of this new informa-tion. The purpose of this section is mainly to generate discussion in a training session and, as it was not included in the first version of the exercise, there are no results available for this section. The entire instrument is tied together by a simplified statistical and epidemiological model which is adapted from that developed by Creese and Gentle (1974) for their management game. The statistical model is shown in table 2.2.

There are a number of points to be made concerning the validity and inter-pretation of the results from the monksbane exercise. The instrument only measures the degree to which people respond to the various values. It does not identify a person's ranking of those values. It can show that somebody has high preferences for two particular values but gives little clue as to which one would predominate if there were a conflict between them.

Table 2.2 The statistical model underpinning the monksbane and feverfew instrument

	Monksbane	Feverfew
Incidence of the disease per 1,000 of the population per year	0.225	2.3
% of those screened who will still die of the disease	5%	38%
% of those unscreened who will die	100%	57%
% of the population that can be screened at given levels of expenditure		
£10,000	5	30
£20,000	10	51
£30,000	15	63
£40,000	20	72
£50,000	25	79
£60,000	30	86
£70,000	40	92

Formula

Formula for calculating lives saved for a given expenditure	$L = Ipx (Mu-Ms)$
L	Number of lives saved
I	Incidence of the disease per 1,000 population
P	total population (200,000)
x	% of the population screened
Mu	% of the unscreened group dying of the disease
Ms	% of the screened group dying of the disease

Source: Based on a model and simulation in Creese and Gentle (1974).

Monksbane and feverfew has two other main limitations. First, its content is too specific to one part of the public sector, the health service. Second, the open and narrative structure of monksbane makes it difficult to assess whether the meaning that respondents take from its various sections is the same as the meaning I thought I had encoded within them. Some other problems with the interpretation of results from monksbane stem from its longitudinal design and from its simulated nature. The longitudinal design assumes that people do not feel the need to be consistent, and are happy to revise their opinion as they move from section to section. The problem is partly that people may stick to their decision in section 1 throughout the exercise because they do not wish to be seen dithering. The bigger danger is that a cumulative anchoring and adjustment effect will develop as they proceed through the instrument so that changes become increasingly marginal towards the end of the exercise, irrespective of their actual ratings of the values. The simulated nature of the instrument is likely to result in respondents revealing espoused values rather than the ones they might actually apply. The notion of espoused values, or values that individuals would like to be known to hold, is a form of competency value. Competency values, ideas about the proper ways of doing things, may be more important than people's ideas about justice and equity. As will be argued in the conclusion of the book, incompetence is a greater fault for public officials than flawed beliefs about social justice.

Results from the exercise

As monksbane and feverfew was designed as a management development tool, the results obtained have come from groups of public sector middle managers with whom I was working as a management trainer in the late 1980s. The instrument was always used at the beginning of a training session with no preliminary tutorial input which might have affected the way in which people responded. In the first round of the exercise's use it was completed by seventy-five middle managers. When the results were analysed and the responses categorised as high, medium or low the distribution emerged as shown in table 2.3.

It can be seen from table 2.3 that the most popular heuristic was individual need. Fairness and utility show a similar pattern of response. The majority of middle managers gave both of them a medium response and only a small percentage rated them highly. Deservingness received a generally low response and ecology received an overwhelmingly low response. A simple weighting scheme, which gives a low response a weight of 0, a medium response a weight of 1 and a high response a weight of 2 enables the values to be put in rank order for the whole group (see table 2.4).

The seventy-five people surveyed using monksbane can be divided into two main subgroups, Social services and health service middle managers,' on the one hand, and mixed profession local government middle managers, on the other. There is a small overlap between the two because the local government group includes a few social services staff. As monksbane was completed anonymously it was not possible to separate these staff out. Monksbane was also completed by a small group studying for the Diploma in Management Studies (DMS) which included a majority of public sector middle managers. It is possible consequently to study the responses of these different groups to the value heuristics. This has been done by using the actual decisions made

Table 2.3 Responses to the value heuristics: % of managers responding high, medium or low to each value heuristic

Value heuristic	High response	Medium response	Low response
Utility	14.7	48	37.3
Individual need	37.3	45.3	17.4
Deservingness	18.7	18.7	62.6
Ecology	12	13.3	74.7
Fairness	12	57.3	30.7

Note: n = 75.

Table. 2.4 Ranking of middle managers' heuristic preferences

Heuristic	Rank	Weighting
Individual need	1	90
Fairness	2	61
Utility	3	58
Deservingness	4	42
Ecology	5	28

in monksbane rather than by the classification of responses as high, medium or low. The variables used are:

1 mean expenditure in section 1 (utility);
2 mean expenditure in section 2 (individual need);
3 mean decrease in expenditure in section 3 compared with section 2 (deservingness);
4 mean increase in expenditure in section 4 compared with section 3 (ecology);
5 mean increase in expenditure in section 5 compared with section 4 (fairness);
6 percentage of positive responses to section 6 (fairness).

The values named in the brackets are those for which the variables are held to be a measure of response. The results obtained from the three groups of middle managers are given in table 2.5.

Table 2.5 Analysis of the responses to the value heuristics by the three sub-groups in the sample of middle managers

Sample/variable	All managers	NHS and social service managers	Local govt managers	DMS managers
Mean exp. on sec. 1 (utility)	22.7	25.53	16.79	10.77
Mean exp. on sec. 2 (ind. need)	30.2	34.04	23.75	20.77
Mean decrease in exp. on sec. 3 (deservingness)	−6	−6.81	−4.64	−4.2
Mean increase in exp. on sec. 4 (ecology)	1.67	1.81	1.43	5.38
Mean increase in exp. on sec. 5 (fairness)	5.27	5.21	5.35	1.9
% positive response to sec. 6 (fairness)	31	34	25	23

Notes: Health and social services n = 47, local government n = 28, DMS n = 13.
Total public sector middle managers = 75, total n = 88.
All financial figures expressed in £000s.

These figures show that the three groups were similar in their responses to ecology, deservingness and fairness. The one exception perhaps was the DMS group's greater response to ecology; but the sample size for this group is very small and it may not be significant. There was, however, a greater difference in the responses to utility and individual need. The local government group was less responsive to need and more responsive to utility than the health and social services group. The DMS group was, in turn, more responsive to utility and less responsive to need than the local government group.

There could be many explanations for these results. One possibility is that the culture of local government (excluding social services) had a more utilitarian bias than that of health and social services organisations. Another factor could be the mix of professions represented in the two samples. Those in the health and social services groups are mostly from the caring professions, nursing and professions ancillary to medicine. One could perhaps predict that the professional training of these groups would stress individual need. The local government group contains a greater number of people from the 'analytic' professions such as architects, quantity surveyors, planners and administrators, who may have a greater utility component in their training. It is also interesting to speculate whether the management training received by the DMS group, with its private sector emphasis on optimisation, explains their high response to utility.

Although these results from monksbane are not representative or scientifically valid, the samples are too small and are not random, they do suggest that the value heuristics were a recognisable aspect of public sector managers' thinking about resource allocation and priorities. If they were not, then the exercise simply would not have worked as a management training technique. But it did work, and the exercise does provide information about the kinds of information and values that managers use when allocating resources.

The results presented above give a snapshot of the thinking of some public sector middle managers; before market principles had had considerable impact on their thinking. I have continued to use monksbane and feverfew as a training exercise. But as most of the courses on which the instrument has been used are mixed ones, including public and private managers, results cannot be given for a recent sample of public managers.

Decision making and the heuristic use of values

The findings from the monksbane and feverfew exercise suggest that, first, values about resource allocation are used heuristically by managers, and, second, that managers have different preferences between the heuristics. In short, the claim is that managers have ideas about the proper allocation of public services and resources which they use to edit and filter the available information concerning any particular decision they have to take. So, to give a practical illustration, if a manager has a preference for deservingness, but not for utility, evidence about the moral failings of a client will be taken into consideration, but data about the likely cost benefits of providing that client with a service will be sidelined. Once this has been done, a decision can be made by an inductive, and probably intuitive, leap from the springboard of the chosen heuristic. This is very different from the process that the rational model would propose and in the final section of this chapter I want to put into focus the differences between the heuristic and the rational decision making models. In particular, the ways in which values are treated within the heuristic approach will be contrasted with their treatment within the rational model. The concept of the heuristic approach includes aspects of the incremental, emergent and informal styles of planning and decision making discussed earlier in the chapter.

Formal theories suggest that values have a peripheral and evaluative role in decision making. The emphasis in these prescriptive rational theories is on the mechanism for the evaluation of iterations or options. When such decision techniques are used, possible solutions to a problem or alternative policy options are checked against the requirements of an ideal solution. The values or goals embedded in an ideal solution are a relatively unregarded area. Illustration of this claim can be found in the range of management science techniques available to decision makers. In optimisation models, such as linear programming for example, the value goal of the optimisation of output, within the parameters of the constraints, is implicit in the mathematical methods and it is taken for granted. In option evaluation techniques, such as multi-attribute utility testing, values are simply treated as an input to the system, in the guise of weighted choice criterion or performance standards. In Johnson and Scholes' (1993: 273) use of MAUT, to evaluate strategic options, the criteria are predetermined. In the academic field of public choice, which also draws its impetus from economic theory, the emphasis is on the technical problems of summating individual preferences (something of an academic conundrum since the publication of Arrow's theorem (Bailey 1995: 104)). If a means could be found of doing this, despite Arrow's proof of its impossibility, it would provide a way of avoiding direct consideration of values. Public choice theorists are concerned to account for political behaviour without recourse to the idea of values. This involves the use of algebra and mathematical models in attempts, for example, to describe people's demands for relational goods (which is a jargon term for social relationships) through an objective function (Uhlaner, reported in Stretton and Orchard 1994: 179). In Uhlaner's model people who co-operate with others are said to be seeking sociability, or relational goods, just as people desire any commodity. Once sociability is defined as a commodity then people's desire for it can be analysed using the notion of the rational egoist and econometric models of supply and demand. As Stretton and Orchard note:

> the suspicious simplicity of defining giving and taking alike as 'egoist', and collapsing such diversely selfish, co-operative and altruistic purposes into the single concept of 'relational goods', [is the reason

why] ... Uhlaner followed her admirable opening page about human sociability with thirty pages of algebra and games theory.

(Stretton and Orchard 1994: 179)

The ambition of formal technique is to master and minimise value differences and debate.

The role of values in formal theories of decision making can be analysed in more detail by focusing on the subjective expected utility (SEU) technique for decision evaluation (Wright 1984). According to this approach, when people make decisions they ought to define a matrix of possible future scenarios, which includes both the alternative decisions they could take and the different circumstances they might find themselves in. Their next step should be to evaluate the options according to their implicit value to the decision maker and in the light of the probability of the differing circumstances which might apply when the decision is implemented. The technique therefore uses a five-stage sequence for decision making. First, the nature of the decision is mapped out by identifying the possible options. The situations in which these options might be acted upon are then defined, and probabilities are assigned to them. Penultimately, utilities (or values) are attached to these outcomes. Finally, all the analytic elements are consolidated arithmetically to arrive at a best answer.

Let me give a simple example to illustrate this procedure. The hypothetical problem I will use is choosing where to go on holiday in Britain. Assume there are three possible options, a seaside holiday, a countryside holiday in a national park or a holiday in one of the holiday parks that boast sub-tropical swimming paradises which maintain a constant high temperature (whatever the weather outside). The circumstances in which these options have to be evaluated inevitably refers to the variability of British weather. For ease of illustration three weather conditions are defined and their likelihoods are expressed as probability numbers. All this information is shown in table 2.6.

The third stage of the SEU process is represented by the figures in the matrix. These are subjective utility figures which express the different values the decision maker puts on all the possible outcomes. The higher the number, the more that situation is valued. Stormy weather in the countryside is preferable, according to this decision maker, to similar conditions at the seaside. In the last stage the figures are manipulated to produce the subjective expected utility

Table 2.6 An illustration of subjective expected utility technique

	Storms	Dull drizzle	Fine and sunny
Probabilities/options	0.2	0.5	0.3
Holiday park	90	80	70
Seaside	10	50	90
Countryside	15	60	80

of each of the three options. In the case of the holiday park option the calculation is $(0.2 \cdot 90) + (0.5 \cdot 80) + (0.3 \cdot 70) = 79$. The SEUs of the other two options are 54 and 57 respectively. As the holiday park scores highest, that is the preferable option. From a strict perspective this analysis should be applied to all possible options. The satisficing approach sacrifices some of the rational purity of this sequence by only testing a limited number of options, but it still uses values evaluatively. The satisficer evaluates single options iteratively until a good enough solution is found rather than evaluating a large set of options to identify the best solution.

SEU can stand vicariously for all formal and rational decision making methods, and it can be used to illustrate how values figure in such techniques. The first observation is that there is a clear distinction in such techniques between judgement and evaluation. Judgement means assessing the probabilities of future circumstances and does not involve value considerations whereas evaluation does involve values. To use SEU people must apply judgement before they evaluate and make a mentally discrete use of their preferences and values each time they make a decision, keeping them out of the way until the time comes to make an evaluation of the options. Intuitively this seems unlikely, and predictably researchers have found SEU to be a normative rather than an empirical theory (Wright 1984).

Simon (1983) went as far as locating SEU in Plato's heaven of ideals, implying that actual decision making is an ill-focused shadow of the theory. In particular, and this is the second observation on the role of values in formal decision making, he criticised the sleight of hand by which values are brought into consideration.

> The SEU model finesses completely the origins of the values that enter into the utility function; they are simply there, already organised to express consistent preferences.
>
> (Simon 1983: 14)

SEU implies that values are brought out at the end of the mental process unsullied by the preceding analytic thoughts. And their role is to discriminate between a series of possible outcomes. Other writers, from different academic fields, have emphasised the poverty of this approach to values in decision making by exploring the ways in which people reason about ethical and value-based dilemmas. Writers such as Snell (1993) have stressed the importance of argumentation and debate about the selection of appropriate values, or principles of ethical reasoning, in decision making.

The third observation on the role of values in formal procedures is that they are seen within a consequentialist rather than a deontological perspective (Mackie 1977: chapter 7). Deontology is the study of principles; it implies that one ought to do what is right even if the action might cause unwanted social or political consequences. Consequentialist approaches to ethics, in contrast, judge the correctness of an action according to the extent it will help achieve a valued end or goal. From this perspective a value is seen as a continuous variable that can be maximised, and therefore the proper concern of a decision maker is to obtain the most of a value that can be achieved. But the deontological perspective is concerned with principles and doing the right thing irrespective of that action's consequences. In this case, a value is a discrete and not a continuous variable, a value, in the guise of principle, has either been met or it has not. An example can be given from multi-attribute utility testing. When this technique is used, as has been discussed, a final utility score is calculated for each of the options and the one with the highest score is regarded as the best. Now it may well be that one of the performance standards is the extent to which the options would make staff's jobs tougher or less satisfactory. Within MAUT an option could score poorly against this criteria but still score favourably overall because it rates highly against other criteria. If a deontological perspective were applied, however (and the principle adopted was that things should not be made worse for staff), then the decision maker would argue that, although an option scored favourably in aggregate, we should not choose the option because it has failed to satisfy a crucial principle.

The fourth observation is that formal methods proceed by a process of elimination rather than design. Rational methods can only be used where the problem can be structured; and the most common structure is a list of options or alternatives from which unsatisfactory options can be identified and eliminated. The last remaining option, as the evaluation proceeds, is the optimum choice. There are some management science techniques, such as simulation or Monte Carlo methods, which do not operate by elimination. But it is characteristic of these methods that they do not generate optimum solutions; they merely, but interestingly, forecast the practical consequences of taking certain decisions.

Decision making by design, rather than by elimination, is similar to the 'Ready-Fire-Aim' approach reported by Peters and Waterman (1982: 119). Using this process involves taking initial actions on a problem based on nous or intuition. The feedback that results from that action is then used to decide whether the action should be continued, modified or abandoned, and this in turn leads to a continuing cycle of trial and error. This style of thought fits easily with the idea of heuristics, a term which includes amongst its manifold definitions the idea of trial and error. In monksbane and feverfew, for example, the structure of the exercise allows respondents to iteratively change their mind as additional information and its value consequences are presented to them. There are certain requirements for this kind of decision making; there should be an emphasis on minimising risks and trying to arrange that actions can be undone if they are not useful. Actions, from a design approach perspective, should expand the range of future possible actions and not restrict them. These ideas of incremental decision making are ubiquitous, particularly in the area of public policy making (Lindblom 1959; Dryzek 1983), but they have seldom been seen as a serious challenge to the bullet pointed procedures preferred by trainers and text book writers.

The argument of this chapter is that values are used heuristically rather than evaluatively. Such use emphasises cognitive expediency, focusing on usable, rather than on optimal or satisficing, solutions. It also suggests that values are the basis of heuristic thinking in the case of resource allocation decisions. Used heuristically, values are the starting point of decision making. They act as a filter or editor which selects from all the available material and allows people to arrive at solutions compatible with their beliefs. The contrast between this view of decision making and the formal, rational view is generalised in table 2.7.

The argument pursued in this chapter can be summarised as follows:

- that, despite arguments that officials and managers should not be involved in policy making and decisions involving the balancing of competing values, there is a general agreement that officials and managers do have the right to engage in debates about values;
- many argue that officials' and managers' involvement with values should be restricted to applying them in formalised and mathematical techniques for decision making and policy analysis;
- that research has suggested that officials and managers use values in a much more argumentative, intuitive and political manner in their work;
- that values are used heuristically in the process of decision making;

Table 2.7 The contrasts between the rational and the heuristic approaches to decision making

The rational approach	*The heuristic approach*
Values enter at the end of the decision making process	Values are used at the start of the decision making process
Values are used as yardsticks for formal evaluation	Values are used to filter and categorise the available information
Values are taken as a given	Values are the subject of argument
Values are variables to be maximised	Values are principles which can trigger a veto
Emphasises the quantity of options evaluated	Emphasises the quality and flexibility of options
Uses a process of elimination	Uses a 'design' process moving incrementally towards an ill-defined end
Analysis	Synthesis
Uses procedures and algorithms	Uses informal cognitive processes
Formal	Intuitive

- and that the values/heuristics used by officials and managers can be identified as:
  - individual need
  - deservingness
  - fairness
  - utility
  - ecology
  - personal gain and competence.

The rest of the book will explore the allocation of public services and resources to look for the traces and consequences of the value heuristics discussed in this chapter.

ADDENDUM
MONKSBANE AND FEVERFEW

A diagnostic instrument
about values in public sector resource allocation

Introduction

In this questionnaire you imagine yourself to be a manager responsible for screening programmes for two diseases: feverfew and monksbane.

You have a total budget of £70,000 (£70k) to spend on these two programmes. In this questionnaire you will be presented with some initial information and asked to say how you would divide up the budget between the two diseases. On the subsequent pages you will be given additional information, and for each additional piece of information you will be asked to review the use of the budget available to you.

- All the information you will be given is mutually consistent, i.e. information at the end of the questionnaire will not invalidate earlier information.

- Answer the questions in order.

- Once you have answered a section please do not return to it later and change it.

- There are no 'right' answers to the questions in this questionnaire. It's all a matter of your own values.

- Please make your allocations of the budget between monksbane and feverfew in units of £5,000 (£5k), i.e. £0, £5k, £10k and so on.

Section 1

The graph below tells you the number of lives that will be saved as a consequence of different levels of expenditure on the two diseases. The graph is based upon sound research conducted by the Paracelsus Epidemiological Institute. You need have no doubt about its accuracy.

The result of splitting the £70k equally between the two diseases, for example, would be:

No. of lives saved as a result of spending £35k on monksbane   7
No. of lives saved as a result of spending £35k on feverfew   <u>59</u>

Total no. of lives saved   <u>66</u>

Feverfew and monksbane affect men and women equally and also affect the same age group and social classes.

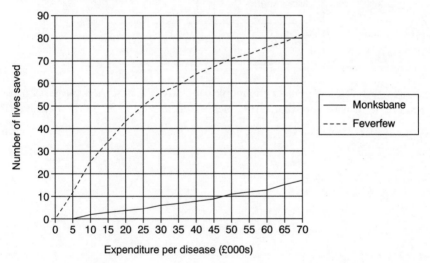

Relationship between money spent on each disease and the number of lives saved

How much of the £70k do you think ought to be spent on monksbane?

£

When you have written your decision in the box please turn over to the next page.

Section 2

Monksbane is a much more dangerous disease than feverfew. If people with early signs of the disease are not identified through screening and treated, there is a certain (100 per cent) chance they will die of the disease. Feverfew, on the other hand, can be fatal but the chances are smaller. If sufferers with feverfew are not identified and treated there is only a 57 per cent chance that they will die of the disease.

There have been great advances in the medical understanding of monksbane and only 5 per cent of people treated die from the disease. The death rate amongst patients treated for feverfew is 38 per cent.

Assume that currently no money at all is being spent on monksbane. How much of the £70k do you think ought to be spent on monksbane and how much on feverfew, as a result of the information given on this page?

Monksbane	£
Feverfew	£

If the figure you have put in the monksbane box is £10k or less please turn to section 3b. If it is more than £10k, please turn to section 3a on the next page.

Section 3a

Feverfew is a disease that can be caught by anybody. Monksbane, however, is much more likely to be contracted by people with certain habits and lifestyles which they have chosen to adopt. Another characteristic of monksbane is the tendency for sufferers to be of a particular personality type. They are of a choleric disposition: aggressive, demanding and ungrateful. This relationship has been well researched by the eminent group of scientists from St Barty's who have recently published their work on personality and disease. This relationship has always been well known in popular folklore. It is the origin of the disease's name since sufferers were the bane in the life of monk almoners and hospitallers in medieval monasteries.*

Bearing in mind this information, how much do you now think ought to be spent on monksbane?

£

Please turn to section 4 when you have put your decision in the box.

Note: *Adam of Barnsley (1372) *De Naturae et Nomine Opus Malleficarum.*

Section 3b

Monksbane is a disease that can be caught by anybody. Feverfew, however, is much more likely to be contracted by people with certain habits and lifestyles which they have chosen to adopt. Another characteristic of feverfew is the tendency for sufferers to be of a particular personality type. They are of a choleric disposition: aggressive, demanding and ungrateful. This relationship has been well researched by an eminent group of scientists from St Barty's who have recently published their work on personality and disease. However, this relationship has always been known in popular folklore. As Victorian doggerel had it:

'e's a gringer and as poisonous as yew is the man what's got feverfew.*

Bearing in mind this information, how much do you now think ought to be spent on feverfew?

£

Please turn to section 4 on the next page when you have put your decision in the box above.

Note: *F. Smith Jr (1978) *Semiotics and Ethnomethodology of Disease in Victorian England*, California: Albertus Publishers.

Section 4

A recent television programme in the 'Medicine and Society' series has high-lighted the problems of monksbane sufferers and it has caused a tremendous increase in the donations received by the MRC (Monksbane Research Committee). This money is only available for research and cannot be used for screening or treatment. There is a very powerful national pressure group representing the needs of monksbane victims and they have the ear of several key members of your Community Health Council (a consumer watchdog body). In addition, your organisation employs a number of consultant medical staff who have made their reputations developing treatments for monksbane.

There is pressure from these groups to spend *more* on monksbane than you are currently spending, i.e. that is more than you have agreed to spend on monksbane in any of the previous sections.

Bearing in mind this new information, how much of the £70k do you now think ought to be spent on monksbane?

£

When you have entered your decision in the box please turn to the next page.

Section 5

Your research indicates that the percentage of the population that can be screened for each disease, and therefore the proportion of sufferers from each disease that can be identified and treated, is as shown in the following table.

Amount spent on screening (£K)	% of feverfew sufferers identified	% of monksbane sufferers identified
10	30	5
20	51	10
30	63	15
40	72	20
50	79	25
60	86	30
70	92	40

This means that an expenditure of £10k on feverfew and £60k on monksbane will enable you to treat 30 per cent of the sufferers from both diseases. To put it in other words, people with the two diseases will have an equal chance of being identified and treated.

Assume that at present the £70k available is split between the two diseases as follows:

Feverfew: £40k.
Monksbane: £30k.

Bearing in mind this new information, how much of the £70k do you now think ought to be spent on monksbane?

£

Please turn to the next page when you have written your decision in the box.

Section 6

It would be possible to treat the £70k budget for feverfew and monksbane as a combined budget and not allocate it between the two diseases. That means you would treat feverfew and monksbane sufferers as they presented themselves through their GPs until the budget ran out (if it did).

Would you take up this option to run a combined budget and work on a first come/first served basis?

Please tick the appropriate box.

Yes	
No	

Section 7

What is your current allocation of the £70k between the two diseases?

Monksbane [   ]   Feverfew [   ]

If you are planning to spend most of the £70k on feverfew, complete this section.

You have just been told that someone very close to you is suffering from monksbane.

How would you now allocate the budget between the two diseases?

Monksbane		Feverfew	

If you are planning to spend most of the £70k on monksbane, complete this section.

You have just been told that someone very close to you is suffering from feverfew.

How would you now allocate the budget between the two diseases?

Monksbane		Feverfew	

Monksbane and feverfew: an interpretation

People have preferences about the criteria to be used in resource allocation whether they are involved in decision making, in the implementation or are on the receiving end of the policies. These different criteria, or heuristics, can be classified under the following six headings.

1   *The deservingness heuristic*: This heuristic divides resources between groups and individuals according to the resource provider's classification of them as either deserving or undeserving. This is a moral judgement. Groups or individuals who are thought to have created their own problems or to be demanding and difficult are often labelled undeserving.

2   *The individual need heuristic*: This heuristic responds to individual needs. It is not concerned with the overview of a service but with meeting the needs of individuals. Needs are identified and ranked in importance by using professional judgement. It does not make moral judgements about individuals.

3   *The fairness heuristic*: This heuristic is more concerned with treating all clients fairly than with the provision of services to individuals. Fairness is about standardisation and equal access to services by all clients. Its aim is to avoid accusations of unfairness. Fairness can be planned or created by arbitrary means (such as queues) in which all have equal probability of receiving service irrespective of their background and situation.

4   *The utility heuristic*: This heuristic is concerned with maximisation of output, that is to say, with efficiency and effectiveness. It deals with the notion of the common good rather than with individual need. Generating the greatest amount of 'good' is more important than the way it is distributed amongst the community.

5   *The ecology heuristic*: This heuristic allocates resources by taking into account the demands of the various interest groups involved with the service. The greatest weight will be given to the most significant or powerful groups. The success of the allocation is measured by the extent to which it meets the needs of these groups, not according to objective or professional criteria.

6   *The personal gain heuristic*: In the case of this heuristic resources are allocated in a way that will create personal gain for the staff involved. In extreme cases this gain could be financial, but more often it will be a gain in power, job satisfaction, working conditions, or the achievement of a personal objective.

Scoring and interpretation of monksbane and feverfew

Evaluate your answers by working through the boxes below.

Section 1

How much did you decide to spend on monksbane? ☐

- If it is zero (£0) you score *high* on *utility*

- If it is £20k or less you score *medium* on *utility*

- If it is more than £20k you score *low* on *utility*

Section 2

How much did you decide to spend on monksbane? ☐

- If it is £15k or less you score *low* on *individual need*

- If it is more than £15k but less than £35k you score *medium* on *individual need*

- If it is £35k or more you score *high* on *individual need*

If you answered section 3b ignore this box.

Section 3a

How much did you decide to spend on monksbane? [ ]

- If this is the same amount as you decided in section 2 you score *low* on *deservingness*

- If you have reduced the amount on monksbane by a third or less compared with the amount in section 2 you score *medium* on *deservingness*

- If you have reduced the amount spent on monksbane by more than a third compared with the amount you spent in section 2 you score *high* on *deservingness*

If you answered section 3a ignore this box.

Section 3b

How much did you decide to spend on feverfew in section 2? [ ]

How much did you decide to spend on feverfew in section 3b? [ ]

- If the amounts are the same you score *low* on *deservingness*

- If you have reduced the amount spent on feverfew by a third or less compared with the amount in section 2 you score *medium* on *deservingness*

- If you have reduced the amount spent on feverfew by more than a third compared with the amount in section 2 you score *high* on *deservingness*

Section 4

How much did you decide to spend on monksbane? ☐

- If this is the same as you spent on monksbane in sections 3a or 3b you score *low* on *ecology*

- If the amount is £5k more than you spent in sections 3a or 3b you score *medium* on *ecology*

- If the amount is £10k or more greater than you spent in sections 3s or 3b you score *high* on *ecology*

Sections 5 and 6

How much did you decide to spend on monksbane in section 5? £ [   ]

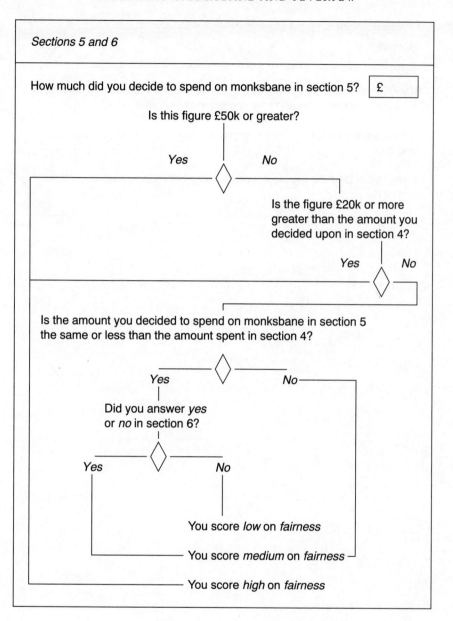

Is this figure £50k or greater?

Yes　　　*No*

Is the figure £20k or more greater than the amount you decided upon in section 4?

Yes　*No*

Is the amount you decided to spend on monksbane in section 5 the same or less than the amount spent in section 4?

Yes　　*No*

Did you answer *yes* or *no* in section 6?

Yes　　*No*

You score *low* on *fairness*

You score *medium* on *fairness*

You score *high* on *fairness*

Section 7

If you increased the sum spent on the disease which affects you personally, then you score *high* on *personal competence* and *gain*

If you kept the allocation the same you are *low* on *personal competence* and *gain*

If you decreased the allocation you are *very low* on *personal competence* and *gain*

3

THE APOLOGETICS OF PUBLIC SECTOR ORGANISATIONS

Six resource allocation heuristics have been identified which, in this chapter, will be studied in more detail. The chapter is called 'The apologetics of public sector organisations' because the values discussed are the basis of many of the justifications of the public sector. Public sector organisations can claim they are more effective than markets, as a means of allocating public services, because they institutionalise the values embedded in the resource allocation heuristics.

Each of the heuristics will be reviewed in turn, and in each section the heuristic will defined more carefully than has so far been done. Examples of the application of the heuristics will be taken from the literature and used to explore the complexities and implications of the different values. The heuristic values are not only found in modern British public administration. Whilst the welfare state was an invention of the postwar era, the question of resource allocation has always been an issue for governments and, consequently, the range of heuristic values has always been available to politicians and administrators. Most of the illustrations in this chapter come from contemporary experience in the UK but, to give some idea of the application of the heuristics in other times and places, examples from the politics and administration of India in the nineteenth century and the early twentieth century are given. This choice of other time and place is not as perversely eclectic as it might seem, there are many links between the Indian and the British systems of public administration.

On a technical note the reader will become aware that the term 'professional' is used frequently in this chapter and the next. This term is a source of great controversy for organisational theorists; however, it is used here only in a descriptive sense to mean those staff in the public services who need a formal qualification to be able to work in their chosen field. It is therefore a shorthand expression for doctors, nurses, librarians, surveyors, civil engineers, environmental health officers, and so on.

Deservingness

The medieval salt cellar is a symbol of the heuristic of deservingness because its position on the medieval trestle marked the dividing line between the worthy and the unworthy. The deservingness heuristic similarly divides people into two moral classes, the deserving and the undeserving. When resources are being distributed according to the deservingness heuristic, the favourable allocation is given to the former and the unfavourable portion to the latter. Deservingness as used in social policy is an Edwardian concept. This traditional view saw the provenance of all poverty in individual moral failure and indolence. The growing depersonalisation and alienation of social life, caused by nineteenth-century industrialisation, made this view untenable and a distinction was drawn between the deserving poor, brought low by social and economic factors beyond their control, and the undeserving poor, whose failure was of their own doing. When pensions were first introduced in Great Britain in 1909, for example, it was on the basis of deservingness, and there were clauses to ensure that the feckless did not receive them (Bruce 1968).

New possibilities for morally classifying people have emerged during this century. People can be allocated to moral categories according to whether they are, on the one hand, greedy, truculent and ungrateful or, on the other, meek, humble and full of gratitude. Political ideology also offers opportunity for moral classification. Groups can be classified as deserving or not according, for example, to their relationship to the means of production. The proletariat in consequence are either, depending upon preferred political ideology, deserving, because they are victims of forces beyond their control or they are undeserving, because they have failed to learn the lessons of Samuel Smiles by moving themselves up through the social strata by dint of hard work. The final moral criterion is group membership. The deserving person is one of us; the undeserving person is an outsider.

Deservingness concentrates upon the moral autonomy of people and allocates services and resources accordingly. In its negative aspect deservingness implies a sense of moral superiority on the part of the decision makers. Such was the case in the British empire in the early twentieth century. It was at this time (1927) that Katherine Mayo published a book which caused a storm of protest because it attributed the poverty, disease and ignorance found in India to the early sexual incontinence allegedly encouraged by Indian social customs. She ended her second chapter as follows:

> Given men who enter the world physical bankrupts out of bankrupt stock, rear them through childhood in influences and practices that devour their vitality; launch them at the dawn of maturity on an unrestrained outpouring of their whole provision of creative energy in one single direction; find them, at an age when the Anglo-Saxon is just coming into the full glory of manhood, broken nerved, low spirited, petulant ancients; and need you, while this remains unchanged, seek for other reasons why they are poor and sick and dying and why their hands are too weak, too fluttering, to seize or to hold the reins of Government.
>
> (Mayo 1927: 38)

If politicians and public administrators had views such as these about the people they administered, then any resources directed to such subjects could only have been an act of charity, provided out of benevolence to the undeserving. Mayo's statement is cruelly prejudiced but it was made only seventy years ago. It can be contended that this type of argument, perhaps less extreme, is still in use in resource allocation. The arguments, if not the language, are not far removed from more recent theories such as the cycle of deprivation (Joseph 1975), which stressed the inadequacy of some parents of large families. In a more recent policy debate, about the funding of treatment for sufferers from AIDS, similar moral criteria could be detected. Academic writing on the subject has been concerned with whether the treatment of AIDS sufferers is cost-effective and with the opportunity cost of such treatment (Eastwood and Maynard 1990). But there were arguments put forward, particularly in the press, which suggested that AIDS patients should receive 'less eligibility' treatment because they had visited the illness upon themselves through homosexual behaviour or drug abuse. It is, perhaps, the effect of deservingness that accounts for the different public perceptions of the plights of haemophiliacs, who acquired the disease through the necessary treatment of their primary illness, and that of homo-sexuals who, more likely, acquired it as a result of chosen behaviours. Whilst the government was initially curmudgeonly in the question of compensation for haemophiliacs, who had become HIV positive from being treated with infected blood products, public opinion clearly thought they should be compensated quickly (Mihil 1990). There was a popular temptation to see haemophiliacs as deserving, and homosexuals as undeserving, and to fund their programmes accordingly.

The validity of the deservingness heuristic is contingent upon the validity of the moral precepts used in its application. This is why its use, as in the case of Mayo and the funding of AIDS, is always a matter of controversy as the justice of the ethical standards being used is challenged. Another recent example was the controversy sparked by John Redwood's condemnation of young single mothers who were living on state benefits and were showing no interest in entering into a stable relationship (Wintour and Schwarz 1993). The debate which followed was about the validity of the ethical standards Redwood had applied.

Deservingness has a positive as well as a negative aspect. It can lead to people receiving better than anticipated services as well as cutting back on provision. It is deservingness which causes staff to give more effort and atten-tion to the deserving client than is actually required by their employers. At a more general level it may well have been moral criteria which led the early direct labour organisations in local authorities to build council housing to a high standard and to become self-conscious exemplars of good employment practices (Langford 1982). Public care of the deserving may be exemplary, but it can also be condescending. Raymond Urwin, who designed model workmen's dwellings for the employees of manufacturer and reformer Joseph Rowntree, decided that space given to a parlour would be better used by incorporating it in a bigger and lighter living room/kitchen.

> There can be little doubt that until any cottage has been provided with a living room large enough to be healthy, comfortable and convenient, it is worse than folly to take space from that living room where it will be used every day and every hour to form a parlour, where it will be used only once or twice a week.
>
> (Aslett and Powers 1986: 265)

The deserving British workman actually proved undeserving in their irrational attachment to their parlours; and when Urwin designed houses for munitions workers in 1916 he was obliged to leave room for parlours.

The focus of the deservingness heuristic on behavioural choices, which cause people to bring incapacity or misfortune upon themselves, has been given a formal economic description by LeGrand (1984, 1987, 1991) and discussed by Pereira (1989), in relation to the problem of equity in healthcare. He argues that:

> if an individual's ill health results from factors beyond his or her control then the situation is inequitable; if it results from factors within his or her control then it is equitable.
>
> (LeGrand 1987: 114)

The analysis is shown graphically in figure 3.1, which plots an individual's condition of health (h) against the volume of health-harming activities such as overeating, drinking, smoking, working in a stressful environment (q). It is assumed that it is possible for an individual to trade off between the two. But for each individual there is also a boundary of constraint which defines the feasible area in which choices can be made; this may vary between individuals. For two individuals, A and B, the choice boundary is the same and is represented in the figure by RT. A and B have different preferences between health and harmful activities, both of which can provide utility or pleasure and these are shown by the two indifference curves Ua and Ub. The exercise of these preferences and the equilibrium points that emerge show that A has a lower health status than B but this is equitable because it is the consequence of free and informed choice. However, a third individual (C) is introduced who is, according to LeGrand, poorer and whose health therefore is likely to deteriorate much more quickly as he or she engages in health-harming activity. The choice boundary for C consequently is reduced as described in the diagram by RX. The preference order shown by C is the same as B's but, because of the different choice frontier, C's equilibrium point at h_c reveals that C will have worse health than B. LeGrand argued that the difference in health status between B and C is inequitable because it arises by chance as shown in the

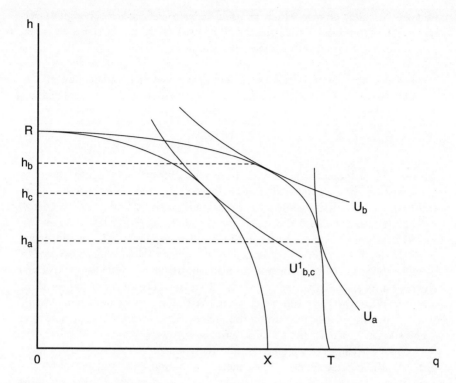

Figure 3.1 Equity as choice
Source: LeGrand (1991).

different choice sets available to the two people. Clearly, in this analysis, A is undeserving, when compared with B, but C is deserving when compared with A and B. The analysis makes the point well that deservingness and undeservingness are relative and not absolute categories.

Research has been published which shows how the use of the deservingness heuristic can find a place in public sector organisations. Social security benefits offices were an interesting case. The staff were often young non-graduates with very little training when compared with, say, qualified social workers. Stevenson, reported by Brown (1975), argued that they are a hybrid group whose training attempts an uneasy combination of bureaucratic and professional styles. The predominant ethos in benefits offices, however, is an administrative one focused on the implementation of policy rules. But as Howe (1985) discovered, during research in a Northern Ireland supplementary benefits office, staff also used a deservingness criteria when determining need. The nice, polite and quiet clients were seen as deserving and the ungrateful and truculent were regarded as undeserving, especially in relation to the granting of single payments. (Since Howe's study, single payments have been replaced

by loans, a policy change which in itself seems to reflect a deservingness perspective.) Howe argued that this labelling was done on the basis of moral
evaluation rather than on evidence. For staff:

> the average client is not perceived as a pawn manipulated by an
> oppressive and complex system, but as someone who actively and
> cunningly exploits it; he is someone who requires restraint rather than
> encouragement.

(Howe 1985: 64)

This view had the consequence of placing the obligation to identify need on
the client and not on the staff. In the ritual of the client interview therefore,
staff responded to the requests for benefits made by the clients but did not seek
to identify further benefits they might be eligible to receive. The interview was
mostly concerned with acquiring information from the client, not imparting
it. Similarly, the counter staff did not hand out the available explanatory leaflets
as willingly as Howe thought proper. Such an ideology and culture explained
the antipathy staff felt towards professional social workers. DHSS staff believed
social workers saw their role as determining the extent of need, and finding
ways of meeting it, not restraining the greedy. Social workers, no doubt, were
seen as a soft touch by the social security staff.

Some of the causes of a preference for deservingness were suggested by Howe.
One was the official management concern to minimise the number of fraudu-
lent claims. This bias led to the suspicion that fraud was rife. 'Everyone's doing
it; it gets into your head that everyone is doing it', as one officer reported to
Howe. Staff were encouraged to study claimants' demeanour for clues of mal-
feasance. But, predominantly, deservingness was adopted by staff as a defence
against the pressures of their jobs. Constant, unremitting and demanding contact
with clients could be coped with by restricting real effort and concern to the
deserving. If, to the lack of time, was added heavy workloads, low pay, lack of
management appreciation of staff, rapidly changing regulations, 'foul breath,
foul manners, foul language' and even, occasionally, violence from clients, then
a morally discriminating response from staff was a necessary defence mechanism. It reflected the staff's belief that they were not dealing with clients whose
only role was to be passive, but were involved in a negotiation with tricky and
manipulative people. The heuristic of deservingness was an ideological statement of the benefit office staff's independence and status in relation to the
client. An independence that for them could not be buttressed by the symbolism
of professional qualifications.

The use of deservingness has also been identified by researchers studying
housing services. One of the consequences of the use of deservingness is that
eligibility is not assessed solely on the basis of need. For example, it was found
that housing visitors' assessments of housing needs could be affected by their
view of the householder's standards of cleanliness and tidiness (Lambert *et al.*

1978). This insight returns us to the Edwardian origins of deservingness. Samuel reports on his mother's reaction to the 'slummers', charitable ladies of good background, who used to visit the poor in the East End of London early this century.

> My mother used to be top of [their] list, being a cripple, that appealed to them. The children had to be all lined up for the ladies to look at, and if you were clean you got more money.
>
> (Samuel 1981)

In an American study housing inspectors were found to be equally responsive to household tidiness and better disposed to complaints made by co-operative tenants and less responsive to those made by aggressive and demanding tenants (Nivola 1978). A preference for polite and tidy people makes it particularly likely that those working with the sick will be prone to using the deservingness heuristic. As Titmus noted:

> in being querulous and ungrateful, demanding and apathetic in turns, we are in fact behaving as ill people. The demands that people make on society are greater when they are ill than when they are well.
>
> (Titmus 1963: 124)

If dealing with difficult clients is a trigger for the use of deservingness, then we might expect to see evidence of it in schools and classrooms and there is research which suggests that this is the case. Educational researchers working on the ORACLE project into classroom interaction in primary schools, for example, received:

> the abounding impression ... that the personal and social behaviour [of the pupils] is not viewed by the teachers with the same detachment as they view progression in reading or maths or any other area of the curriculum. Cognitive skills can be seen as rather impersonal entities, and teaching techniques and learning materials can be considered dispassionately. Not so it appeared with personal and social behaviour which seemed to be viewed by many teachers as cause and consequence of their continuing relationship with the children.
>
> (Ashton 1981: 78)

Primary teachers, it appears, evaluated their pupils' behaviour (as opposed to their pupils' cognitive development), through the child's status as a morally autonomous and participating individual. These evaluations could lead to teachers adopting the deservingness heuristic. The ORACLE project found that the use of deservingness (although they did not use the term) affected the judgements teachers made about children's abilities, in a way that could be identified, by comparing these judgements with the results of objective testing. The researchers found that the ability of children classified by teachers as 'solitary workers' and 'quiet collaborators' were overestimated relative to that of the 'attention seekers' and 'intermittent workers'. The latter groups were both underestimated on independent study skills, although only 'intermittent workers' were underassessed on basic skills (Jasmin 1981). It would seem that the degree of co-operation (a deservingness criterion) that teachers received from their pupils affected their assessments of those pupils. The deservingness heuristic is adopted in the classroom, as in the social security office, as a response to unremitting contact with difficult clients. Teachers' negative reactions to children assessed as undeserving were not found in their allocation of time, attention seekers inevitably received more of a teacher's time, but in the nature of their response to children. Those deemed undeserving and slow received less immediate feedback to their questions, less praise and more criticism. Teachers also tended to rephrase questions that 'bright pupils' found difficult whilst for 'slow learners', in the same situation, they tended to merely repeat the question verbatim in a way that reinforced the pupil's sense of inadequacy. Such behaviour on the teachers' part created an expectancy effect amongst the difficult children which caused them to respond by becoming more disruptive (Galton and Delafield 1981). Professional staff, like non-professionals, are service deliverers in direct contact with clients. Their professional training insists upon an absence of emotional response to clients but the pressures of demanding contact with the difficult ones can override this precept and cause them to apply a deservingness heuristic.

Individual need

The individual need heuristic, in contrast to deservingness, is an attempt to replace moral judgement with dispassionate assessment of clients' needs. It is the heuristic that underwrites the occupational ideologies of professional staff in the caring professions. To quote from a publication of the Royal College of Nursing:

> some patients may find it hard to communicate, others may be unco-operative, or in hospital through their own inadequacy – to put it bluntly nurses must never show that matters.
>
> (RCN 1986)

There is an irony here. Deservingness attributes an independent moral status to individuals and then uses the consequences of that freedom to discriminate between them. The need heuristic attempts to remove that discrimination but in so doing reifies people and demeans their moral status. The concept of need in this discussion is restricted so as to exclude a client's wishes or desires. To use Daniels' (1981: 152) formulation, some of the things we claim to need fall into a special category which gives them a weightier moral claim involving the distribution of services. In his analysis such special category items have two characteristics. First, they are objectively describable, which means that needs can be ascribed to people who do not know they have them or who even claim that they do not have such needs. Second, weightings can be given to such needs irrespective of the client's own preferences. From the perspective of the need heuristic, clients are not seen as moral agents but as packages of objectively defined conditions which can be ranked. The allocation of services, if the need heuristic is applied, should be proportionate to this assessment of need.

Those who use the individual need heuristic reject concern with the subjective experience of need. It can be objected that this charge is unfair and that many professionals are as concerned with a client's subjective feelings as with their objective condition. There is much concern within the caring professions with maintaining the dignity and independence of clients by personalising services. It is increasingly recognised that there is a difference between the objective conditions, or pathology, of a situation (let us say a disease) and the subjective experience of it. An area of academic study has developed, around the idea of measures of well being, to provide a counterweight to the objective description of need (Briscoe 1982). But these studies have tended to provide objective measures of subjective feelings or enumerated subjective measures of feelings (e.g. how much do you worry about being lonely? – on a scale of 1 to 5). This sort of data can easily become incorporated into a wider objective assessment and so subjective feelings become objectified. The clients' emotions become schematised into an assessment of need. Under a need heuristic subjective experiences are an aspect of objective need and not the key to the provision of services. This may well be because objective data facilitate a practical approach. A doctor may feel that more good can be done by concentrating on the pathology of a disease than by getting involved in the uncharted territory of the patient's experience of it (see the correspondence on disease and the novel: *Times Literary Supplement* 1986). Similarly, social workers working with the elderly tend to concentrate on practical, objective help for their clients rather than on their psychological needs (Rushton and Briscoe 1981). Nevertheless, where there is dissonance between objective need and the client's subjective desires, under the need heuristic, need will dominate. This is a particular problem when dealing with elderly clients. Surveys have shown that they are often 'satisfied with conditions that seem objectively deplorable to others' (Abrams 1978; see also Gray 1997: 126). The need heuristic would lead a professional to want to change these conditions but this would then conflict with the equally professional requirement to respect the wishes and dignity of the client.

In those public sector professions where need is the dominant heuristic there is an emphasis during professional training on the assessment of need. This is seen as an expert, diagnostic process rather than as market research. There is also, in these professions, a continuing search for methods of assessment which put a patina of objectivity on what must be an essentially subjective exercise of professional judgement. The use of dependency and rating scales, such as the points systems used to determine housing need, or used by occupational therapists to decide how capable people are of looking after themselves in their own homes (McIntosh and Young 1990), are examples of such techniques. Dependency and rating scales help when making decisions about individual cases as and when they arise and perhaps when making limited comparisons with other proximate cases. There are technical problems in devising such scales, however. Culyer (Culyer and Wright 1978), for example, has shown how the use of ordinal and cardinal rating scales can produce different rankings of clients' needs.

The use of triage in hospital accident and emergency (A&E) departments is another example of a needs assessment technique (Blythin 1983; Parmar and Hewitt 1985). It is a system for prioritising need that was first developed to deal with battlefield casualties during World War I who were classified as emergency, urgent or delayed cases. In the triage system, used in one A&E department, people arriving by ambulance or as walking wounded have their problem categorised as one of twelve conditions, and judged as urgent or nonurgent, by a trained triage nurse. Triage is an assessment system for ensuring that the specialised services of an A&E department are directed to those who most need them. If some patients, as a result of triage, found themselves waiting a long time for treatment for a trivial complaint, it was not a denial of their need but a recognition that other sources of healthcare, such as their GP practice, might be a more appropriate source of remedy for their need. Triage illustrates the use of objective assessment as one of the characteristics of the individual need heuristic.

There are two forms of the individual need heuristic. The first, and the one which has been discussed so far, is that of the service deliverers; the second is the administrative application of individual need. The professional application is concerned with individuals and not with populations. As Whitmore and Fuller (1980) noted in their review of priority setting in social services, 'much social work activity and thinking still appears to be predicated in the irreducible individuality of each case', even in a situation where declining relative resources require greater prioritisation. Another characteristic of professional interpretation of need is the emphasis it places on the quality of the individual service provided as the key aspect of service evaluation. As Jones has argued:

> Professional public administrators often focus on services as products which are subject to quality control standards, rather than as services as scarce commodities to be divided up by groups who disagree, at least implicitly about who should receive what level of service.
>
> (Jones, quoted in Webster 1982: 72)

This tendency can be seen very clearly in nurse management where evaluation is viewed as a concern for quality assurance and the devising of techniques for monitoring it (Jenkinson 1981; Willis and Linwood 1984). Quality assurance is concerned with doing things properly, with maintaining professional standards. People with an individual need orientation will be less at ease with quality systems, such as total quality management (TQM) for which one definition is:

> an integrated, corporately led programme of organisational change designed to engender and sustain a culture of continuous improvement based on customer-oriented definitions of quality.
>
> (Joss and Kogan 1995: 13)

Joss and Kogan researched the implementation of TQM in a number of pilot site hospitals. They found in general that only 1–5 per cent of consultants turned up to TQM training events and that it was impossible to secure their attendance at quality improvement team meetings. As they concluded:

> highly trained professionals, used to administering their own quality criteria, will need convincing of the need for generic and systemic forms of quality assurance.
>
> (ibid.: 155)

The notion of quality incorporated within the individual need heuristic is a very particular and limited vision.

It follows from an emphasis on individuals and service quality that people operating within the need heuristic are less concerned with the pattern of distribution of their services among all, actual and potential, clients. Staff can only respond to the needs they know about. The individual need heuristic requires a referral system in order to operate and so groups who are vociferous in their self-referral may obtain more of a service than more needy groups who are not knowledgeable enough, or motivated enough, to self-refer. This effect has been noticed in consumer advice services which are used more by higher income groups than by lower income groups who probably live in areas where trading practices are more invidious (Stewart et al. 1976). One report has suggested that many severely handicapped elderly, without friends and relations, are living in the community without help because the social services departments do not know about them. It is the friends and relations of people with needs who draw attention to those needs; and if the needy have few such contacts they are not brought to social services' attention (Audit Commission 1985). The irony of individual need, as a means of distributing services, is that it can create a pattern of service provision within a population which is in inverse proportion to the distribution of need.

The administrative form of individual need differs from the professional form. Although a concern for individuals has been identified as a characteristic of the need heuristic, it does not, in its administrative form, always take an individual person as its focus. The provision of many public services requires little direct contact between clients and service providers. In practice, professionals in these services work with a nominal, ideal-type, vision of the clients for whom the service is provided. This notion of the idealised individual who is the focus of planning and allocation is similar to that of the 'intelligent general reader' who is the alleged focus of attention in the world of non-fiction publishing. In this situation it is easy for the notion of need to become transferred to the service itself. In library services, for example, professionals may assume that their users have generalised characteristics such as the desire to inform themselves so that they can properly fulfil their democratic duties as citizens. The mission statement of the Library Association (1996) confirms this view and opens with the clarion call: 'The Library Association asserts that libraries are fundamental to the maintenance of a democratic society, culture and civilisation.' This vision of the user justifies the service deliverer's wish to provide a comprehensive range of cultural and informational services. Emphasis on an ideal type of client makes the service itself the unit for the assessment of need, as the needs of individuals become a constant. It is like buying a birthday present for a child. We all know that, stereotypically, they like Lego or computer games and when we choose presents for them all we have to do is find the gaps in their collections of these things and buy gifts that plug them. Similarly, need in a library becomes an assessment of the gaps, in the range of information sources or in the collections, as identified by professionally qualified staff. The standardised vision of the user is perhaps broken down into a few broad categories, such as children and the disabled, which in turn form the basis for service planning and the segmentation of collections and services. The transferral of the notion of need from client to service reinforces the emphasis on the quality of service that typifies the individual need heuristic.

There is a further consequence of allocating resources in terms of nominal and standardised images of clients. The needs of standardised clients can be aggregated by multiplying up the needs of the average client. This was an approach that conscientious Indian civil service (ICS) officers frequently used in the administration of their districts in the nineteenth century. J. H. Kerr (1962) was the collector of Darbhanga district in northern Bihar in north India and in 1904 he published the settlement report on the district. These reports were written primarily to set the rate of land tax for the district, but their compilers also used them to survey the economic and social conditions of the population. A major problem in Darbhanga was famine. Kerr collected a wide range of statistics on, amongst many other things, the outturn of crops per acre, the market value of the crops, the cost of cultivation and the net profit of the cultivators. He was able to work out the minimum land holding needed for the subsistence of a cultivator and his family. When this was compared with the mean size of holdings it was clear that the average family could subsist in a normal year but had no reserves to see them through a drought year. These forms of calculation are still essential to government planning but in the West the calculations are likely to be made with reference to a relative rather than to an absolute definition of poverty (Runciman 1966).

A characteristic of the calculative approach to the identification of need is the number of statistical assumptions and guesstimates that have to be made. In order to work out the capacity of field labourers to survive drought years, for example, Kerr had to make a series of guesstimates. The first was that only 7 rupees (Rs) out of the average cost of cultivation of Rs15 went to pay hired labourers, because most landlords were petty and resident and did much of the field work themselves. Applying his assumption of Rs7 per acre as the cost of hired labour to the district's cultivated area gave a wage pool of Rs55,776,382 which, after a few other statistical deductions, was available to be distributed amongst the 2.3m cultivators and labourers of the district. The resulting net income per cultivator/labourer was Rs21–8 per head when the minimum needed to keep an individual in modest comfort was Rs15. Kerr concluded:

> A considerable portion of the district must, in an ordinary year, earn little more then the minimum, and any serious increase in their numbers, or a bad year, must inevitably be followed by a reduction in their standard of comfort.
>
> (Kerr 1962: 171)

The purpose of these calculations was to determine the extent to which government might have to fund famine relief in the district. I have a suspicion that the statistical proclivities of the ICS founded an administrative tradition that continued to pervade the British public sector in the twentieth century. As an anecdotal example of this, when I was working as a management services officer in local government in the 1970s, much of my work entailed the statistical calculation of needs. In one project I was concerned to identify the numbers of education welfare officers (EWO) needed to meet schools' caseloads of truanting pupils. This involved correlating the proportion of pupils on a school's roll who had an absence problem, with a relative deprivation index score of their school's catchment area. The regression line obtained was used to produce a staffing formula to ensure that each education area had the correct quota of EWOs.

Work measurement techniques are tools for applying the heuristic of individual need. This perhaps would seem a strange conclusion to many professional staff for whom the images of work study, the clipboard and the stopwatch, were a traditional source of apprehension. The function of work measurement is not to assess cost effectiveness but simply to calculate the level of resources necessary to meet a pre-determined level of need. In nursing dependency systems such as GRASP and the Ninewells system, nurses make a professional assessment of their patients' need for care and then the work measurement systems transform these assessments into staffing levels (Willis and Linwood 1984). From the 1970s to the 1980s there was a shift in the attitude of professional staff towards work measurement. Initially it was seen as a threat to jobs and to staffing levels, but as cost cutting pressures increased, systems such as GRASP came to be seen as ways of protecting staffing levels against government-inspired cuts.

Nursing is one area where the administrative view of individual need has taken root. But this has not happened in all public services. In social services, for example, many directors of social services have claimed that their knowledge of needs at the community or aggregate level (as opposed to knowledge of the needs of individual clients) is 'patchy' and 'extremely incomplete on a population analysis basis' (Wistow et al. 1996: 54). In social services the professional perspective on individual need has remained dominant. It is probable that the balance between the administrative and the professional view of the individual need heuristic varies across the range of the public services.

The ways in which need is measured have been discussed. But how is the heuristic used to allocate resources, particularly when resources are inadequate in relation to needs? The first question concerns the relative status of needs. The classic view of the individual need heuristic is that all needs are equal and all ought to be met. The purpose of need assessment is simply to decide how much resource is required to meet the need. This is clearly seen in a curriculum objective for a school written during the 'Red Book' exercise on the entitlement curriculum 11–16.

> Education must respond equally to the needs of all individuals. The needs of individual people may be different but any one need is of no greater importance than any other. Different needs are not met by giving equality of resources. The aim should be to make education equally valuable to all individuals and to do this it must respond proportionately to the needs of the individual.
>
> (Department of Education and Science 1983: 78)

This interpretation eschews any form of prioritisation of needs, and it attempts to avoid the fact of limited resources for providing services.

Under the aegis of the individual need heuristic the correct response to limited resources is to lobby and campaign for more. This response is at the core of the service ethic in the public sector. The demand for more resources to meet increasing levels of need has been a consistent theme in the history of the public services. In the 1990s the refrain has been mostly heard in relation to the funding of education and the NHS. The reaction of ministers to this demand has become as much a cliché as the demand. They argue that problems cannot be solved by throwing money at them and that more creativity and better targeting of resources are the solutions to the problem. Schools, they argue by way of illustration, don't need more resources, they need to take more managerial responsibility for themselves by assuming grant maintained status and by changing their teaching methods.

The political debate about the level of resourcing has had an academic parallel. It is often argued that need is an incapacitating concept because it sees meeting needs as an end in itself. Culyer (1976), a health economist, believed this approach caused people to forget that the meeting of needs is merely instrumental in achieving an outcome. He defined meeting a need as a means to an end; and as it is the end that should be valued, the choice of means is a technical, and not a value-based, decision. But instead, he suggested, many professionals came to see means, such as more hospital beds and more surgical operations, as intrinsically and not instrumentally good.

> One of the principal dangers of the language of 'needology' applied to instruments is that it encourages a particular form of sloppy thinking, namely the denial of the substitutability of alternative means in attaining an end, or at least, a denial of the legitimacy of considering that the most effective means of meeting an ultimate need may be too costly and that possibly to adopt a less effective means, or indeed, no means at all might be the proper course.
>
> (Culyer 1976: 14)

The notion of a means being too costly implies it has a high opportunity cost in relation to the aggregate well being of the population. The notion of individual need, however, is predicated on individuals' rights to services and benefits and not on the maximisation of good within the society. Culyer's accusation that needology ignores outcomes is correct. The individual need view does take results into consideration, but it only requires that there is some beneficial impact for the individual, and not that there is a maximisation of outcome for a population. It is only required that the impact is positive; it does not need to be large or cost effective (Roach et al. 1988). This is not a demanding criterion, most services provide some benefit.

Culyer's second criticism, that needology is insensitive to the use of alternative methods, is less fair. A rights-based response to need does not create a right to a particular service; it only requires that some appropriate response is made. Although, in practice it is easy enough for practitioners to forget the distinction between outcome and services, the individual need heuristic does not preclude the health economist's interest in substitutability of means. As Barr (1985) points out, in formal economic terms, neither a utilitarian concern for cost effectiveness, nor an individual rights concern with a response to need, have a monopoly over concern with the efficient use of resources. The individual need heuristic can be applied in a way that is sensitive to the need for economy. This means that staff should be careful to use the cheapest way of meeting a need.

Under the individual need heuristic all needs are equal. But needs are only deemed equal once they have been accepted by the professionals as a need. The distinction between valid and invalid needs in relation to public service provision is an important rationing device within the application of the individual need heuristic. The constant re-evaluation of this dividing line is a major activity for professional staff. The question of the validity of needs was raised in 1991–3 when social services departments were preparing internal markets for the delivery of social care. As part of these preparations social workers had to produce individual care plans for all clients. This raised the problem of how to deal with unmet need, which arose when an assessment said a client needed a service which, for reason of lack of resources or whatever, the department was not prepared to provide. Such discrepancies could easily occur because, as one social services director said, 'how do you define unmet need?; it is as long as a piece of string' (Wistow *et al.* 1996: 58).

If there is thought to be inadequate resources to meet the amount of need, then the users of the need heuristic favour lobbying for more resources. But, if this is unsuccessful, then their response is rationing by tightening up the definition of need (by redrawing the line between valid and invalid need) and restricting those who can enter into the category of the needy (Scrivens 1979). This process preserves the belief that all needs are equal in their right to a response whilst providing the individual need heuristic with a system for prioritising and structuring need. The recognition that populations as well as individuals have to be considered brings us to the next heuristic.

Fairness

Fairness is concerned with impartiality between individuals. Like need it is focused on input rather than output. But whereas supporters of individual need would argue for more resources when need outstrips budget, the proponents of fairness would be more likely to consider ways of doling out existing resources equally. Fairness emphasises the importance of giving everyone equal access to services or at least an equal chance of access. This opens up the possibility of using arbitrary mechanisms for allocating scarce resources. People who apply the fairness heuristic are interested in the standardisation and consistency of services to clients. One of the clearest definitions of fairness, as it is been defined here, can be found in a medieval Islamic story quoted by Russell.

> A child and an adult both of the True Faith are in Heaven, but the adult occupies a higher place. God explains that the man has done many good works whereupon the child asks why God allowed him to die before he could do good. God answers that he knew the child would grow up to be a sinner and so it was better that he die young.

A cry rises up from the depths of Hell: 'Why O Lord did you not let us die before we became sinners?'

(Russell 1985)

The Lord was obviously working on an *ad hoc* basis dealing with individuals as they appeared before him for judgement. For some reason this child was noticed and saved whilst many others were not, a lapse on God's part that those in hell naturally thought unfair. Fairness therefore must operate according to universally applied rules. Either all potential sinners die young or none. If we move from the celestial to the human sphere, then it is clear that rules must be devised without regard to the particular circumstances of the people drawing them up. John Rawls (1972: 136) refers to the 'thick veil of ignorance' in a thought experiment in which he argued that the rules of resource allocation must be drawn up in ignorance of the status, rank, abilities, needs and merits individuals will possess in the social system, if they are to be impartial. Given the constraints of the thought experiment, people will devise rules that they could live with whether their position in society were to be privileged or unprivileged. The application of fairness therefore forgoes the knowledge of individuals that is essential to the individual need heuristic. As Rawls has pointed out, in an uncertain game such as the thought experiment one chooses a minimax strategy. For example, if a person has to decide how to cut a cake for distribution between three people they will cut it unequally if they know they will have first choice of the portions, but will cut it equally if they do not know the order in which people will choose their slice.

The fairness heuristic consequently evinces no interest in the probabilities of, or in taking chances on, likely outcomes. Fairness is about the method of distribution and not its outcomes; it simply insists that managers create and use rules that will ensure procedural justice. For public sector staff it is about ensuring that, when the outcome or impact of services is known, criticism can be defused by referring to the fairness of the method of allocation. This is a low-risk option for staff. Making forecasts about the consequences of action is difficult. If public managers try to use services as a tool for social engineering they may find that the results of their actions are not what were anticipated. It is safer therefore to treat everybody equally, since they are more likely to be criticised for a noble attempt at social engineering that goes wrong, than they are for treating everybody fairly and having no great ambitions. Fairness is a consequence of having to deal with populations rather than individuals and having no confident knowledge of the consequences of action upon that population.

The queue and the input norm are common forms of fairness in the allocation of public services. They are normally used together; input norms provide the strategic and tactical distribution of resources whilst the queue provides a mechanism for operational service rationing. Input norms specify the amount of resources to be provided in terms of number of population. Mostly they are in the form of so many resources for so many thousands of heads of population. In the 1970s, for example, school staffing was determined by an input norm which related the number of Burnham points a school had (Burnham points were the numbers of pupils on roll weighted according to age) to the numbers of staff. The system worked on forecasts of pupil numbers in schools and, in the case of teaching staff, a fixed pupil–teacher ratio was used to determine the number of teachers required. In the system of the time the local education authority (LEA) would also determine the balance of ancillary staff, clerks, laboratory technicians, library assistants, etc. needed within each school. In the 1990s schools' budgets are still determined by an input norm. A school's budget is still (largely) determined by the numbers on roll and their age (Bartlett 1993: 128–9). The main difference is that the school, not the LEA, decides how that budget is to be allocated across the various heads of expenditure.

The queue provides a mechanism for fairness through randomness. As long as there is no one jumping the queue then everyone in it is being treated fairly. If services have to be rationed, this is one way of doing it that does not discriminate against individuals. Many GP surgeries for example have, in at least a few surgeries during the week, an open appointment system. This means that a patient can come to see the doctor, without an appointment, and will be guaranteed a consultation as long as they don't mind waiting until the doctor is free. This system is fair because it treats everyone the same. Everyone has an equal chance of a long or a short wait; it depends upon whether it turns out to be a busy or a quiet surgery.

Queues, however, are only fair in their treatment of the people within the queue; there may well be unfairness between queues. This is the problem I always face in the supermarket. I choose the queue that appears shortest but then the till breaks down or the customer in front drops all their shopping on the floor and I end up waiting longer than people in the other queues. Many retail organisations, such as banks, have tackled this problem by using a common queuing system in which all the customers are in one unified queue, and when people reach its head they go to the next free cashier. Similar problems occur in public sector services and hospital waiting lists are a good example. Waiting lists have long been a contentious political issue and one which is now measured by performance indicators. The Brighton Healthcare Trust (1995) has put its waiting list information on the Internet and it reveals, not surprisingly as the pattern would be the same in other hospitals, that the length of wait is different for different specialities and consultants. They have posted the consultants' names on a list which showed that, as of the 31 December 1994, if you needed ENT treatment and had been referred to H. Elcock the average wait until your first outpatient appointment was 36 weeks and only 54 per cent of patients were treated within 3 months. If you were referred to J. Weighill, however, you would only wait 16 weeks for the outpatient appointment and 83 per cent of patients were treated within 3 months.

Clearly, patients on the first list might think themselves unfairly treated compared with those on the second. Madhok (1995) has researched the variations in wait times between consultants and has suggested that, for high volume routine surgical procedures such as inguinal hernias, common waiting lists should be maintained at departmental level rather than for individual consultants. This would mean that everybody needing a particular surgical procedure would be put on the same chronologically ordered list and would be treated by whichever consultant was working when their turn came. Madhok pointed out that most of these operations are, in any case, performed by junior doctors and not by the consultants. He argued that the procedure would be administratively feasible and would reduce some of the stresses which arise from the waiting list system. Queues are not infallible as a mechanism for promoting fairness in the allocation of services and resources, but once in a queue you are assured equal treatment with others in the same queue.

Lotteries, or other arbitrary means, are another form of allocation mechanism that are acceptable from the perspective of fairness. It was noted in chapter 2 that in the Cave Rescue exercise the drawing of lots was a popular method of decision making. In practice, arbitrary means are not so common in the public services in the UK. But examples can be found in other times and places. This provides an opportunity for taking another illustration from the history of India in the nineteenth century. Maine, in his classic work on village communities, mentioned the impact on those village communities, who operated a communal system of land ownership and cultivation, of the large irrigation canals built in the Punjab by the government of India. He pointed out that:

> The common life of the group or community has been so far broken up as to admit of private property in cultivated land, but not so far as to allow departure from a joint system of cultivating that land.
>
> (Maine 1881: 109)

His interest was in the way that such communities, which themselves controlled the order and form of cultivation by minute regulation, negotiated rights of access to the water provided by the irrigation canals. Under the official system for using irrigation water the government agreed with the village community to provide a certain amount of water for a certain increase in revenue; and it was then up to the village community to distribute the water amongst its several families. Often the detailed rules they drew up to allocate the water were regarded as immemorial custom even though there had been no source of irrigation in the past. But, more particularly as regards the argument about fairness, there was no thought amongst the villagers that the distribution of water should be regulated by any implied or expressed contract amongst them which related to their proprietary share of the village:

rather than have a contract or agreement, it would appear to them to be a much more natural and reasonable arrangement that the distribution should be determined by *casting lots*. Authority, Custom or Chance are in fact the great sources of law in primitive communities, as we know them, not Contract.

(ibid.: 110, my italics)

The reference to the primitiveness of such communities is arrogant but the illustration does show the possibilities of using arbitrary means as a way of deciding the allocation of public goods. There is a feeling in western societies that only windfall or *bonne bouche* goods or services should be distributed by lot. If a school, for example, were to be unexpectedly sponsored by an industrial company to send some students to an international conference then it would probably be seen as acceptable to choose delegates, from those eligible, by drawing lots. It would probably not be seen as acceptable if the people who needed hip operations because of their arthritis were chosen in this manner. Except, of course, when a patient actually has their hip replacement operation will depend upon which hospital and which consultant they are referred to, and that is not dissimilar to a lottery.

The fairness heuristic is often used to extend the need heuristic by looking at the allocation of services in relation to the distribution of need within a population. The individual need heuristic causes individuals to be considered only as they become known to the service providers, it is not concerned with the interpersonal distribution of a service. The fairness heuristic is a statistical extension of the need approach. It aims to ensure that clients with the same level of need have equal chances of receiving services and that the more needy are not denied services because less needy have already monopolised the available resources. This problem is another aspect of the use of queues which can cause people in some queues to receive their services before people in other queues, but with greater need, receive theirs.

This problem is well known in institutional services such as residential homes. Homes will often take in less needy clients in a particular time period because there are no needy in the queue and they need to take in clients to maintain an efficient bed occupancy figure. When in the next time period clients with needs greater than the clients already admitted arrive, they cannot be taken in because the home has no vacancies (Local Authorities Management Services and Computers Committee 1977). This concern for equality of treatment in relation to need can be seen in one reported attempt by a social services team to deal with the problem of prioritisation (Whitmore and Fuller 1980). Their analysis started from the perception that need cannot be defined independently from the resources available to meet it. The system they used to prioritise the allocation of services involved collecting three sorts of information about a range of typical social work problems. First, information was sought on the intrinsic merit of the problem (the level of need), second, on the kinds of professional response feasible within the constraints of available resources and, third, on the incidence or frequency of the problem within the team's area. The possible professional responses to these problems were divided into the minimum adequate response (which would be used in the case of low priority problems), the maximum feasible response (which would be applied to high priority problems), and the maximum desirable response (which is the service that would be provided if more resources were available). The implications of this system are, first, that, if clients cannot receive all the service that they merit, then it is important to ensure that all clients, with similar needs, receive consistent responses. Second, that there should be some relationship between the incidence of problems within the community and the allocation of resources. Both of these are fairness considerations related to the issue of equal provision between clients.

The system developed by Whitmore and Fuller was an attempt to avoid the possibility, born out of professional autonomy, that some clients would receive the maximum desirable response and others, with the same needs, receive only the minimum response: either because they were assessed when resources had already been allocated to others or because they were assessed by different professionals using variant professional standards. The team produced their own system of case classification by consensus which represented an important move away from the social worker's preferred heuristic of individual need. But the need heuristic could still be seen powerfully at work in the priority setting exercise; because one of the purposes of collecting data on the incidence of problems was to use it to argue a case for increased resources. If the case for more resources were successful, all clients could receive a full service, rather than a reduced service fairly distributed.

An example of the application of the fairness criterion, as an extension of the need heuristic, can be found in the Audit Commission's (1985) review of residential social services for the elderly. They began their analysis by estimating the average number of elderly people in residential care per thousand population and by categorising their degree of physical disability. They found 11:1000 in care, with severe or very severe disability, and 6:1000 in care with moderate disability. These groups were named the core group and the optional group, respectively. The ratios were then used as input norms to identify whether a particular social services department had high or low residential provision for the two groups. Their analysis was based on the quadrants shown in figure 3.2. The Audit Commission then posed different strategic questions of the social services departments who were located in the four quadrants.

- *Quadrant* A: these authorities would seem to be making adequate provision for the core group but managers in this quadrant would have to ask if there were any special local factors indicating a higher than average number in the core group.

Summary of national residential reference framework
Number/1,000 elderly in residential care

Level of physical disability	Core in residential area	Optional in residential care
Very severe	3	
Severe	8	
Moderate		6

Source: study team estimates

Policy questions suggested for sample authorities
Residents per 1,000 elderly

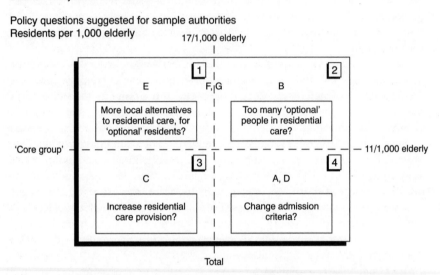

Figure 3.2 Framework for analysing provision of residential services for the elderly

Sources: The Audit Commission for Local Authorities in England and Wales (1985: 23–5).
Crown copyright, reproduced with the permission of the Controller of Her Majesty's Stationery Office.

Note: The letters A to G in the above diagram represent the seven local authorities that participated in the study.

- *Quadrant B:* these authorities are providing higher than average facilities for both core and optional groups. The strategic questions for this quadrant would concern whether some of the optional client group could be better provided for in the community.
- *Quadrant C:* these authorities may not be providing adequate facilities for the core group.
- *Quadrant D:* these authorities may be blocking their facilities with the optional group and excluding core clients.

This analysis was concerned with the fairness of the distribution of residential facilities between different local authorities and between those with severe and moderate needs for residential care. It created average national norms for provision, which were adjusted to take some account of local demographic circumstances. If an authority provided less than 17:1000 places for the total elderly patients and 11:1000 for core group elderly, then policy questions needed to be asked because people in these authorities were being treated unfairly in relation to clients in other authorities. The report did not judge effectiveness by the proportion of need within the community which was met. The test was simply whether an authority was doing as well as others in meeting, or failing to meet, need.

After dealing with the relative provision of authorities, the Audit Commission then enquired into the fairness of the distribution of services between the core group and the optional group and particularly raised questions where the optional group received relatively high provision and the core group relatively low. Utilitarian concerns inevitably creep into the kind of policy analysis used in the study. It was argued in the report, in connection with the analysis of residential services, that a distribution of resources skewed towards the optional group was not cost effective because homes became filled with people, 'who could be better cared for with less intensive, less expensive community service' (Audit Commission 1985: 18). In its analysis of community, as opposed to residential services, the Commission moved more directly into an application of the utility heuristic by looking at the relative costs and benefits of the two types of care. They raised the question, for example, of whether the large amount of money spent by some authorities on community services for low dependency elderly was justified by its preventative effect in reducing future demand for residential care (a utility criterion); or was it justified on the individual need grounds that it improved the quality of individuals' lives? This is to jump ahead of the argument but it is useful to stress at this stage that any analysis of a particular service is unlikely to restrict itself to one particular heuristic. Local authority residential provision for the elderly has been much reduced since the publication of this report as part of the general policy shift from institutional care to care in the community.

One particular contribution of fairness to decision making about resource allocation is its provision of a mechanism for dealing with situations where legitimate demands on services outstrip the capacity of resources to meet them. In this situation the individual need heuristic would demand that more resources be made available; the utility heuristic would insist that services were rationed to minimise the amount of need in the population not met. This would mean that some clients could lose all of their services and others none. From the point of view of fairness, in contrast, it would be argued that the loss of met need should be equalised between individuals. That is to say that one person's rights to have their needs met should not be infringed more than another's. In concrete terms this would lead to the demand that an organisation cutting budgets should cut everybody's budget by the same percentage, or '10 per cent off all round'. Fairness, in summary, is about spreading resources equally within a population, especially in relation to the distribution of need. It is not concerned with the outcome or impact of those services or even with service take up. That is the province of the next heuristic.

Utility

Forecasting the impact of service provision is central to the application of the utility heuristic. Utility is concerned with allocating resources in a way that maximises the common good (or beneficial impact of services). Those who apply this heuristic are less conscious of the interpersonal distribution of services. To use Jeremy Bentham's terminology, utility is concerned with doing the greatest good for the greatest number. Thus, under Pareto's criterion of efficiency, a policy change which makes at least one person better off without making anyone worse off is desirable. This rule could mean, for example, that a librarian could decide to put a disproportionate share of additional resources into libraries in an affluent area, at the expense of inner city libraries, because, according to Luckham (1971), the usage rate (and hence the assumed amount of benefit achieved) is higher in areas where the higher socio-economic groups live. Under the aegis of the utility heuristic the important issue is the maximisation of the quantity of good done. But, as Sen says:

> the trouble with [utilitarianism] is that the maximising the sum of individual utilities is supremely unconcerned with the interpersonal distribution of that sum.
>
> (Sen quoted in Barr 1985: 177)

Utility is the heuristic that underwrites much of management theory and management science in particular. Within the field of management science cost–benefit analysis (CBA) both epitomises the utility heuristic, and identifies its limitations. CBA is designed to identify and measure all the consequences of a policy, not simply the immediate ones. In public sector jargon it analyses final as well as intermediate outcomes. The ratio between the cost of a policy and its benefits (measured in monetary terms) becomes the criterion for choosing between a range of alternative policies. If achieving the greatest amount of good from a particular sum of resources is the purpose of utility, then CBA has to do two things. First, it has to determine what the specific consequences of a policy will be and, second, it has to evaluate the worth of those consequences in financial terms.

However, Alan Williams, in his review of CBA (1972), identified a range of management science techniques, of which CBA formed only a part. The first group he defined was systems analysis. These were techniques which sought to describe and model situations in a quantitative manner. Such analyses can be effectively done even when different inputs and outputs are measured in different units. The second group of techniques was concerned with cost effectiveness. These techniques produce models which are designed to meet an explicit policy analysis objective, as opposed to those in the first category which are scientific in intent. They are used to ask 'what if . . .' questions and to investigate policy trade-offs. They value all the inputs in cost terms but use other measures for the outputs. The next category was CBA proper, and this differs from cost effectiveness studies by expressing both inputs and outputs in commensurable, financial, terms. The example of a CBA analysis of a school drop-out programme reported by Garrett (1972: 127) is typical of many studies which claimed to be CBA (but which, in Williams' terms, are properly cost effectiveness studies), in that it showed a few of the outputs in cash values but most were described in words together with a + or − sign to show whether they were regarded as positive or negative.

By way of contrast to this narrative style of benefit description the development of QALYs, in health policy studies, represents an advance in the measurement of outcomes. QALY stands for quality adjusted life year and the technique was tested out in a project looking at allocation of development funds to medical specialities in the North Western Regional Health Authority (Gudex 1986). The purpose of the project was to develop measures of the survival rate and the quality of life achieved after various medical treatments, such as haemodialysis and scoliosis surgery in patients with neuromuscular illness. The use of QALYs needs rigorous systems analysis work on the survival rates and prognoses for treatments. These data were obtained from the medical research literature. The quality of life of a patient was measured by assessing patients against a matrix of values. This matrix has two dimensions, disability and distress. The different combinations of these two dimensions were rated on a scale which runs between 0 (dead) and 1 (healthy); so for example, slight disability at home and work with mild distress was rated at 0.986 whilst confinement to bed with severe distress was rated at −1.486, i.e. worse than death. The ratings were obtained from a sample of respondents including patients, nurses, doctors and healthy volunteers. QALYs can be obtained by rating and summating the average patient's expectation of quality of life in the years of survival after the treatment. But the study also investigated the costs of each treatment which meant that costs per QALY could be obtained. Haemodialysis produced a cost per QALY of £9,075 whilst for scoliosis surgery the cost was £194. The researchers recognised a number of limitations in their methods, for example, the exclusion of various aspects of quality of life in the rating matrix, but they argued that in any rational analysis of resource allocation such analyses ought to be taken into account. QALYs, at least in this aspect of healthcare, make the possibility of the scientific application of utility (or at least a health maximisation criterion) look feasible. There have been many criticisms of the QALY approach, as reported in Pereira (1989) and Baldwin et al. (1990) but it is an application of a cost effectiveness approach that cannot be ignored.

Full-blown cost–benefit analysis studies are restricted to large civil engineering, infrastructure projects such as airports, motorways, by-passes, environmental planning and health and safety policy. Pinkus and Dixson (1981) reported two CBA studies. One related to a flood prevention scheme for Towcester and the other concerned with alternative by-pass routes for Faringdon. In both cases there were still important qualitative considerations which had to be identified and listed separately from the cost–benefit ratios. It is precisely these issues which, in the 1990s, have become the focus of criticism of CBA. The argument about the building of the Newbury by-pass raised questions in some people's minds about whether the cost–benefit analysis paid enough attention to environmental issues and to the impact of the road on wildlife (Tickell 1995). The problem of valuing environmental benefits was also to the fore when the Environmental Agency was established. Its founding statute required it to make assessments of costs and benefits when fulfilling its role. One commentator remarked that if this was interpreted as the application of CBA then:

> the agency is in danger from its inception of being saddled with an absurd and discriminating monster and of becoming bogged down in wrangling over the cash value of various parts of the environment.
>
> (Adams 1995)

Most CBA studies, because of the problems of defining the cash values of impacts, are presented as aids to decision making and not a substitute for it. From the above analysis it can be seen that the failure of CBA to completely quantify the evaluative stage convincingly does not mean that management science has no part to play, or that managers cannot apply the utility heuristic. The less ambitious forms of management science can still assist the manager who sees the maximisation of the common good as a proper, if not simple, end. Detailed systems analysis and operational research cannot replace the exercise of judgement about the relative weighting of benefits but they can assist by clarifying and systematising data and information relevant to the problem. Pinkus and Dixson, for example, distinguish between the analyst and the decision maker. It is the decision maker's job to:

> synthesise the solution derived from the mathematical model, which is based on quantifiable objectives, and the more subjective criteria which relate to the problem to reach an overall decision.
>
> (Pinkus and Dixson 1981: 283)

Simulation modelling, which is a less demanding form of management science, can do much to provide data on the consequences of policy, particularly in systems such as outpatient clinics where there are queues for services (Moore 1980: 323). In these applications management science systematises professional judgement and observations into sets of formal relationships which can be mathematically manipulated. A key role of management science therefore is the enhancement of judgement about outcomes, ultimately through such techniques as knowledge-based expert systems. But this form of scientific approach does not attempt to convert decision making into a purely technical process. People to whom the utility heuristic appeals may yearn for the possibility of resource allocation by technical algorithm but the current incapacity of technique does not mean the utility heuristic cannot be used.

J. R. Kemm (1985) used a utilitarian approach in a discussion of the ethics of food policy. He was interested in identifying the ethical issues involved in modifying the eating habits of the population through regulation, facilitating measures (such as differentially taxing foods) and through education. He argued that a policy is ethical if it produces more beneficial outcomes than harmful ones. This decision rule is utilitarian in spirit but breaks the rule that no one should be made worse off. But his suggestions about how policy makers might analyse issues are also interesting in light of the limitations of technical and objective means. He stressed the interconnections between subjective and objective thinking in assessing the outcomes of policies. The three stages in this process are:

1   Determining the inherent goodness or badness of an outcome. This is a value decision such as that involved in stating that dental mottling is less bad than carcinoma of the colon.
2   Measuring the probability that the desired outcome will be achieved. This is a scientific and objective activity.
3   Assessing the degree of certainty with which the probability of the outcomes have been estimated.

This third element includes objective measurement of certainty by such statistical methods as confidence levels. But it also includes the subjective element of calibration (Wright 1984). Calibration is the extent to which people making probability judgements know their own limitations. A well-calibrated person knows what they know; others are likely to be either over- or under-confident in their exercise of judgement.

Making utility judgements therefore is both an objective and a subjective process. The subjective element emerges, as Kemm reports, in the ethical difficulties that utility's concern for populations rather than individuals produces. How, for example, should moderate good for the majority be compared with great harm to the minority? Fortifying chapatti flour would provide some health benefit for most chapatti eaters; but for the rare individual with vitamin D sensitivity it might cause serious vitamin D toxicity. The ethical problem can be exacerbated by the fact that the majority may not be aware that they have received benefits from the fortified flour. To give another example, if food policies increase the amount of fibre in the diet this will benefit people by protecting them from diverticulitus. But they will not be aware of this. But those who suffer from boborygmus or flatulence will be in no doubt that they have suffered. In view of these problems Kemm seems prepared to forgo Pareto optimality.

> Most would take the view that a very small harm to a very few individuals could be outweighed by a sufficiently large benefit to a sufficiently large number of individuals.
>
> (Kemm 1985: 291)

Technique can provide an objective framework within which subjective assessments, using the utility heuristic, can be made.

Kemm replaces the calculation of cost–benefit analysis with rigorous debate of the ethical implications of the advantages and disadvantages of a policy. There is another form in which utility can be applied in decision making without striving for the full formality of utility calculation. This approach attempts to maximise utility by creating a proportionality between inputs and outputs to public services. The idea developed from work on programme structures which were part of the PPBS mechanisms developed in the 1960s and 1970s. A programme structure is a hierarchical diagram which attempts to assess the contribution of means to ends (figure 3.3). Programme structures are drawn up for particular policy fields, for example, the protection of the environment. At the top of the programme structure is placed the goal of the policy, normally couched in terms of the programme's impact on the quality of life. Below this level in the diagram are the main programme areas which will contribute to this goal; they could be, visual amenity, air quality, conservation and recycling, and so on. Then each of these areas is in turn broken down into the various activities that will make a contribution to it. In general, progress from top to bottom of a programme structure involves asking the question: how do we achieve the objectives set? Progress from the bottom to the top is made by asking: why are we undertaking this activity? The idea of contribution is central to the construction of a programme structure. Each activity within it has to be justified by its contribution to the next level in the structure.

Some of the proponents of programme structures (Waddington 1977: 219) developed systems of mathematical coefficients which showed the degree of contribution that each activity made to the objectives in the next highest level of the structure. Obviously some activities on a given level would make a greater contribution than others. It is not a hard logical step to then argue that the funding of each activity should be proportional to its contribution to the programme's overall objectives. This approach can be illustrated from work done in the early 1980s on the curriculum of schools. The work was published in a document known colloquially as the 'Red Book' on the entitlement curriculum. Its analysis was based on a programme structure for education (Department of Education and Science 1983). The programme structure was based on the 'eight areas of experience'. All the subject teaching of a school, according to this process, had to be analysed in terms of its contribution to

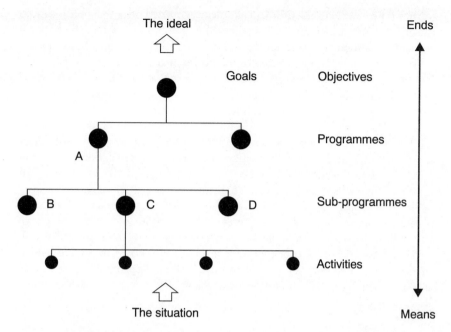

Figure 3.3 A programme structure

each of the eight areas. The maths department might be judged to make a significant contribution to the scientific area of experience but much less to the spiritual area. The Red Book included the suggestion that the allocation of time in the school's timetable to each academic subject should be in direct proportion to its contribution to the programme areas. So, if a subject was judged to make a 40 per cent contribution to the spiritual area of experience, which in turn made a 20 per cent contribution to the school's overall educational goals then that subject should receive 8 per cent (0.4 · 0.2) of the timetabled hours (Department of Education and Science 1983: 81–2). In the cross-disciplinary spirit of the programme structure a subject could win points by contributing to several areas of experience.

The method just described is based on some major assumptions, not the least of which is that the rate of marginal benefit derived from giving different subjects extra time is the same for all subjects. But the method did represent a serious attempt to apply utility's concern with maximising beneficial outputs to school timetabling. This example has been discussed in some detail because it represents an interesting attempt to base resource allocation on utility thinking. One particular aspect that is worth specifying is the use it makes of judgement and subjective assessment. In the Red Book proposals the contribution coefficients are not measured, they are subjectively judged. Overall, the method is one in which subjective judgements are put into a numerical form so that they can then be arithmetically manipulated. The specific proposals on the entitlement curriculum were superseded by the introduction of the national curriculum, although debate on the balance of subjects within it continues.

For most people the application of the utility heuristic is an entirely subjective process in which consequences are assessed according to professional experience and judgement and not by an objective process of arithmetic and measurement. Acceptable mechanisms for measurement do not exist. Utility as a heuristic does not match up to the economists' or the philosophers' theories of utilitarianism, but it does nevertheless represent another and distinctive approach to making resource allocation decisions. This conclusion means that the assessment of utility will be prey to the errors of subjective judgement. But it will still place emphasis on the achievement of a greater common good.

Utility is defined by its calculative intent and not by the method or nature of the calculation. It is this instrumental focus that causes many people to object to utility-based thinking. White made a fierce attack on the crude utilitarianism of writing on education management. She noted that management writers emphasised the importance of virtues like co-operation, good morale and teamwork. But she was horrified at these writers' motives for valuing these characteristics:

> they clearly see these personal qualities as of instrumental value – valuable insofar as they promote the ends of the organisation.
>
> (White 1987: 86)

In her estimation such qualities should be valued for themselves and because they contribute to, and recognise, human dignity.

Neither does utility, as a heuristic, imply agreement about what the good is. The policy makers will seek to maximise the good as they see it, and historically utilitarianism has had an authoritarian patina. This tendency can be illustrated by the public debate, which lasted many years in the early part of the nineteenth century, over the sources and mechanisms of revenue collection in the Indian provinces ruled by the East India Company. James Mill, the father of John Stewart Mill the philosopher, was at the centre of this debate and through him the utilitarian philosophy of Bentham and the economic theories of Ricardo became the dominant forces in the argument about Indian land revenues. As with all utilitarian enterprises there was a strong belief in the power of calculation. The Ricardian theory of rent hypothesised that, as populations grew at a faster rate than food production, marginal land would increasingly be taken into cultivation. At the margin, on the last quality of land, the capital employed would only be able to reproduce itself and yield the ordinary prevailing rate of profit. But all the better land which had been taken into cultivation earlier would be producing a higher return, and in Ricardian terms the difference between the rate of return of the marginal land and the return on all other land was rent. It was possible, according to the utilitarians, to measure the level of rent if careful cadastral and agricultural surveys were made. (It was for this reason that later in the century Collector Kerr, as we have already seen, was busy making surveys of his district.) A further implication of Mill's analysis was that, in those parts of India where the rent had not already been alienated to private landlords, the state (or the East India Company in this case) could take the whole of the rent as revenue. There was an added advantage that, according to the theory of rent, such a source of revenue would not constrain economic growth because it was not a tax on wages, capital or commerce. The supporters of this argument then recognised they had a special duty in deciding how this rent fund should be spent. As Holt Mackenzie argued in 1820:

> but holding 9/10ths. of the clear rent of the country as a fund to be administered for the public good, the government may, I think, justly be regarded as under a very solemn obligation to consider more fully than has hitherto been usual, how it can dispose of that fund so as to produce *the greatest sum of happiness*.
>
> (Stokes 1959: 113, my italics)

There was a clear authoritarian and paternalistic strand in the thinking of these utilitarians. They believed they had a mission to transform India, but this mission could only be achieved by strong government. They would decide how the revenue fund should best be spent. This strain of thought, deriving from Hobbes, can be found in Bentham's own writings, in which he argued that the will of the executive should not be checked by constitutional or popular devices (ibid.: 72, 79). This is the point at which utility differs from the next heuristic to be discussed. The ecology heuristic is predicated on the need to involve a wide range of groups and interests in the exercise of executive power.

Ecology

The supporters of the utility heuristic believe that the activities of an organisation can be objectively evaluated. The apologists for the ecology heuristic take a very different approach. They see clients as morally autonomous agents who are not passive recipients of services, but are, themselves, resources within the resource allocation process. The expressed demands of people become an integral element in policy planning. They are pluralists who assume there will be many different points of view that have to be accommodated in service planning.

The ecology heuristic is concerned with identifying the different perceptions of the many groups involved with a service and trying to create a consistent policy from that variety. Ultimately this concatenation is achieved by giving more weight to the views of those who are most closely involved with the service. In other words, an ecological resource allocation is one which meets the expectations and aspirations of the most significant interest groups. But such allocations also have to meet the minimum requirements of all the interest groups. If they do not, then those disregarded groups will seek to make themselves more significant to the organisation and so reach a condition in which the decision makers have to listen to them. This section is largely concerned with identifying how this criterion of involvement with, and significance to, an organisation or group of policy makers is interpreted and applied.

The importance of listening to the recipients of services can be illustrated by Eddison's (1973) analysis of physical planning decisions. He argued that, typically, such decisions were made on a professional basis by experts who interpreted the common interest or good. This position, he asserted was becoming untenable as belief in a single public interest diminished. Conflicting interests, opposing values and opinions as to what was in the public interest were emerging. He illustrated this change in perception by quoting from a document produced by a planning pressure group in the City of Cambridge.

> Government of the people by the people ... How are we to stop short changing the people of Cambridge? There is a very simple answer – listen to what they are saying and pay heed to it. Cambridge Planning Interface urges the Planners to come out of their hard professional shells and listen to what people living here want their town to be like. If the rest of the world wants Cambridge preserved let it say so and pay the price. But the Planning Authority represents each one of us living in the town and the County; it does not, as has so often been maintained, hold Cambridge in trust for the rest of the world.
>
> (Eddison 1973: 127)

If, in this example, the Cambridge Planning Authority had responded to these demands they would certainly have been viewing their residents as important contributors to their planning activities. But the difficulty for any public authority in such a situation is that, however much the residents may deny it, the residents are not the only interested group in the future of the city. To be ecological the authority would have to find some way of reconciling the differing demands of (to use the polemic's terms) the residents and the world.

Public housing is a particular area in which attempts have been made to provide a public service on an ecological basis. Policies and programmes were developed to make the management of housing estates much more flexible and responsive to the tenants as stakeholders. These included consumerist initiatives involving the use of tenants' charters; PEPs under which maintenance services were decentralised to make them more responsive to tenants' needs; exit strategies which allowed tenants to choose a new, private sector landlord and programmes for encouraging tenants' associations to take a more active role in the management of their estates. Stewart and Taylor (1995) carried out a review of these initiatives and concluded that they had largely been unsuccessful because estate tenants were disempowered and their voice was not powerful enough to make an impact on those who managed the estates. It is clearly not enough to say that the ecology heuristic is about listening to stake-holders. Stewart and Taylor (1995: 66) argued that tenants' groups need to be empowered, by giving them access to basic welfare rights and by building their self-esteem before they can acquire an effective ecological voice.

The ecology heuristic increasingly underpins evaluations of public services. Smith and Cantley (1985) used an approach, labelled 'pluralistic evaluation', to monitor services provided in a new psychogeriatric day hospital. They opted for a subjectivist, or phenomenological, epistemology for their study. In the investigation the perceptions of different groups about how well the service met their needs, as they interpreted them, became the key information in deciding whether the hospital was doing a good job and how services needed to be developed. A number of interest groups concerned with the hospital were identified such as doctors, nurses, social workers, patients, patients' relatives, administrators, and so on. Then six different criteria of success used by the interest groups were isolated. They were:

1   *free patient flow*: preventing blocked beds and 'silting up';
2   *clinical cure*: improving the patients' clinical condition;
3   *integrated service*: good communication and liaison with other related services;
4   *impact on related services*: provision of support to other agencies concerned with this client group;
5   *support of relatives*: the relief of the strain put upon relatives who have to care for aged people;
6   *quality of service*: concern for ethos and excellence in the way the service is actually delivered.

I have simplified the above criteria a little but from the perspective of the developing argument, the important fact is that the different interest groups viewed the six criteria differently.

> Some groups of staff and relatives employ some criteria and some others. Some employ several criteria and some adopt a more single-minded stance ... In practice different criteria are used in different ways by different groups at different times in different contexts for different purposes with different effects.
>
> (Smith and Cantley 1985: 44)

In short, the researchers found disagreement about the relative weighting between the six criteria. They could produce a very useful evaluative analysis of the hospital but could not produce an overall evaluative judgement about it. It all depended on who you were within the system.

The key issue for those who use the ecology heuristic is how to produce an allocation of resources that is responsive to a mass of conflicting expectations. One solution would be to use democratic mechanisms. But majoritarian voting mechanisms are conflict-avoidance techniques rather than a means of reconciling conflicting views. Oppenheimer, arguing from an analysis of Prisoners' Dilemma games, claimed that:

> no democratic system, majoritarian or otherwise can be developed so as to be mechanical and non-manipulable.
>
> (Oppenheimer 1985: 248)

The point is that redistributive issues represent a zero sum game with many players, that is, a game in which the cake to be divided up is of fixed size. Some games are stable which means that for each player there is always the same best ploy. But games involving redistribution are likely to be unstable, so that the players have a choice of moves and the game cannot move into a stable equilibrium. If, in a democratic system, there is a wish to come to an equilibrium, i.e. make a decision, then the game has to be manipulated if inaction and indecisiveness are to be avoided. Oppenheimer is writing from within the field of public choice theory; from this perspective it is axiomatic that democratic mechanisms for identifying the preferences of the population do not necessarily lead to rational results. As in Condorcet's Paradox, democratic methods can mean that individual rationality would result in collective irrationality (Mackenzie 1967: 142).

It does not appear that democratic devices could provide the necessary mechanism for equitably resolving value conflict. Given this difficulty, Oppenheimer and other writers turn to another possible method of reconciling conflicting demands, which is ethical arbitration. Oppenheimer's argument is that the postulates of public choice are incompatible with notions of justice. If, then, the public sector officials believe they are concerned with justice in their resource allocation decision making, they must take on the role of ethical adjudicator between the competing expectations of interest groups. If public choice cannot be the final arbiter then public officials must be.

This is a view that Stewart (1984) takes in her interesting analysis of the problem in relation to public sector personnel management. She identified three main groupings (or stakeholders) impinging upon personnel managers, each of which attempted to impose a 'decisional premise' upon the personnel managers. First, the public sector unions sought to impose a 'collective negotiations' premise. The substantive views they wished to put forward varied with time and circumstances. Their demand was that their views were acted upon. The second group were the personnel professionals who favoured a merit premise. This proposed that people should be recruited, developed, promoted and evaluated according to their technical competence at the job. This was essentially a utility heuristic interested in maximising output from employees.

The third interested party was formed from disadvantaged groups in society who wished to see an equal employment premise implemented. This group argued a case of need which they believed ought to be met by affirmative action; they were therefore fighting for the application of a need heuristic.

Personnel managers were caught within this arena of competing claims. Stewart argued that the manager could not abdicate responsibility in this situation but had to act as an ethical agent, filtering and comparing these claims and demands. She then proposed a series of ethical precepts which managers should use in performing this role. The first was that emphasis should be placed upon avoiding injury to the interest groups rather than on doing good. Above and beyond this principle the manager ought to respond to the needs of a particular group because of the Kew Gardens principle. (The geographical reference is to the public gardens in New York where a murder was witnessed by passive bystanders, and not to the British botanical gardens.) This proposed that action was necessary where:

- there was a clear case of need;
- the agent was close to the situation in terms of 'notice' if not space;
- the agent had the capability to help the one in need;
- no one else was likely to help.

The Kew Gardens principle is a straightforward application of the individual need heuristic. If managers carry out ethical adjudication, one way to do it is to use their own values, in Stewart's case the individual need heuristic, as a standard.

If, on the other hand, managers want to treat the interest groups ecologically then a different mechanism for reconciling conflicting expectations will need to be developed. Ethical adjudication remains central to the operation of the ecology heuristic, but the method of adjudication favoured by proponents of ecology owes nothing to any of the other heuristics. Such a mechanism, if it is to remain ecological, must be based on some aspect of the interest groups themselves. This suggests the Aristotelian notion of distributive justice which views justice as an equality of ratios (Aristotle 1969). According to Aristotle there should be an equality of proportion between, 'the merit of men' and the share of resources they receive. The philosopher accepted that merit can mean different things. It might mean wealth, quality of birth or intellectual and moral status. In the ecological approach, however, it is a group's importance to the service-providing organisation that determines merit. Watson (1995: 273–4) applied this approach to a modern organisational setting and, building on population ecology theory, developed it under the heading of resource dependency. From an ecological and resource dependency perspective interest groups are seen as contributors (internal or external, as in the case of the day hospital discussed earlier) to the organisation and active participators in its activities. This perception can cause boundary setting problems. Are school children, for example, within or outside schools' organisational boundaries? A constituency's participation and contribution will not necessarily be cash, it could be an investment of time, interest and effort. The extent to which a particular group's requirements should be met therefore will depend upon its merit in the eyes of the organisation or, rather, the importance of its contribution.

Hickson's *et al.* (1971) strategic contingency theory of intra-organisational power, although it was not particularly designed to account for external constituencies and interest groups, provides one framework against which the relative ecological merit of groups might be assessed. It rates groups according to their relative power, influence and non-substitutability to the organisation. In particular:

- the extent to which a constituency can create or control uncertainty for the organisation;
- the extent to which the constituency's relationship with the organisation is indispensable;
- the extent to which the constituency's actions and decisions can impact upon the organisation.

Within the workings of the ecology heuristic these ratings should then be used to ensure that, in the distribution of services and resources, the constituencies have their expectations met in proportion to their contribution. The most powerful should receive most but all the constituencies should (if possible) have their minimum requirements met. Circumstances change of course and the relative ecological significance of the constituencies will be fluid. At different times different constituencies will become strategic or dominant. Ecology is a heuristic that is concerned with organisational survival and this means that senior managers will change their policies and stances as constituencies rise and fall in their significance for the organisation.

For many public service managers the ecology heuristic simply looks like political expediency or playing politics, and hence a bad thing. Though perhaps a marketing person might see it as reacting to customer preferences and hence a good thing. A case can be made for saying that the ecology heuristic is a proper, and not simply an expedient, response. According to Oppenheimer's analysis collective or public goods foster rational ignorance. The cost of such goods are shared between all members of a community and the impact an individual can have on the service is minimal; in the end she or he has only one among many votes. The cost and effort involved in becoming knowledgeable about the service are not rewarded and it is rational to remain ignorant.

> One is confronted with characteristics which engender rational ignorance throughout the process of politics from pressurising to propagandising and implementing. It may be that some groups can

organise themselves to overcome some of the difficulties, but then similar problems are usually created within the group.

(Oppenheimer 1985: 244)

In this situation people simply absorb the costless information or propaganda that is available from the government and the media. In short, they are manipulated by the flow of easy information and such rational ignorance can lead to amorality and apathy. Surely, then, if constituencies manage to organise and become knowledgeable and increase their merit and contribution at the cost of irrational effort, public service organisations ought to respond to them. This is still essentially an argument from merit. But it suggests that ecology can be given a justification other than one of expediency. When public organisations respond to ecological pressure this may not be simply a pragmatic movement but a recognition of the merit the constituency has earned by mastering their subject and their brief.

An example from Indian history can be used illustrate ecological thinking and to identify some of its deformations. The story concerns Frank Lugard Brayne, an ICS officer in the 1920s, who developed a mission to bring about 'village uplift' in the Punjab. His concerns were practical, he wanted to improve the quality of everyday life by encouraging such things as improved sanitation, the addition of chimneys to the huts and houses of villages and the use of his favourite device, the *bhoosa* box, which was a form of slow hay box oven. In his book *Better Villages* (Brayne 1945) he also discussed the political arrangements needed to encourage village uplift. He noted that in each district there were many associations, the Red Cross, health centres, the Boy Scouts, which could contribute to the process. He wanted to bring them all together:

> to make the best of everyone who has any contribution – work, money or ideas – to offer to the solution of rural problems . . . in every village there are associations and societies which will enable the villager, individually and co-operatively, to express his views.
>
> (ibid.: 180, 183)

He thought that such associations should be brought together as a subcommittee of the *Dehat Sudder* Committee which was a kind of semi-official voluntary services council. But he was also of the belief that paying membership of this committee was essential; in other words having a say in the committee's actions was based on making a contribution, preferably financial, to it. There are in these proposals the three main components of the ecology heuristic. First, it recognises the existence of diverse interest groups or constituencies; second, there is the suggestion that the extent to which the *Dehat Sudder* committee would listen to any group would be affected by their merit in the committee's eyes, assessed by the degree to which they offered work, ideas and subscriptions; third, and implicitly, the committee would have the task of creating a plan of action through adjudication for all the schemes and projects proposed by the associations and societies. Brayne's reputation could easily be resurrected as an early proponent of the communitarian view of politics that has come into fashion in the 1990s (Etzioni 1993; Walker 1995).

But Brayne's work also suggests how easy it is for the ecology heuristic to deform itself into the application of different heuristics. This claim needs explanation. Brayne had been brought up as an assertive evangelical Christian (Dewey 1993). He saw many solutions to the problems of the villages but he, as did Mayo in the book *Mother India* quoted earlier, believed the Indian peasant to be too fatalistic to want to improve their lot and to use sensibly the improved earnings that resulted from the digging of the Punjab's irrigation canals (Brayne 1945: 5) mentioned in an earlier example from Indian history. The moral arbitration role, that officials applying the ecology heuristic fulfil, can become the exercise of autocratic will, and this was how Brayne saw his task. As an evangelical he knew what needed to be done and by persuasion or coercion he would get everyone to see it his way.

The use of coercion can lead to a kind of anti-ecology heuristic: instead of the public officials trying to meet the aspirations of the interest groups and constituencies, these groups try to convince the public official that they have met *his* expectations whilst, in practice continuing to do things in the way that suits them. Brayne's subordinate officials, in particular, were very good at window dressing. When Brayne went on tours of inspection in his district a narrow corridor of villages was cleaned up for him to inspect. As one official described the process:

a great deal was done in the course of a few hours, and although chimneys were impossible we managed to get a few [magic *bhoosa* boxes] installed.

(Dewey 1993: 96)

The ecology heuristic becomes its converse whenever the person at the centre of the ecological web sees their role as changing the expectations of the constituencies rather than reacting to them.

In view of the above analysis a distinction needs to be made between the recognition that constituencies exist, and are important to policy making, and an ecological response to the constituencies. People working with heuristics other than ecology may still recognise the importance of the constituencies to the evaluation of the organisation's success; but they will decide to manipulate them or to change their views instead of responding positively. Dearlove (1973), who studied local councillors in the Royal Borough of Kensington and Chelsea, and Weiner (1962), who studied pressure groups and policy making in India, have described the mechanisms that public sector organisations use to control the demands made upon them by constituencies. The tactics mostly involved controlling the access of interest groups to the policy makers. This leads to spiralling games playing as the interest groups seek to overcome the barriers to access and the policy makers barricade themselves more deeply behind big desks, ante-rooms, kitchen cabinets and PAs. Therefore, although ecology is political, it should not be confused with acting politically to gain influence and power to achieve the implementation of one's own purposes.

To summarise: ecology like utility is concerned with consequences and not with the intrinsic rightness or wrongness of actions. But, unlike utility, ecology is concerned with subjective instead of objective consequences. People who use the ecological heuristic have to make an ethical arbitration between competing demands based on their perception of the merit (in relation to the organisation) of the various interest groups or constituencies. Ecologically the correctness of a resource allocation is judged by the perceptions of it held by the constituencies. Ecology responds to the phenomenological environment of the organisation and not to its positivist environment. In plainer words the ecologically minded officer or manager is more concerned with what people think than they are about the 'facts' of the situation. People who use this heuristic need to be tolerant of ambiguity, and intransitive in their preferences, to cope with the changing relative merit of the constituencies. This contrasts with both deservingness and need which require a transitive set of values. Ecology, finally, views clients and constituencies as active moral agents who play an important role in the provision of public services.

Personal competence and gain

Personal gain and competence is a heuristic which, when applied to the allocation of resources, causes the decision to be made so as to benefit the decision maker. But the benefit can be of two very different kinds. The first is the sense of worth and self-esteem that can come from having done a job properly. This implies that the decision has been made using appropriate methods and that no short cuts, which offend against the decision maker's beliefs, have been used. The second sense relates to personal advantage. In this sense the decision makers allocate resources in a way that brings some material or personal benefit to them – this may be an increase in organisational influence, professional satisfaction, something which eases the burden of daily life, cash or a bottle of whisky. Personal gain does not necessarily imply gain for the decision maker because they may value being able to help their friends or family, but it does imply that decisions are made according to private rather than public considerations.

The competence aspect of personal competence and gain is concerned with the individual's beliefs about the proper methods to be used to make resource allocation decisions. According to this heuristic, a resource allocation is not judged by the justness of the decision but by the correctness of the methods used to arrive at it. People of course will have their own conceptions of procedural correctness. For many managers in public organisations the highest competency accolade is to be seen as an effective political operator. Others, contrarily, might complain that a decision had been made on political grounds and that not enough emphasis had been given to facts and formal evaluation. But, whatever the principle that is applied (and Edwards *et al.* 1981 list the main ones), the characteristic of this heuristic is the desire to avoid the shame caused by the use of unsatisfactory methods.

The personal gain aspect of the heuristic could lead someone to persuade themselves to adopt a particular resource allocation because it offers, *inter alia*, job satisfaction, excitement, opportunity for professional growth, power, improved promotion prospects, comfort and diminished stress, convenience or monetary rewards (including bribes). Whilst bribes may be relatively rare in public organisations, the allocation of resources to satisfy private agendas, research suggests, is not. For example, investigations into the work patterns of peripatetic staff, such as environmental health officers, reveals that they often arrange their pattern of daily visits to suit their personal convenience (Webster 1982). Perhaps, for example, their inspection visits are programmed around the need to collect some dry-cleaning at 3 o'clock in the afternoon. Personal gain is ubiquitous. It probably lies behind the preferences about work location shown by social work students who were asked where they would like to practise. The top three preferred locations were Devon, Somerset and North Yorkshire. The West Midlands and the London boroughs were the least favoured areas (Collison and Kennedy 1985). At a more general level it has been noted that, within the NHS, it is difficult to disentangle what is seen as good for the service from what is seen as good for the professions within it (Brown 1975: 234).

People may use other heuristics to disguise or rationalise the application of the personal gain criterion. But the discernible presence of the personal gain heuristic in a person's arguments and justifications does not mean that other values incorporated in their thoughts and statements are invalidated. A lecturer, for example, may decide to introduce a new piece of curriculum into his or her teaching because it will be valuable to the pupils, but also because it will reduce the boredom of teaching over-familiar material, and provide an opportunity for professional development. There is no necessary harm in such conjunctions if the clients' interests are not compromised. Even if personal gain does distort decision making it does not necessarily amount to fraud or corruption. But Hepworth (1995) pointed out that the increasing use of rewards based on the performance measurement of managers creates dangers. This was particularly true of managers working in discrete managerial units which have no involvement in policy making. He argued that, instead of working towards the public interest, new public managers are tempted to make decisions which maintain their job or influence and which increase their performance-related pay. Negotiating targets which it is convenient to work towards and which can be easily measured is an example of the influence of the personal gain heuristic but it is below the threshold of corrupt behaviour.

118

However, public officials can cross the dividing line. The case of the Inland Revenue official who was found guilty of taking bribes provides an interesting example. He ran a specialised team of investigators set up to detect tax evasion amongst high rolling business people. To achieve his targets for the amount of revenue to be retrieved, he argued, he had to adopt the lifestyle of, and become friends with, the people he was investigating. If this involved accepting hospitality, gifts and money from them, then this was acceptable as long as he secured a larger payment to the Treasury from them. Although the jury thought differently and found him guilty of corruption, his self-justification was, as Hepworth might have predicted, that achievement of his targets made his behaviour efficient rather than corrupt. The use of market criteria of success can lead to behaviour which, when compared with the traditional public service ethic of detachment, may seem corrupt.

Many critics of public organisations have long argued that privileging the interests of public officials over that of the public has been a distinguishing mark of public organisations. This view is clearly seen in the theory that public organisations are subject to unconstrained growth. As Lane puts it:

> The hypothesis that bureaucrats maximise their own utility, and that their personal utility is a strict function of bureau size is a simple one.
>
> (Lane 1995: 65)

Others argue, in contradiction of the hypothesis, that in periods of retrenchment bureaux do reduce in size and that many bureaucrats consequently give a greater priority to security than they give to growth. In this scheme of things the bureaucrat will press for stability rather than growth (ibid.: 66). But, for the purposes of the argument being made, it does not matter whether bureaucrats' preference is for growth or stability, the significant observation is that in both cases they are putting their personal wishes ahead of the public interest.

Personal gain can be seen in the practice of public administration in the Indian sub-continent during British rule. There were never many English officials in India, in relation to the size of the country, and it was inevitable that most of the administration was done by Indian officials. In many administrative districts jobs as public officials became the *de facto* property of families (Frykenberg 1965). Washbrook and Baker (1975) in their study of the politics of south India found that the local administration of many districts was in the hands of particular caste associations. A caste association was a political and social association set up to protect and advance the interests of a particular caste. Towards the end of the nineteenth century caste associations and service families began to extend their influence from a local to a provincial stage. By the 1890s, for example, members of the Vembakkam Sri Vaishnava Brahman family held official posts throughout the Madras presidency and they had begun to hold annual family conferences in order to preserve their official and familial unity (ibid.: 159–60). In such situations it was inevitable that nepotism would

119

be important in recruitment to public jobs and that the administrative system would be bent to the advantage of the caste association.

The belief that political or administrative office is best seen as a source of advantage for one's family rather than as a public service or duty can easily become commonplace. This perception is not of course only found in the sub-continent. The payment that some MPs received for asking parliamentary questions is indicative of the same attitude. The Nolan Committee found that 30 per cent of MPs were holding paid consultancies and that this had contributed to the decline in public confidence in politicians. The report concluded that 'people are not always as clear as they should be about where the boundaries of acceptable conduct lie' (Committee on Standards in Public Life 1995a). Nolan's seven principles of proper public conduct, i.e.

- selflessness
- integrity – not being under any obligation to other people
- objectivity
- accountability
- openness
- honesty
- leadership,

can be used to define the heuristic of personal competence and gain. The first three principles are mirrors which give a reversed reflection of the behaviour of someone who seeks personal gain, the last four are aspects of virtue in public decision making which someone seeking personal competence should emulate.

4

THE RHETORIC OF RESOURCE ALLOCATION

Arguments about how priorities should be set
and resources allocated

The rhetorical perspective

The value heuristics that have been identified and described in chapters 2 and
3 are not, in themselves, complete ethical or philosophical positions; rather,
they are rhetorical material and devices which people can use in their arguments and debates about public sector resource allocation and service delivery.
They provide the themes from which people compose arguments in their
attempts to make sense of their work and their organisational worlds. The
analysis in this chapter is based on a rhetorical perspective and on a belief that
it is important to identify the arguments used, and the language games
that are played, by the participants in the arguments.

Humpty Dumpty, in Lewis Carroll's *Through the Looking Glass* can act as the
starting point for a brief review of the rhetorical perspective.

> 'When I use a word,' Humpty Dumpty said, in a rather scornful tone,
> 'it means just what I choose it to mean – neither more nor less.'
>
> 'The question is,' said Alice, 'whether you can make words mean
> so many different things.'
>
> 'The question is,' said Humpty Dumpty, 'which is to be master –
> that's all.'
>
> (Gardner 1970: 269)

The arguments over resource allocation and priority setting are constructed
from words, such as equity, fairness, effectiveness, which may have many meanings and the issue is, who is to be master in setting the meaning within any
particular group or debate. This chapter will give an account of some of the
battles for control of meaning but it will also describe how the question of
mastery may be a more personal one, as individuals, trying to create their own
interpretative schemes, tussle with the definitions of words that others seek to
impose on them.

Controversies about the meaning of terms are compounded by the tendency for proper names, in the managerial world, as well as in Humpty Dumpty's (Gardner 1970: 263), to take on universal meanings while ordinary words acquire a contingent meaning. By such devices does a brand name such as Xerox imply any form of photocopying while everyday words such as 'supervisory' and 'process' can acquire a ™ mark and represent a particular five-stage model for managing staff which is sold through the media of training seminars and audio tapes. Both illustrations exemplify the single process of people exercising mastery over words and, perhaps, using words to obtain mastery over other people.

Language games have four aspects which will be highlighted in this chapter. They are dialogic, they are rhetorical, they are changeable (arguments and attitudes change as the circumstances of the arguments alter), and they have some of the characteristics of story telling. The use of the term dialogic refers to the tendency for all thought to take the form of an argument (Billig 1996: 46–54, 190–1). A thought can only exist if there is a position to be argued against. Even if people are thinking through an issue quietly for themselves the process will be conversational, involving an internal dialogue with anticipated interlocutors. As Watson has put it:

> To think and to speak is to engage with counter-thoughts and counter-arguments. It is part of the process whereby we negotiate reality with others through the cultural medium of discourse and through which we justify and make sense, to ourselves and to others, of what we do.
>
> (Watson 1994a: 25)

It is probable that these disputations may become habitual, indeed, the resource allocation heuristics are elements of debate which have become inflexible through persistent and clichéd use, but no matter how predictable, debate retains a Manichean character.

The rhetorical nature of language games indicates the importance of the use of language as a device for persuading others. People try to persuade others, or at least have the last word in a conversation, through the inventiveness and the power of their arguments and by the skill they use in presenting the arguments. One common example of a presentational device is the urge to rename things when their value is challenged. In the early 1980s, for example, ministers often set off on QANGO (quasi-autonomous non-governmental organisations) hunts. They wanted to cull QANGOs because they were seen as a source of bureaucratic waste and ineptitude. By the early 1990s, in contrast, QANGOs were seen as a way of achieving managerial efficiency in the public sector because they represented an empowering driving down of decision making to the lowest possible managerial level. This change in the politicians' evaluation of them came to be reflected in their new names. In the health sector for example, the new QANGOs were called trusts, a name with a powerful emotional undercurrent. The persuasive use of such tricks, tropes and trimming is inherent in all our communication. Watson, for example, has taken a banal, and short, piece of managerial banter and identified the unself-conscious use of seventeen rhetorical figures by the speakers (1994a: 184–6). Others (Swales and Rogers 1995) have dissected the rhetorical nature of more formal communications such as mission statements.

Protagoras was an early Greek rhetorician who had a distaste for oratorical fancies, but the argument about the relative worth of style and content is always present whenever the term rhetoric is used. The emphasis in this chapter is on the Protagorean rhetoric of argumentative invention rather than on the rhetoric of tricks and tropes (Billig 1996: 3). There are several stages in the classical rhetorical process which include *inventio*, the construction of the points and arguments to be used in a debate, and *elocutio* which is the persuasive style in which the arguments are presented (Yates 1969: 20). It is the subjects of the argument that will be considered in this chapter, and not the manner of their presentation.

Billig (1996: chapter 7) identified a third characteristic of language games that will be referred to. It is the tendency for arguments and attitudes to change shape and focus as a debate unfolds. The phenomenon may be explained by considering the nature of attitudes. The definition of attitudes has reached a point where they are seen as a possession, as something a person has or owns. A person's set of attitudes therefore is like a collection of fine china or a schoolboy's collection of free toys from McDonald's. The collection is made up of tangible and discrete objects which stand witness for the things that their owner values. Once attitudes are seen as an unchanging set of things, then it becomes possible for the opinion researcher, standing outside the department stores with their Likert scales and clipboards, to count and measure them. Billig puts attitudes into a different light. He argues that they only exist in relation to matters of controversy and that they are a stance that is taken on a matter of public debate (Billig 1996: 207). One implication of this view is that attitudes are things people are prepared to get into arguments about, and Billig offers some experimental evidence that people's attitudes can arise out of debate. Someone may become engaged in a debate without any initial strong feeling one way or another, but as positions are taken and arguments made, they can easily form attitudes under the pressure of rhetorical attack (ibid.: 208). The general conclusion to be drawn is that attitudes are not simple and monolithic things that have a fixed and permanent place in people's thoughts. Rather, they develop and adapt as people face new circumstances and fresh arguments. At times people can experience a gap between their general attitudes (e.g. 'I approve of staff development') and their specific beliefs ('This course I am on is awful'). Tensions such as these can change the shape and form of attitudes.

The final characteristic of language games that will be raised in this chapter is the importance of story telling. This is not to say that language games are mendacious. It is simply to recognise the power of myths and stories to help people deal with the contradictions and disjunctures that they experience in life. As Kirk, following Lévi-Strauss, puts it in his study of the Greek myths:

> The function of myths, then, is to make such contradictions bearable, not so much by embodying wish-fulfilment fantasies or releasing inhibitions as by setting up pseudo-logical models by which the contradictions are resolved, or rather palliated.
>
> (Kirk 1976: 83)

A more recent example of this rhetorical process can be found in Silverman's study of patients' families in a paediatric cardiology unit. Many of the relatives told Silverman (1993: 182–3) that they felt that the presence of so many medical staff in the room at the time of their first outpatient appointment made it very difficult for them to ask questions of the doctors. Yet, when he analysed the transcripts of these consultations, he found that on average parents asked more questions when there were more medical staff present than when there were less. He theorised about why parents should draw attention to this feature when it appeared in practice not to cause them problems. The answer he proposed was that the parents were presenting their experience in the form of a story in which the issue of the number of medical staff was a dramatic way of expressing the pressure they found themselves under. In following through this analysis he adopted the idea of *moral tales* from other sociological research because he did not want to see his findings as a simple misunderstanding on the part of the parents he had talked to.

> Instead we came to see parents' accounts as moral tales . . . Our respondents struggled to present their actions in the context of moral versions of responsible parenthood in a situation where the dice were loaded against them (because of the risks to life and the high-technology means of diagnosis and treatment).
>
> (Silverman 1993: 200)

It would appear that one aspect of our language games is the way we construct stories which help us come to terms with the pressures we live and work with and which enable us to maintain our own ethical self-image. In management terms the accounts managers give of themselves in their appraisal interviews may well be a form of moral tales (Jacques 1992).

Controversies about resource allocation take place at many levels. At the first level there are the internal debates people have with themselves about the proper means of allocating resources. But beyond this level there are a number of public debates that need to be reviewed. When I began researching these questions in the early 1980s, before the Thatcherite explosion of markets, quasi-markets and internal markets within the public services, the emphasis was on the arguments between public officials about which criteria for resource allocation and priority setting should be used. These debates occurred both within and between organisational levels. While it could be the case, in a social services department for example, that professional staff took a different view from that of top management, it was also likely that there were internal debates within both of these groups (Miller and Munn-Giddings 1993). During the late 1980s and the early 1990s the subject of the discussion changed to the relative merits of bureaux (or hierarchies) and markets as mechanisms for allocating resources and services. Whereas, in the earlier phase, the argument had been about which values public officials should apply, in this latter phase the controversy focused on whether public choice, as expressed through the mechanism of a market, should not transcend the decisions of officials. The arguments no longer concerned internal issues. They became externalised and directed to the design of appropriate mechanisms for avoiding the officials' heuristics. In the 1990s when many public services are provided by privatised companies or by local public spending bodies (such as TECs and grant main-tained schools), the issue has become whether the mechanisms of the market are sufficient to maintain proper levels of conduct and whether they are adequate to protect the customer from exploitation.

The discussion of the rhetoric of resource allocation in this chapter will be placed in the context of four arenas of argument. Each of these arenas could illustrate all of the four characteristics of language games already discussed but, in order to highlight the points, each arena will be used to exemplify a particular aspect, as shown below.

- *Personal arguments about resource allocation*: rhetoric as story telling.
- *Arguments within public sector organisations about the appropriateness of different heuristics*: the development of arguments and attitudes within the context of an unfolding debate.
- *Arguments about the relative merits of public sector organisations and markets*: the dialogic nature of rhetoric.
- *Arguments about the effectiveness of market mechanisms*: the persuasive nature of rhetoric.

Agonising as individuals

The Resource Allocation Preferences Survey (RAPS)

Individuals have their own internal arguments about how resource allocation decisions should be made which often belie the assertiveness of their public utterances. In this section some of these arguments will be illustrated and the use of story telling as part of language games will be used to explain the processes involved. The RAPS (resource allocation preferences survey) questionnaire was designed to capture a little of the flavour of these individual debates. It was written after the monksbane and feverfew instrument and was intended

125

as a questionnaire that could be used for training and research purposes. RAPS is a traditional attitude measurement instrument for use throughout the public sector. The use of a questionnaire does not imply acceptance of the traditional view of attitudes as fixed mental objects, or agreement with the view that given conversational cues will always trigger standard forms of words in response (Billig 1991: 190). Strong views, according to Billig, are adapted and reformulated as a person discusses them and so their expression can be typified by variability and novelty. People will describe their views from different perspectives as an argument unfolds and turns in on itself, just as a three-dimensional image on a computer screen can be rotated and viewed from unusual standpoints. RAPS cannot capture the intricacy of such patterns and it cannot identify novelty because it uses predetermined statements, but it can throw into relief the variability of people's views on resource allocation.

The first version of RAPS was a long, fifty-statement, questionnaire. The statements were sorted into groups of five, each of which had statements categorised as belonging to each of the five resource allocation heuristics. The respondents were asked to rank the statements by distributing ten points between the five statements. The more they agreed with a statement, the more of the ten points they allocated to it. The intention was to make respondents think about the statements in relative terms and avoid the temptation of rating every statement as a good thing.

The first version of RAPS was piloted on a small group of eighteen middle managers from the public sector. The results indicated a high degree of randomness in the way people responded to the statements. That is to say, statements which all, supposedly, expressed the same belief were not always scored the same by respondents. This ought to have been anticipated because the statements attempted to express complex values through a vocabulary with many layers of, not always consistent, meaning. The analysis meant that about twenty-five of the statements could be jettisoned because they could not bear the strain placed on them.

However, there was still a degree of inconsistency amongst the remaining statements, although much less than in the rejected statements. The amount of variation was different for each of the resource heuristics. Individual need showed much more variation than the statements which defined the utility heuristic. This led to a close examination of the statements; and the possibility emerged that the statements associated with each heuristic could be classified into two types. Some were broad expressions of a belief, without context or constraint. These can be called expressions of espoused values. Other statements, however, related to hard cases. These tended to be set, at least nominally, in a real-life context where decisions were difficult and the consequences were hard. Mostly this second class of statement referred to situations of budget stress where cuts or redundancies were necessary. The remaining statements in this 'hard case' category were extreme descriptions of the heuristics such as people might adopt when their values were being strongly challenged.

Following this analysis a new version of RAPS was written. It is given in an addendum to this chapter. This questionnaire contains twenty statements and respondents are asked to rate each statement independently and in turn. Half of these twenty statements are judged to be expressions of espoused values and the other half contains descriptions of value preferences in hard cases. There are two analysis sheets in the questionnaire. One sheet assesses the respondents' preferences about resource allocation in general terms whilst the other analyses their preferences in hard cases.

The implication of the construction of RAPS is that, in this case at least, people's value preferences are contingent on their situation. The introduction of this variable of course makes the construction of a valid and reliable questionnaire difficult. The problem is caused because the structure of the questionnaire requires us to believe that, on this particular issue, people have two pre-prepared packages of attitudes, one for general public consumption and one for use in difficult cases. This is like shopping in the supermarket: there on the shelf is the upmarket glossily branded product which will be bought when you want to make a show, and then there is the own brand cheaper alternative for use in straitened times. But, as has been discussed earlier, research suggests that people will have many views, some of which they will not have clearly articulated, and which they will reveal selectively according to the nature of the argument they are involved in. It is accepted therefore that RAPS can only give a view in which the contrasts have been heightened, as in a landscape as seen through a Claude glass which painters used to enhance the contrast between light and shade. Nevertheless, despite this constraint, a pilot test and an analysis of the internal consistency of the test data from this second version of RAPS suggested that the questionnaire was valid within its limited objective.

The RAPS questionnaire was completed by 106 middle managers from health authorities and local authorities. They were not the same people as those who completed the monksbane and feverfew instrument, but like them they were participants in middle management training programmes. The questionnaire was always completed at the start of a session so that subsequent tutorial input or group discussion did not affect the participants' responses. The results are given in table 4.1. The espoused results will be discussed first and if the results are put in order of rank, the preferences of the middle managers can be clearly seen as in table 4.2.

It is suggested, later in this chapter, that individual need and utility might be the characteristic heuristics of middle managers. This is clearly what the results suggest, with individual need claiming the top position. The pre-eminence of individual need is easily explained. As was discussed in relation to the monksbane and feverfew results, almost all public sector middle managers in local government and the health services began their careers with professional training and professional practice from which they will have acquired a belief in individual need as a trigger for the provision of services. It is to be

Table 4.1 Analysis of middle managers' responses to the Resource Allocation
Preferences questionnaire

Resource allocation heuristic	Mean scores for espoused values	Mean scores for hard case values
Individual need	3.45	6.42
Fairness	5.13	8.71
Utility	4.83	5.0
Ecology	5.74	4.60
Deservingness	7.42	4.60

Notes: n = 106.
Rating scale 1 = this expresses my preferences very well, through to 10 = this does not express
my preference at all.

Table 4.2 Middle managers' heuristic preferences: 'espoused values'

Rank		Heuristic
Most preferred	1	Individual need
	2	Utility
	3	Fairness
	4	Ecology
Least preferred	5	Deservingness

expected, in a questionnaire concerned with espoused values, that those beliefs
acquired early in a career will continue to figure importantly in any public
expression of values. But the results also suggest that these middle managers
have successfully accumulated, in addition to their professional beliefs, an acceptance of the managerial value of utility. Ecology and deservingness are at
the bottom of the rank order.

The results for middle managers' preferences in hard cases, however, are very
different from those for the values they espouse. The rank ordering of the
resource allocation value preferences reported in response to this category of
statements is shown in table 4.3. The impact of hard cases on people's expressed
views is to evince less concern for individual need and fairness but more for
deservingness and ecology. In hard times, the results from this questionnaire
would have us believe, middle managers think that allocation decisions should
be made in relation to the worthiness of the subjects of such expenditure
(deservingness) and in relation to the ecological influence that these subjects
can bring to bear. In short, middle managers become more political than rational
in their priority setting. The questionnaire suggests that in principle middle
managers do not think that moral judgements about clients should affect decisions about need and priority. But when resources are scarce they show a
preference for helping those who help themselves (thus relegating the undeserving to a lesser priority) and for giving priority to vigilance against the abuse

Table 4.3 Middle managers' heuristic preferences in 'hard cases'

Rank		Heuristic
Most preferred (joint top)	1	Deservingness
	1	Ecology
	3	Utility
	4	Individual need
Least preferred	5	Fairness

of expenditure. It is worth noting that in the hard case results all the heuristics become less popular. The average score for all the espoused value statements is 2.65 while that for all the hard case statements is 2.94. This would suggest that managers find all of the heuristics harder to apply in extreme circumstances. But, when managers see themselves as under pressure, deservingness becomes relatively more popular, followed by ecology with the next greatest increase in popularity.

A move from espoused value to hard case values in people's responses to the questionnaire makes relatively little impact on the ratings of the utility heuristic. It becomes a little more unpopular in hard cases but the amount is too small for it to be statistically significant. Utility, it seems, is a heuristic for all seasons, a staple value. From the anecdotes managers tell, utility seems to be a criterion that public sector managers accept but without enthusiasm and so, as in quiet reflection they dislike it but accept it, so in hard times there is little additional angst associated with its use. Fairness and individual need, however, are abandoned under pressure. The decline in the rating of individual need is probably explained by its status as a residual value left over from the early days of individuals' careers. Its function is to remind the individual that there was a time when their values were pure. This is a luxury that has to be abandoned when managers are trying to cope with resource stress. The decline in the popularity of fairness is more difficult to explain. One possibility relates to the way the application of the fairness heuristic would seek to share out the pain of resource stress evenly. In hard times this is not a recipe for survival since it maximises complaint and opposition.

One of the main findings drawn from RAPS is that people under pressure become more ecological, and hence more political, in their rhetoric and actions. They also become more responsive to the deservingness criteria and so discriminate between people on moral criteria. The results from RAPS are almost too neat to be true, and there has to be a suspicion that the clarity of the outcomes may be more the result of some bias built into the questionnaire than a reflection of people's views. But other research published in the literature suggests that the phenomenon identified by RAPS may not be uncommon. Ferlie and Judge (1981) provided some useful research findings in a study of budget decision making in social services departments. They hypothesised that reductions in budgets would lead managers to use more rigorous, utilitarian and management science-based, techniques in their efforts to find where budget cuts should be made. Their findings, however, falsified the hypothesis. They found that budgetary retrenchment did not appear to result in greater rationality in social service department budgeting, but quite the reverse as 'recurrent crisis budgeting tends to neither the synoptic nor rational but aims solely at preventing total collapse'. The emphasis on survival in organisations facing budget reductions creates a situation in which managers give greater emphasis to the political stakeholder ecology of their organisations; and this may be interpreted as giving more play to the ecological and deservingness heuristics.

Watson's (1977) discussion of the role of LIFO (last in first out) as a criterion for deciding who should go when an organisation makes redundancies can also be used to throw light on how people in difficult circumstances choose heuristics. In order to make this argument it is necessary to identify LIFO with one of the resource allocation criteria identified in chapter 2. This is not a straightforward task. LIFO is not fair in the way it is defined in this book because it does not give to each employee an equal probability of keeping or losing their job. It seems that LIFO is essentially a moral criterion based on the belief that people who have invested the longest amount of service have generated a sense of obligation towards them on the part of their employers. They are the most deserving of keeping their jobs and therefore LIFO may be interpreted as an aspect of the deservingness criteria.

Watson identified, in his studies of personnel managers, that those who had no actual experience of managing redundancy expressed a preference for utilitarian criterion (get rid of those who have least contribution to make) or individual need criterion (make redundant those who can best recover from it) in making redundancy decisions, while those who had managed redundancy preferred LIFO. This can be interpreted as meaning that those who have no practical experience of redundancy see it as a hypothetical situation and apply their espoused values, whilst those who have had to make people redundant see it as a very hard case and apply pragmatic criteria. He suggests that in a situation where managers have to make decisions about redundancy they are 'men in the middle' who have to respond to pressures from both top management and from the trade unions, and that for such people LIFO emerges as an ecological compromise that meets the needs of both these groups. It provides the top managers with the reduction in numbers they require and uses a criterion that is felt to be acceptable by the unions. It may also have been that the welfare orientation of many personnel managers in the 1970s would make them receptive to the deservingness claim of people who had been in the organisation for many years. This analysis of Watson's argument suggests, as do the results from RAPS, that in difficult situations managers apply criteria based on ecology and deservingness. As a postscript to this argument it is interesting to speculate on the reasons why, between the 1970s and the 1990s, LIFO appears to have lost out to utilitarian criteria as a decision rule for deciding who is to lose their jobs. It may be because the ecological balance between top management and the trade unions, that led to a preference for LIFO, has shifted dramatically in favour of the employers in the intervening years.

Evidence of the impact of financial pressure on managers' resource allocation values can also be found in the research carried out by Jick and Murray (1982). They concluded that managers who are faced with demands for budget cuts will respond according to their own estimation of the influence they wield in their organisation. If they see themselves as relatively powerful they will oppose the cuts. The way in which they pursue this opposition will depend on their interpretation of the motives for the cuts. If they believe that the demands for cuts are based on sound analysis and believable data, e.g. a change in the demographics of the client population, then they will conduct their fight against the cuts with the weapons of rational argument and data, which are both designed to show that the original analysis was faulty. If, on the other hand, they believe that the demand for cuts is based on political whim or bias they will fight them by mobilising power in support of their budgets and the values implicit in them. Anthony and Herzlinger (1975: 249–57) give an amusing catalogue of the political ploys that public sector managers may use in defence of their budgets or in their bids to increase their budgets. In situations where the budget holders regard themselves as powerless in relation to the budget providers, or they are merely worn down by endless demands for cuts, they will acquiesce in the budget restrictions.

Jick and Murray also identified a number of organisational cultural characteristics which might predispose managers to see budget cuts as being based on analysis rather than politics. These included the availability of advance information about likely cuts or whether announcements about cutbacks were only made in crisis conditions. A belief amongst managers that the organisation was good at providing them with feedback, that it had good consultative procedures and clear policies and procedures also predisposed them to see a cut as rationally grounded while the absence of such beliefs bent them towards a political construction of the cut (Jick and Murray 1982: 154). So, while their model does not imply that all managers in hard times adopt ecological and deservingness criteria, they do provide an interesting psychological calculus which explains why many might.

This cultural analysis of managers' reactions to resource cuts can be made into a rhetorical analysis by standing it on its head. As it stands, the argument is that managers will absorb the organisational culture by the stories and anecdotes they tell each other about the way senior managers make decisions. The more the stories stress the informality and the 'point scoring' aspect of decision making, then the more will managers respond to senior management's announcements as if they were politically based and thereby strengthen the culture of political game playing. The satire on joint decision making shown in figure 4.1 is a good example of the genre. But, if looked at from a different angle the analysis could proceed as follows. Middle managers are told they must cut their budgets, they respond in a political rather than a rational manner.

This causes them some discomfort as this is not the way managers are supposed to behave. They begin to form and tell stories which explain how unfair and difficult senior managers are and which imply that, though they are reasonable and mature people, it is impossible for them to behave in this way in the face of such appalling behaviour from their superiors. To use the term introduced earlier in this chapter, the managers create moral tales which maintain their sense of being responsible in the face of pressures to be otherwise. Silverman (1993: 200) noted the importance of 'atrocity' stories to maintaining an individual's self-image. He reported the work of Webb and Stimson (1976) on consultations with medical general practitioners. They noted that when asked to give accounts of the consultation they told stories in which they behaved actively and sensibly whereas the GPs were routinely shown to be insensitive and of poor judgement.

> By telling 'atrocity stories' ... patients were able to give vent to thoughts which had gone unvoiced at the time of the consultation, to redress a real or perceived inequality between doctor and patient and to highlight the teller's own rationality.
>
> (Silverman 1993: 200)

Hard times and budget cutting are circumstances that illustrate the story telling aspect of language games. I am not trying to make a point about cause and effect. It is not the case that the atrocity stories are caused by the demands for cuts, they are, however, a way by which people come to explain and interpret their own behaviour. And, of course, the idea that rhetoric and culture are in some ways the opposite of each other is inaccurate. Clearly the stories that people tell may become part of the organisation's cultural stock and may well influence how people in the future respond to cuts. Rhetoric and culture are interdependent.

The main conclusion from this part of the chapter is that people agonise over which of the resource allocation heuristics they should use in particular circumstances. It is certainly the case that the complexity of these personal debates is greater than presented by the results from RAPS. RAPS proposes a simple structure which contrasts espoused values with hard case values. It is unlikely that there are only two levels in the structure of people's values. As with Peer Gynt's onion, it is possible to continue stripping away the layers and never find a core. But even the notion of a structure of values may be going too far: the resource heuristics are probably no more than a discursive resource from which people weave different patterns of values as their context and conscience suggest. From a rhetorical point of view the interesting issue may be the way people tell stories to justify their actions rather than an alleged inconsistency between espoused and practised values. RAPS then gives a very ill focused picture of these personal debates with too strong a contrast but it does at least provide a glimpse of the complexity.

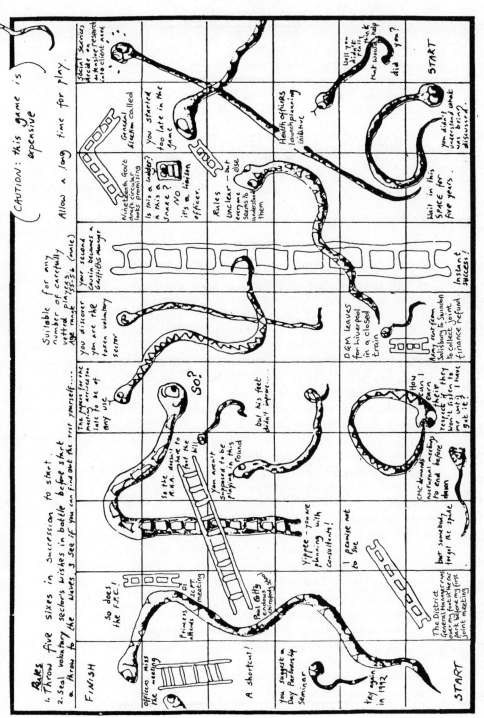

Figure 4.1 The joint planning game

Source: The Newsletter, Community Care in Wiltshire, July–August 1986.

Arguments within public sector organisations

In the period from the reorganisations of the NHS and local government in 1974, through to the first half of the 1980s the key debates about resource allocation took place within the public sector and were focused on the criteria that public managers and politicians should use when setting priorities. In other words, there were arguments about which of the heuristics identified in the previous chapter should hold sway in decision making. The main groups involved in the arguments were the hierarchical levels, or domains, within public organisations. The intention in this section is to describe the polarities of the argument in terms of the hierarchical status of the participants. This section will also be used to illustrate the way in which people's attitudes and preferences can adapt and modify according to the circumstances they find themselves in.

Arguments about heuristics and values

First, it will be useful to clarify the nature of the controversies which separate the proponents of different heuristics. There is a danger when trying to answer this question of, 'squeezing everything into dichotomies', which was Bacon's judgement on a structurally minded Renaissance grammarian (Padley 1985). But it is an unavoidable consequence of the rhetorical approach that things must be seen in terms of argumentative polarities. With this in mind it is suggested that the first five heuristics (individual need, fairness, utility, ecology and deservingness) can be analysed in relation to two dichotomies. The first is taken from Dworkin's (1977) distinction between principle and policy. According to Dworkin's definition a case derived from principle assumes that people have a moral right to a thing, irrespective of whether the organisation or agency involved has any official view as to what is desirable for those individuals. Rights may be natural and universal or they may be part of a contract of mutual obligation, but they are met or granted, not because of their consequences, but because it is right to do so. Service allocation according to principle is not goal based whereas a policy-based allocation is. An argument of policy is concerned with the public benefit of doing one thing rather than another. If I can relate this distinction to two technical terms from the philosophy of ethics, policy is consequentialist whilst principle is deontological. In Dworkin's words:

> I call a policy the kind of standard that sets out a goal to be reached, generally an improvement in some economic, political or social feature of the community (though some goals are negative, in that they stipulate some present feature that is to be protected from adverse change). I call a principle a standard that is to be observed, not because it will advance or secure an economic, political or social situation deemed desirable, but because it is a requirement of justice or fairness or some other dimension of morality.
>
> (Dworkin 1977: 22)

134

The second dichotomy that will be used is one which distinguishes a subjective and an objective view of people. From the first perspective people are seen as self-directing, morally accountable and autonomous agents. A view from the second perspective reifies people and sees them as collections of objective conditions or as members of statistically aggregated populations. The first perspective gives a view of the social world dominated by individual actions and motives whilst social trends and historical forces are seen as the moving forces from the second perspective.

This distinction is similar to an analysis of modern ideologies made by Kochen and Deutsch (1980: 6) which is based on work by Marien. They characterised two perspectives on post-industrial society, termed service society and decentralism. The service society advocates take an objective view, the decentralists take a subjective focus. The former favour technique and order, the latter prefer self-determination, plurality of values and moral freedom. Kochen and Deutsch's characteristics of the two ideologies are shown in figure 4.2 which gives a leftist

	SSAMs as:	Decentralists as:
SSAMs see:	Scientific	Nihilistic, apocalyptic
	Objective	Romantic
	Quantitative	Antiscience
	Professional	Antiprogress
	Harnessing technology	Ineffective
	Bureaucrats	Moralistic
	Interdependent in the global community	Hedonistic
Decentralists see:	Amoral technocrats	Striving for self-sufficiency as the good life
	Elitist experts	
	Reductionists	Independent in small communities
	Middle class welfare	Yearning for return to agrarian life
	Careerists	Acting on their values, freely expressed
	Tools of big government	Ecologically minded
	Tools of big business	Appreciating that small is beautiful
	Ignorant of the real world	Future-orientated

Figure 4.2 How decentralists and service society advocates and members (SSAMs) see themselves and one another

Source: Kochen and Deutsch (1980: 4).

slant to the decentralist ideology. But the decentralist values of smallness, independence and moral integrity would also find adherents on the political right. As George (1985) has pointed out, both the Thatcherite enterprise ideal and the decentralism of the Greens share a common anti-statism. Where they differ is over the specific values they would wish to be dominant in a decentralised society.

These two dichotomies, policy–principle and subjective–objective, can be used to define a matrix for categorising the value heuristics. Any management author ought to feel apologetic about producing yet another two by two matrix. But they are a convenient way of summarising the major characteristics of the heuristics. It is shown in figure 4. 3. The positioning of the heuristics in the matrix needs justification.

As has been discussed in the previous chapter, the individual need heuristic is concerned with individual's rights to services. These rights originate from needs which are determined largely by objective and professional assessment. The individual need heuristic is consequently classified as one based upon principle and objectivism. Utility concentrates on defining, measuring and maximising the objective good achieved by policies. So it is defined as a combination of policy and objectivity.

The fairness heuristic occupies a transitory position between the two heuristics of need and utility. It is objective in that, from its vantage point, clients are seen as elements in a statistical population who have to be treated equally. Fairness has an objective orientation because it is concerned with populations rather than with individuals. Whether the treatment of one person is fair can only be judged in comparison with the treatment of all others. But when the dimension of principle and policy is considered, fairness can be justified by both standpoints. For many people fairness is a matter of simple principle; it is the proper way to behave; for others it is justified because it works. For many years the queue and the waiting list were the main mechanism for access to many public services because they were workable and simple. The debate about the basis of equal opportunities policies, which are an application of the criterion of fairness, can illustrate this dual nature. The argument is about whether the case for equal opportunities programmes and policies should be made on the basis of ethical principle or on the basis of the 'business case' for it. The former implies such policies should be implemented because they are right whereas the latter would argue that they should be followed because they will make organisations more effective (Cassell 1996). Fairness therefore is shown in an intermediary position between principle and policy.

The ecology heuristic provides a subjective view of clients and is concerned with the outcome of the continuous evaluations that stakeholders make of an organisation's activities. It is policy based but is interested in the subjective rather than the objective impact of policies. Someone with an ecological orientation will be happy if a policy is seen to be a success by powerful interest groups. The deservingness heuristic also views people from a subjective position

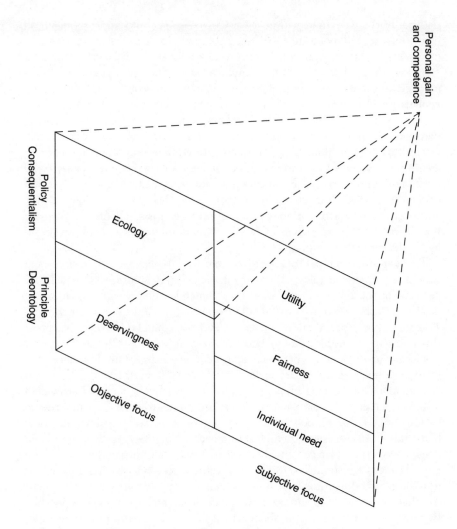

Figure 4.3 The value heuristics of resource allocation

but it is only concerned with whether clients have earned the moral privilege (or right) of receiving services. It is therefore classified by its equal concerns with principle and the subjective autonomy of persons. Personal competence is excluded from the matrix but linked with it. It is shown in the third dimension because its application can be associated with any of the other heuristics in the matrix.

The analysis so far has stressed the epistemological differences between the heuristics. The next step is to consider some concrete examples of how these heuristics might be used in controversies about public services. It is not necessarily the case that, within a particular resource allocation problem, all the heuristics will point to a different solution. In some cases they will be congruent, in others they will form into opposing blocs. To take a particular case: I was once (in the late 1970s) involved with others in a project to decide a policy for the provision of professional librarians to secondary schools. In our analysis we identified a number of key variables concerning the use of school libraries and their need for chartered librarians. Some schools, for example, had purpose-built resource centres and libraries that were centrally located. Others had smaller library premises which were often away from the teaching areas. Some schools had a formal policy for using resource and enquiry-based teaching methods, others did not. Some had spent a considerable proportion of their general allowance on library stock, others had given it a low priority. Although, it is worth noting, even the most generous schools, in terms of library provision, did not come near to the input norm for library books suggested by the Library Association.

The policy that was decided upon was that schools above a certain size would be given a chartered school librarian, if their library stocks were at least 65 per cent of the Library Association's recommended library stock for a school of its size. If the size of the stock could be taken as an indicator of the school's valuation of a library, then a number of heuristics could be adduced to support this policy. First, using a utility heuristic, it could be argued that this policy would maximise the ratio between input and benefit by giving librarians only to those schools which would make use of them. Second, using a deserving-ness argument, it seemed proper to reward those schools who had attempted to help themselves by using scarce capitation monies to keep their libraries up to standard. Those schools which had not done so were undeserving of a librarian. Third, using an ecological approach, the policy met the minimum needs of two particular constituencies, the LEA's school library service (which carried a lot of organisational weight) and those schools and teachers committed to resource-based learning, whilst also keeping relatively happy the constituencies that were concerned with keeping staffing levels and costs as low as possible. By interpreting the arguments about school librarians in terms of the heuristics it can be claimed that the ecology, utility and deservingness heuristics were lined up to support the policy, although in the event it was probably the ecological arguments that carried the greatest weight. Opposed to the policy were the two other heuristics. The supporters of individual need argued that all children in all schools needed the support that a librarian would provide and that all schools should have a librarian added to their establishment. The fairness heuristic could be used to support this stance by claiming that whether a child received the benefit of a school librarian should not be dependent upon whether they lived in the catchment area of a school that was enthusiastic about its library. Fairness would demand that all schools be treated equally. This example shows how the heuristics can be building blocks from which people can build edifices of argumentation. In this case, needs and fairness arguments were ranged against the other heuristics, but other combinations might emerge in different situations.

It is also important to note that it is not always a straightforward task to identify the value heuristics that underlie particular actions and decisions. Let us take another example. A chief dietician explained to me, during a conversation held in the late 1980s, that in the past anyone who was overweight had been allowed to attend obesity clinics for as long as they remained overweight. But the policy had recently been changed, only those clients who contracted to co-operate with the clinic, and who followed the recommended diets, would be allowed more than a few appointments. There are two possible interpretations of this decision in terms of the value heuristics used. The first is that it is a response to the utility heuristic. Under this heading the argument would run along cost effectiveness lines. Scarce resources, such as the time of dieticians, should only be spent on people who are going to co-operate and so benefit. To provide the service to other obese people is simply going to mean that less than the greatest amount of good will be achieved with the resources available. Need, under this analysis, is no longer an adequate trigger for receiving treatment. Similar arguments were being made by other health professionals, such as physiotherapists, at this time. In one case the pattern of giving patients a fixed number of future appointments was replaced by a system in which people's responses to treatment and their need for more appointments was assessed at each attendance. This meant that people who were not responding to treatment did not carry on attending even though the physiotherapy was doing no good (Clifton 1984). The second interpretation of the dieticians' decision is an application of deservingness. Clients who will not adhere to agreements are being troublesome and morally culpable and so ought to be denied further treatment on these moral grounds alone. In practice both of these heuristics could be seen in the decision to restrict the service. In the objective mode the dieticians carried out a detailed survey to identify the costs and the benefits of the service; while, in subjectivist mode, dieticians often reacted with moral indignation when faced with uncooperative clients, jotting down WOT (waste of time) on their patients' case notes.

In summary, the resource allocation heuristics do not have unique policy or programme consequences; a person's policy position cannot be deduced from their heuristic preferences (even assuming that such preferences are fixed and intransitive). This conclusion implies that people incorporate arguments derived from particular heuristics in their discourse because they seem appropriate or persuasive in the social context of the debate. In other words, to reinforce a point frequently made, the heuristics are rhetorical resources.

Arguments between domains

It was suggested earlier that in the 1970s and the early 1980s most of the arguments about resource allocation took place between different groupings within public sector organisations. It will be helpful at this stage to review the literature on domains in public sector organisations to see if it provides evidence about the organisational location of the disputants. One pattern has been suggested by Kouzes and Mico (1979) specifically for human service organisations (HSOs). They argued that these organisations can be divided into three domains: policy, management and service. Each of these constitutes a separate world of values and style. Each domain is internally consistent but their different values put them into conflict one with another. Edmonstone (1982) tested this American-developed model on the NHS and found it applicable in the 1980s. The characteristics of each domain are shown in figure 4.4.

The information in figure 4.4 can be used to identify the resource allocation preferences that the different domains might have. The description of the policy domain uses words – such as representative, participative, negotiating and bargaining – which are redolent of the ecology heuristic, although it does not specifically suggest that the ecological criterion, of significance to organisational survival, should dominate. Rather, it indicates that, in the policy domain, equity is the criterion of success. The term equity implies some kind of justice in the way resources are distributed amongst the electorate and other stakeholders, although the usefulness of the word lies in its ambiguity rather than its specificity (Bjorkman 1985). The characteristics of the management domain encapsulate the utility heuristic with its interest in cost effectiveness; whilst the values of the service domain are close to the need heuristic, concerned as it is, with quality of services, professional standards and client-specific problem solving (the meeting of needs?).

This is a beguiling model: but it has limitations. There are, for instance, some domains missing. The management domain could usefully be divided into two, middle management and top management. The roles of the two groups differ and the distinction between them in public sector organisations is often heightened by the location of middle managers in the 'field' and top management's location in a central HQ. Stewart (1983) has pointed out the value differences that exist between the two. The lack of this distinction in Kouze's and Mico's model became more important in the late 1980s with the increasing use of a division between purchasers (who are centrally based) and suppliers (who are field based) in public organisations.

As is often the case in organisational studies, the manual and the non-professionally qualified staff have been omitted from Kouze and Mico's analysis altogether. They need to be brought in, because in many public services (hospitals, domiciliary services, libraries), they are critical to the delivery of the service. Such staff may have no formal responsibility for resource allocation but they have a powerful effect on service distribution because they deliver it. In any case they will have views on the equity of resource allocation which will affect their organisational role. In local government, where staff were increasingly politicised in the 1980s, the lack of a formal role in policy making for non-professional staff did not prevent a de facto policy role. Staff might have an

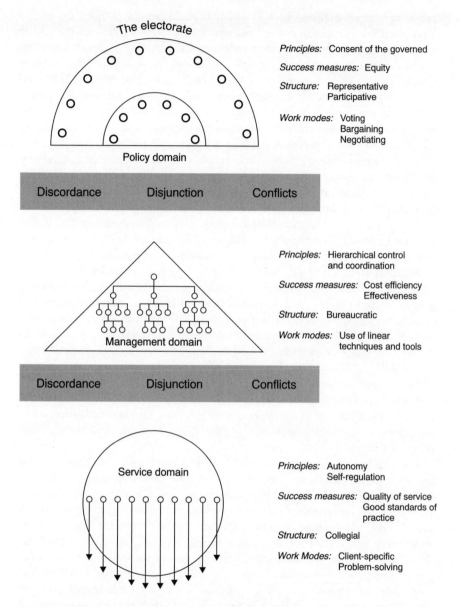

Figure 4.4 The three domains of human service organisations

Source: Reprinted with permission from NTL Institute for Applied Sciences. 'Domain Theory: an introduction to organisational behavior in human service organisations', by Kouzes, James M. and Paul R. Mico. *Journal of Applied Behavioral Sciences*, 15, 4, 449–69. Issn # 0021–8863.

influence with councillors which by-passed that of their chief officers. Laffin and Young (1985) quoted the example of staff who exercised influence on a local authorities through their position in Labour or Conservative party organisations.

Kakabadse (1982) made a cultural analysis of social services departments which was similar to that of Kouzes and Mico. He used Harrison's (1972) division of organisational ideologies into role cultures, task cultures and power cultures as the foundation of his analysis. He characterised the bottom of the organisation (up to social work team leader level) as a task or team culture. The middle of the organisation (up to assistant director level) was described as a role culture and the top management was labelled as a power culture. Inevitably these different cultures operated according to different values. To put my own gloss on his analysis: the task culture could be said to use the individual need heuristic; the role culture operated according to the precepts of utility and top management used ecology as a guiding heuristic. Kakabadse identified conflicts between these cultures, and it fell to the team leaders and assistant directors, he argued, to act as gatekeepers between them.

An analysis with a similar aim to those of Kouze, Mico and Kakabadse was produced by Thompson (1986) in his study of the NHS. Although his starting point was the politics of organisational decision making, and not cultures and ideologies, his delineations of the coalitions within the NHS has some similarities with the descriptions already discussed. Thompson's study focused on the way different groups within the NHS viewed the service's clients and interpreted their health needs. He claimed there was no objective conception of patients' needs but that, instead, there were different political coalitions which expressed a variety of perspectives. In the health service, prior to the introduction of general management in the early 1980s, he identified three major groupings: the political coalition, the practitioner coalition and the administrative coalition.

The political coalition was formed from local and national politicians and members of the health authorities (this list now needs extending to include trust board members). They, Thompson argued, saw the users of healthcare as customers and consumers who had to be kept from major discontent. Theirs was a largely commercial orientation, concerned with keeping the customers happy. The pay off for the political coalition was that customers would pay their taxes and vote for the them, or their political patrons, at the next election. The practitioner coalition was composed of those who delivered healthcare, and they typically saw the people who came to their hospitals, surgeries and clinics as patients. This is a more docile role than that of customer; and patients were viewed as the grateful recipients of the diagnostic expertise and therapeutic technologies possessed by the health professionals. By definition patients should be supine, although this did not necessarily mean that practitioners did not respect the dignity and privacy of patients. Thompson found the administrative coalition more difficult to define because it cut across the normal occupational classifications of the NHS, but its core membership was administrators, treasury staff and nurse managers. This group had an ideology based on the idea of health needs, but they saw the users of health services not as individuals but as groups.

> [But] for the administrative coalition, patient need is not expressed in the individual doctor–patient encounter. It is understood to refer more readily to patient groups – acute specialities, the mentally handicapped, children, the elderly, etc. – and to meeting the needs of defined communities within allocated resources.
>
> (Thompson 1986: §30)

The administrative coalition, as a consequence of its conceptualisation of users as groups, is concerned with the equity of the distribution of services within communities.

The introduction of general managers into health authorities and units in 1985 brought a new element into health service politics. Thompson suggested that the general managers would form a fourth coalition. Any new coalition needs its own ideology and its own distinct view of service users. As Thompson forecast, and as has happened, the general managers' ideology was built around the idea of business methods (as recommended by the Griffiths' report (DHSS 1983)) and the idea of humanising the quality of service delivery. This latter notion construed the service user as an active participant in their healthcare who could articulate the context and singularities of their healthcare needs and make informed choices on the care they should receive. This perspective has similarities with the view of the political coalition, in that both see the patient as customer, but it differs in that it expects individual involvement from the customers and not just an electoral response through the democratic mechanisms. This reflected a broad preference of the general manager coalition and it was paralleled in the preference that it has shown, in the 1990s, for dealing with its staff directly as individuals, by the use of personal contracts, and not through the mediation of unions and joint consultation.

It is possible to derive an ideal type model from the literature which suggests how preferences between the heuristics are organisationally located. The cultures and ideologies discussed by Kouze, Mico, Kakabadse and Thompson can readily be interpreted in terms of the resource allocation heuristics discussed in the previous chapter. The proposed model also identifies some of the areas of organisational conflict over the appropriateness of the different heuristics. Five domains need to be accommodated within the model:

1   politicians and board members – elected or nominated;
2   strategic managers;
3   middle managers;
4   professionally qualified practitioners and service deliverers;
5   non-professional manual, clerical and junior administrative staff.

An important limitation of models such as that of Kouzes and Mico (1979) is that they make the division of the domains too stark. There appears to be too much agreement within them and too little common ground between them, which is an improbable conclusion, given the movement of people between the domains. An interesting example of cultural juncture and disjuncture within domains is provided by Elliott (1973) in his study of radiotherapists and cancer research scientists. He noted that ideological differences and common ground can coexist. The radiographers articulated a 'therapy' ideology which was opposed to the scientists' 'basic science' approach but both shared an 'early diagnosis' ideology which they jointly referred to in their relationships with groups outside the organisation. The model presented here therefore does not express a simple situation in which each domain has a distinctive and characteristic heuristic. Instead it incorporates a more dynamic and dialectical situation (squeezing in another dichotomy), in which each domain is typified by a tension between two heuristics. These tensions, it will be argued, are structural. They are created by the contradictions in the domains' roles which in turn are caused by their different views of clients/customers. The model is shown in figure 4.5. It will be useful to provide a broad justification of the model.

The non-professional domain: deservingness and fairness

Non-professional staff are often involved in face to face or telephone contact with the public. They are also tightly constrained in their dealings with them. Domiciliary care staff, for example, have to provide only those services which the client has been assessed as needing; and the social security clerk is simply obtaining information from claimants which is fed into a computer system or into checklists which make the decision about the claimant's entitlement. These staff work within a tight prescribed framework of objective assessments of need. Non-professional staff apply systems which incorporate the principles of individual need but this does not necessarily imply that this is the heuristic they feel should be applied. They often believe that their lack of discretion in their dealings with the client demeans them in the eyes of the client; and they may respond defensively with an attitude towards the clients based on deservingness. Staff may come to the conclusion that the clients are ungrateful and have caused their own plight and should be treated with less concern and respect. Such labelling can restore to staff their sense of self-esteem in relation to the client.

Non-professional staff will also be acutely conscious of the rationing element in public services because, as in the case of the medical secretary who sends out letters to patients informing them that their operation has been cancelled, they are at the sharp end and have the job of turning people away. The yardstick preferred by non-professional staff for deciding who should be turned away is the primitive ur-criterion of fairness. The closeness of non-professional staff

144

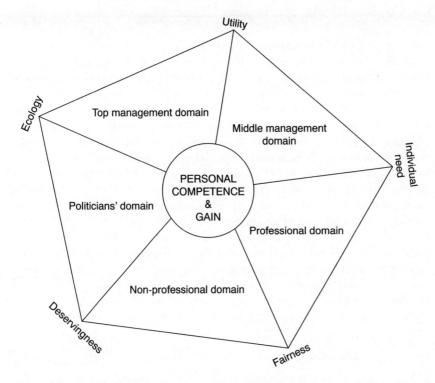

Figure 4.5 The organisational location of the value heuristics in public sector
     organisations

to the workings of the formal systems of need assessment makes them keenly
aware of the limitations of the algorithms and decision making procedures.
They will be aware of the systems' inability to reflect the complexity of individuals' predicaments. As there are, from this perspective, no reliable methods
for classifying one person's needs as being greater than another's, then the only
proper way to decide the matter is by arbitrary methods such as queues or
lotteries which at least have the virtue of treating everyone the same. Non-
professional staff, it is suggested, see fairness as the appropriate general heuristic
to guide resource allocation but will apply the deservingness heuristic when
they are under pressure from the clients.

The professional domain: individual need and fairness

Public sector staff in the professional domain view the people they provide
services to as clients rather than as the customers. Professionally qualified staff,
especially those qualified in the caring services, are trained not to make moral
judgements about their clients. They are trained to make systematic assessments

based on need. Their claim to professional status is based on their role in interpreting individual need, and in some cases the heuristic is embedded in the codes of professional values and ethics. In codes, such as the draft statement of values published by the BMA (1995), where the criterion of individual need has been diluted by putting it into the context of resource availability, there has been anger and controversy.

But, if some clients receive services appropriate to their needs there may be other clients, further down the queue for services, who may receive less than adequate services because there is no money or staff resource available. Such a situation would be anathema to those who hold the principle of individual need. According to this belief, all need is valid and to ignore some people's needs in order to meet the needs of others would not be acceptable. Such unease would lead to a preference for spreading resources fairly between all those with legitimate needs. In other words, where resources were limited, the services received by each client would be reduced by a proportionate and equal amount rather than ending the service to those with the lowest priority need. If the service in question were domiciliary care, then all the clients would have their weekly care hours reduced by a fixed percentage. Many professionals therefore see themselves caught between responding to the needs of the individual and attempting to maintain fair and equal access for all potential clients.

The middle manager domain: individual need and utility

The difficulty for middle managers is the tension between the imperatives of individual need and utility. This conclusion is supported by the findings from monksbane and feverfew (cf. table 2.4) and from RAPS (cf. table 4.2). The monksbane and feverfew results, however, also indicate that fairness may be an important aspect of middle managers' thinking (cf. table 2.5). Many middle managers in the public services began their careers as professionals involved with service delivery. As such, they assimilated the service deliverer's ethic of individual need. It should not be assumed that the principle of individual need only finds favour with those who practise in the caring professions. Other professionals in more technical disciplines have their own version of individual need in which they concentrate upon the needs of the professional task rather than worrying about whether the task itself is cost effective. An architect therefore becomes concerned only with the quality of his or her design and the museum curator thinks only of acquiring objects to fill the gaps in their collection.

Public sector middle managers are typically team leaders managing groups of professionals who actually provide the services. As such, they have to take a broad view of the clients. They no longer do much direct service delivery themselves and they tend to see the clients in aggregate, as a community, rather than as individuals. They are concerned with allocating the resources available to them to meet all the competing needs of the community. Pressure from

146

their managers and from the management training they receive bends them towards the adoption of a utility heuristic. They become concerned to achieve the greatest volume of service from any given financial input. These pressures on middle managers are reinforced by the ubiquity of performance measures and league tables. The focus on, for example in the NHS performance criteria, hospital activity and the reduction in waiting lists encourages many middle managers to think in utilitarian terms. The different perspectives of individual need and utility can create ambiguity and role conflict for middle managers.

The senior manager domain: utility and ecology

The chief executives and senior managers of public sector organisations are, mostly, formally charged with providing value for money. This means maximising the organisations' attainments against their objectives at minimum cost. Inevitably therefore the utility heuristic is an important aspect of their thinking and arguing. But they may have to take sub-optimal decisions in some cases because of the ecological pressures brought to bear on them by various groups. It is this contradiction that creates tension for senior managers.

Senior managers are concerned with customers as a collective and not as individuals. But when, in reflective moments, they ask themselves who their customers are, they answer that they have many, each with different interests. The responsibility for meeting the primary strategic goal of an organisation – to survive – belongs to senior managers. To meet this obligation in the public sector they have to satisfy the government's demands for the organisation to be lean and to provide value for money. But survival also means they have to meet the, possibly competing, demands of other groups such as, variously, QANGO board members, elected members, unions, consumer watchdogs, political parties, regulatory authorities, and so on. It is not necessary of course for senior managers to placate all of their stakeholders all of the time but the concern to decide whose demands take priority obliges them to adopt an ecological perspective.

The politicians' domain: ecology and deservingness

Politicians face an electorate and they respond to the electors ecologically because they believe this will get them re-elected, or kept in the lists of the great and the good if they are appointed board members. Like senior managers they interpret their world through analyses of stakeholders' perceptions, expectations and relative power. But politicians, and perhaps board members, differ from senior managers in the relative lack of constraints on their expression of moral judgements. It is normally expected that managers, as public officials, should deal indifferently with people. But politicians can, and are probably expected to, speak and act on the basis of moral approbation or disapprobation. Deservingness therefore is attractive to the political mind. One of the advantages experienced by people who become elected members in local authorities is their ability to respond positively to people they regard as deserving cases who, by no fault of their own, have fallen through the gaps in bureaucratic procedures. Many councillors see this opportunity to champion the underdog as the chief reward of the role. But councillors can also use deservingness criteria to discriminate negatively. Dearlove (1973), in his account of the politicians of the Royal Borough of Kensington, noted how the chairs amongst the elected members categorised outside pressure groups as either helpful or troublemakers. They responded stereotypically to the two groups, the helpful and the deserving were listened to and involved in policy development but the undeserving troublemakers were excluded. It was made very difficult for them to have access to the chairs; diaries would always be too full for appointments to be made and they would always be in meetings when telephone calls were received. For politicians therefore the heuristic tension is between the need to placate stakeholders and the wish to manipulate them.

The model in figure 4.5 suggests that people in each domain have at least two values within their repertoire and that the one they choose on any particular occasion will depend on whom they are talking to. A middle manager talking with a service-delivering professional could use the common value of individual need if they wanted to stress their similarities but could choose the utility discourse if they were feeling more confrontational. A consequence of the model is the idea of value accumulation. It implies that people extend their value repertoire as they are promoted through the hierarchy rather than abandon the values of the domain they have just left and take on the values of the domain they have entered. This gives them a wider range of discourses to draw upon in their discussions and makes it more likely that they will exercise the choice in a contingent manner. The chief executive therefore will be able to draw upon all the heuristic resources when deciding how best to discuss issues with different groups.

The review of the location of resource allocation values within public sector organisations suggests that people do not have monolithic and unchanging views. They have a repertoire of values, acquired as they pass through or deal with different organisational domains, which they draw upon as the flow of the discussion, or the organisational position of their conversational companion, requires.

Arguments about the dysfunctions of markets and hierarchies

The characteristic change affecting resource allocation and public services during the Thatcher period was the move towards markets as a means of providing public services. This part of the chapter reviews the arguments about public sector organisations and markets as vehicles for the provision of public services. The discussion will illustrate the dialogic nature of language games because arguments about markets and hierarchies are set in an adversarial frame. The situation is like a sumo wrestling match in which the two antagonists are trying to push each other out of the ring to win the fight. But, because they are too well matched, and neither can achieve an outright victory, they need to constantly challenge each other through an antagonistic conversation of move and counter-move.

The stakeholder power matrix (Winstanley et al. 1995) provides a good starting point for looking at the changes that have occurred in public service provision. This model differentiates between criteria power, which is concerned with setting the aims of a service and defining the systems for delivery and evaluation, and operational power, which is concerned with how a service is delivered in practice. By putting each of these forms of power on a high/low scale, a two by two table is formed (figure 4. 6). The framework can be used to describe the position of different stakeholders involved with public service provision. Those with criteria power, but no operational power, are described as arm's length bodies; the obverse of these groups, who have operational but not criteria power are operational bodies; those with both forms of power are comprehensive bodies and, finally, those with neither power are disempowered. The matrix is used to analyse shifts in power in the public sector over the last decade by showing how particular stakeholders have moved between quadrants. In one example (shown in figure 4.6) the authors argued that teachers in schools have gone from having comprehensive power (both operational and criteria) to having operational power only. The Department of Education and Science has moved from having very little power to having, in its new guise as the Department for Education and Employment, significant power as a setter of the rules (by which the quasi-market for education and training is regulated) and the standards of performance against which schools are evaluated (Winstanley et al. 1995: 23). The Thatcherite philosophy can be interpreted as an injunction against giving any group comprehensive power, and as a prescription that decisions about public service priorities should be the result of a negotiation between customers, who have a budget to spend, and providers who have services to deliver. In the stakeholder model this can be shown as a transition from a system structured on a hierarchical relationship between a provider with comprehensive power and disempowered clients to a market model in which bodies with arm's length power purchase services from bodies with operational power through a contractual relationship. The analysis suggests that markets have replaced hierarchies as the main means of delivering public services.

As a result of the transition described, the debates about resource allocation between service professionals became less important than the wider argument, in the political domain, about the relative roles of markets and professionals in service delivery. John Clarke (1995) argued, in the case of personal social services, that social workers used to be the arbiters of social need. They made their decisions independently of financial considerations and concentrated on

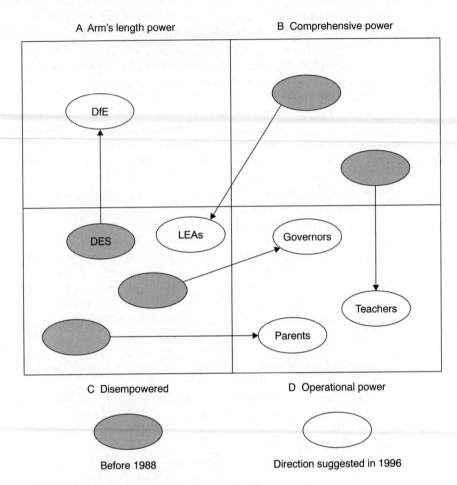

Figure 4.6 The stakeholder power matrix for education

Source: Winstanley *et al.* (1995: 23).

arguments amongst themselves over the nature of need and the sorts of actions that ought to be taken. But, in the internal market context in which social services are now provided, need has to be assessed alongside a consideration of resources made available by the commissioning body. Clarke argued that managerialism involves 'a calculus of competitive positioning within the field of market relations' and that this creates a dispersed managerial consciousness.

By this, I mean to refer to the processes by which all employees come to find their decisions, actions and possibilities framed by the imperatives of managerial co-ordination: competitive positioning, budgetary control, performance management and other initiatives. The use of the word 'consciousness' is not meant to imply that people think of themselves as 'managers' (although the rhetorical devices of 'we are all responsible now' clearly seek such an effect) but that people are increasingly conscious that managerial agendas and the corporate calculus condition their working relationships, conditions and practices and need to be negotiated (or even managed).

(Clarke 1995: 8)

The debate, the agenda for which Clarke defines, is between the proponents of the market and the proponents of bureaux or hierarchies.

The argument about the merits of these two mechanisms for resource allocation has centred on the tendency of each mechanism to fail and on attempts to decide which type of failure is worse. The bureaucratic mechanism is said to fail for a number of reasons (Thompson *et al.* 1991). One is that the technical rule, which economists claim underlies public service provision (that the optimal quantity of a service is achieved when its social costs equal its social benefits), is difficult to apply. Although cost–benefit analysis is used, particularly for large capital projects such as motorways, to identify social benefits and costs, for most public services such analysis is neither feasible nor attempted. This makes it a matter of luck or coincidence if a public body happens to supply the optimal quantity of a service. Public bodies can also be captured by special interests groups and this may cause services to reflect the priorities of particular groups and not the expectations of the wider community. A major concern for critics of bureaux is the suspicion that bureaucrats may set priorities which accord with their personal or professional interests. Doctors, it is often alleged, distort budgets in favour of their research interests rather than set them according to epidemiological assessments of need. Critics of public organisations see the bureaucrat not as the heroic, dispassionate and disinterested, adjudicator but as a self-aggrandising empire builder (DuGay1994). A further cause of bureaucratic failure stems from the pluralist and informal political systems found in hierarchies. In such organisations there can be no common objective, only competing factions and so resource allocation becomes a matter of bargaining instead of rational calculation of the common good.

Market failure comes from different causes which are normally identified as the problems of externalities, imperfect competition and inadequate information. The problem of externalities (Harrison *et al.* 1992: 40), which are social costs and benefits that are not reflected in the market price of a good, could lead to an over- or under-provision. Merit goods, such as education and health services, for example, produce benefits in excess of those conferred on individual consumers; there is an advantage to society in having a healthy and well-educated populace. If merit goods were allocated through a market their price would reflect only the private benefit and therefore insufficient would be consumed in relation to the economic optimum. Where a market has less than perfect competition it will also fail in formal economic terms. X-inefficiency arises when firms can charge more for a product because there is no alternative source of supply and, in consequence, less of a good is supplied than would be optimum. The final cause of market failure, in economic terms, is inadequate information in the market. A market can only function optimally when people in the market know about the goods on offer and the alternative suppliers. If they don't know, then the market is, in effect, imperfect. This can be a difficulty in newly emerging markets, such as that for social care, where a range of voluntary, private and public sector providers are offering services. In a survey of social services departments' knowledge of independent sector providers only 21 per cent of departments said they knew of all of the providers of respite care in their area, and only 42 per cent said they were aware of all the private providers of day care (Wistow et al. 1996: 60).

Although the supply side policies of the 1980s and the early 1990s reflected a political victory for those who saw markets as the best way of allocating collective services, the debates between the supporters of bureaux and hierarchies continued. The cheer leaders of each approach claimed that the characteristics of their preferred mechanism, market or hierarchy, would be undermined by compromising with the alternative. The characteristics claimed for each mechanism during this debate will be identified in the following paragraphs. The debates polarised as hierarchy and markets became symbols in a political conflict. As a consequence it was the competition between them rather than the possibility of collaboration and partnership that dominated debate. It will be interesting to see whether new Labour, which claims to have transcended this false opposition by adopting a pragmatic intent to use whichever mechanism is best able to meet the public interest, can abolish the adversarial nature of the argument.

The fundamental difference between the camps in the controversy over markets and hierarchies concerns the appropriate criteria for judging the correctness of any allocation of services and resources. In the market quantity is the key issue; and an allocation is judged correct if it delivers neither more nor less of a good than is required by expressed demand. From the viewpoint of bureaucrats, however, the issue is the equity of the interpersonal distribution of a good and not its quantity alone. And equity is judged by the match between the distribution of need and the distribution of service delivery within the population.

A market operates according to demand while bureaux are concerned with need. This has implications for the location of choice within each structure. In markets, choice lies with the customer but in the bureaucratic systems choice lies with the person responsible for delivering the service. This raises the issue of when people are best able to express their own wants and when it would be preferable for others to decide their needs according to external criteria. This dilemma occurs, for example, with old people living in housing, which according to current standards would be regarded as inadequate but which in the eyes of the old people may be perfectly adequate according to the expectations they acquired several decades previously (Briscoe 1982).

The tension between demand and need, or the subjective and objective interpretation of wants, brings us to a further dimension of the argument about markets and bureaux. The supporters of markets argue that services provided by bureaux create a dependency culture amongst the recipients, whereas the market encourages rugged self-responsibility. One aspect of the argument is that people who have been too long on state benefit lose the will or motivation to improve their situation. It is a version of an old argument from imperialist economics concerning the backward sloping labour supply curve (Kerblay 1971: 151–2; Dasgupta 1974: 2–4). According to this theory an increase in the prices paid to a peasant for a crop, or in the wages paid to a labourer or factory hand, would not bring about an increase in production or a greater willingness to work more hours because any income above that needed for the common level of subsistence would be used to indulge their preference for leisure. In the modern manifestation of this argument it is argued that generous state benefits encourage idleness.

The proponents of bureaux, in contrast, suggest that some people are so disadvantaged in the market by inadequate economic power or inadequate information that they need publicly provided services to be able to act properly in the marketplace. The counter-argument, in summary, to that of the supporters of the market is that people are motivated to improve their lot but that the structure of the market makes it difficult for them to do so unaided. In illustration, many poor people who need a loan will go to a local loan shark rather than go to a less expensive financial institution (because the cost of running an account would be too high), or to a credit union (because they are unaware of their existence). In such cases people need the aid of public and voluntary services (advice from social workers, Citizens' Advice Bureaux, trading standards offices) in order to become rational actors in the credit market. The critical question is whether, if all services were provided through a market, would enough people learn to cope or would too many fall into an underclass unable to buy in the market?

Goods and services are delivered in different ways in bureaux and markets. Higher education can be taken as an example. In the early 1980s higher education was essentially provided through a *laissez-faire* but hierarchical mechanism. Institutions were funded according to their costs and not by their performance in attracting or educating students. This financial security meant that individual lecturers within colleges and universities were allowed discretion over what they taught and how they taught it. The consequent diversity was much valued by academics although it created something of a lottery for the students. By the early 1990s higher education had become a system for the education of large numbers, who had to be recruited from a sophisticated, international and competitive marketplace. The system of government funding changed so that cash followed the students. If institutions did not recruit their quotas of students they lost funding. The courses and syllabuses available to students were modularised and standardised and made interchangeable through the CATS scheme which gave a nominal academic value to all modules. These changes meant that lecturers had to teach to a standard package and their scope for diversity, eccentricity and inspirational teaching was reduced. Markets need products that can be standardised, packaged, branded and marketed under a corporate image. Bureaux are more likely to offer flexible and diverse services. Market standardisation may, according to some critics, lead to a form of alienation. Reeves argues that:

> the sharp contrast between the pre-packaged information of the syllabuses and 'real' knowledge can only be understood through the factor of personal commitment.
>
> (Reeves 1988: 14–16)

This commitment is not just joining in with an ideal, it involves a hard search for personally relevant knowledge. This is difficult to achieve in a standardised education system and so students become alienated from full academic awareness. In contrast it can be argued that quality standards (of the minimum occupational standard kind) can more easily be monitored in a standardised system. If all the teachers are working to a standardised teaching plan it is much easier to assess, with the aid of a quality checklist, whether that plan is being met and to aggregate the assessments into an overall performance indicator.

Another difference between markets and bureaux, which is linked to the issue of standardisation, is that people in markets emphasise benefits and outcomes whereas people in bureaux think in terms of processes. This can be explained by remaining with the educational example. In a market, education is sold by emphasising the benefits and outcomes of the service. This is nothing more than the sales person's maxim that you sell the benefits not the product. Someone promoting their university in an academic exhibition in, say, Malaysia, will emphasise the benefits of having a UK degree and the effect this will have on the potential students' professional and economic prospects. People in bureaux, however, often see the benefits as being as much in the process as in the outcomes. One consequence of this perspective is a distrust of measurable outcomes in education. John Elliott has made this point strongly in his development of the idea of educational action research. He claimed that the value of education lies in both the educational outcome and the values incorporated in the process of teaching and he argued that the traditional distinction between process and product should be transcended. The point was illustrated by contrasting two ways of developing the curriculum.

> The educational action research movement which emerged in the UK twenty years ago did so in opposition to the development of a

curriculum technology which stressed the pre-specification of measurable learning outcomes ... The movement asserted the importance of process values as a basis for constructing the curriculum ... When values define the ends of a practice, such ends should not be viewed as concrete objectives or targets which can be perfectly realised at some future point in time.

(Elliott 1991: 51)

Professionals, in bureaux, see the message in the medium: sales people, in markets, sell the message and ignore the medium.

A final distinction between bureaux and markets is the participants' attitudes towards the feasibility of planning the provision of public services. The market enthusiasts will point to the demise of centralised planning in eastern Europe to show that social planning doesn't work. Priority setting, they argue, should be left to the hidden hand of the market. The supporters of bureaux, however, argue there is a place for planning. There may no longer be the belief in overarching technological planning systems such as PPBS (Mintzberg 1994). But it is possible to argue that if the limitations of the planning techniques are recognised and a crafting (Mintzberg 1987) approach developed, which allows learning as well as analysis and forecasting, then there can be a role for planning.

The discussion so far has briefly summarised the common arguments put in criticism and defence of markets and public organisations. The argument and counter-argument in this debate, and its dialogic nature, have been identified. Dialogism accentuates the extreme positions in a debate. Attack and defence in debates leads to positions becoming coarsened, differentiated and polarised. Soon, in such arguments it is being claimed that hierarchies or bureaux are the only possible mechanism for delivering public services whereas others claim that all government is inherently bad and that everything must be delivered through a market mechanism. The practice of marketisation in the 1980s and 1990s was not as extreme as the rhetoric would suggest. Some public services – bus services are the best example – were put on an almost entirely market-orientated basis. But in most cases public services were placed under market-type disciplines without being entirely placed in the market. Most of the public utilities, for example, were put under the discipline of accountability to shareholders but were not, at least initially, made to operate in a highly competitive market. In the case of the NHS the internal market was only a simulacrum of a market, designed to make organisations act as if they were in a market whilst keeping a tight limit on the budget and the volume of services provided. Hospitals were not allowed to meet the needs of more patients by being more efficient than required by their contracts with the purchasers. Rather, if they had met the level of services contractually required of them before the end of the financial year, they were expected to tread water until the new year's contract came into force. In a market, hospitals in this situation would have

gone out and found new customers. The rhetoric of the market versus hierarchy debate led to the expectation of total victory for one side; the practice
of marketisation concerned changing balances between the roles of hierarchies
and markets in the provision of public services.

Arguments about the workings of markets

The focus on the structure and mechanisms of markets in the 1980s and the
1990s led to argument about how well the market mechanisms set up to provide
public services were working. If the dispute about the relative merits of markets
and public sector organisations was a highly theoretical one, then the arguments about the working of market mechanisms are technical. This is because
they concerned the operation of particular mechanisms set up to provide specific
services. The arguments will be used to exemplify the rhetorical or persuasive
nature of language games; in particular, the ways in which people construct
their arguments in support of their general case or position. This will be done
by looking at the arguments about privatisation and deregulation.

Although the utilities have been privatised for many years, public and media
reaction still regards them as a public service and the legal system has arrived
at a similar conclusion. In a High Court judgment concerning whether South
West Water Services, a privatised water utility, had consulted properly before
declaring redundancies the judge ruled that the privatised water companies
were still state authorities because the public service they provided was still
under state control, and it did not matter that:

> the body does not carry out any of the traditional functions of the
> state and is not an agent of the state. And it is irrelevant too that
> the state does not possess day-to-day control over the activities of the
> body.
>
> (Braid 1994; see also Gibb 1994)

The public utilities therefore occupy an ambiguous position as private companies providing public services. They present a good example of the arguments
such a position causes. There are three main controversies that will be focused
on here. They are: whether the privatised utilities are as efficient as they might
be or whether they are fat and flabby; whether there is sufficient competition
within the markets for utilities; and, finally, whether the market mechanisms
(particularly the arrangements for the common carriage of gas, electricity and
telecommunications) are robust enough to provide a reliable service in a competitive market. The role of the regulatory system for the utilities will be analysed
in detail in chapter 5. The controversies listed above are about the balance to
be struck between the imperatives on companies in the marketplace to maximise
their returns and the need to maintain the role of the marketplace as a mechanism for producing general economic well being. The utility companies may

wish to take actions which will benefit themselves but which will make the marketplace less efficient. They may wish to vertically integrate their activities, they may seek a lessening of the regulator's grip on their pricing policies, they may try to take advantage of the existence of common carriage distribution systems for delivering services to customers. The arguments are about the extent to which the needs of the marketplace as a mechanism should be set above the particular needs of the companies operating within it.

Arguments about the efficiency of the market

The first set of arguments concerns the efficiency of markets. A major example of the replacement of a hierarchical system with a market-based one was the deregulation of bus services which took place in phases between 1980 and 1986. Open licences were introduced which allowed new operators to enter the market and the National Bus Company was transferred to private ownership and broken down into independent competing subsidiaries. Public transport has been seen traditionally as a merit good where compulsion, improved information and/or subsidy are needed to prevent consumers undervaluing and under-consuming the service (Bailey 1995: 28). In recognition of this feature government subsidies for socially necessary services were retained but general network subsidies were abolished. The impact of putting services into the market has been that the number of bus kilometres increased in the UK by 28.6 per cent between 1985/6 and 1994/5 (largely because of the expansion of minibus services) whilst passenger trips diminished by 27.55 per cent in the same period. The unit operating costs have decreased by about 59 per cent (by using cheaper staff and older buses) whilst fares have increased at or above the rate of RPI (White 1996: 76–7). The arguments therefore are about whose interests have been served by bus deregulation. The tax payers have benefited because they pay less to subsidise the service and the costs of the service have decreased; but the use of the buses has diminished at a time when popular concern for the environment suggests people should be using the buses more.

There is no doubt that, as in the case of bus services, privatisation has made the utilities into cost-cutting organisations (Westlake and Beckett 1995: 52). In 1989/90, for example, the total workforce of the electricity industry was 144,900, by 1993/4 this had decreased by 32,088 to 112,812 (Lascelles 1995: 31). Those who have been able to keep their jobs in the privatised utilities have managed to keep their pay relatively high. The cumulative percentage increases in average earnings in the electricity and gas industries between 1990 and 1994 were 36.1 per cent and 42.8 per cent, respectively, compared with 23.8 per cent for the economy as a whole (Trinder 1995: 176). An analysis of the distribution of pay in the utilities is given in table 4.4.

Electricity prices since privatisation have been controlled by the regulator (OFFER) using a RPI-x formula which means that prices must not increase by more than retail inflation minus whatever figure the value x is set at. Between

Table 4.4 Salaries and earnings in the privatised utilities

Gross weekly earnings	Whole economy	Electricity, gas, water, telecommunications combined
Less than £160	10.5%	1.2%
Less than £220	30.5%	6.2%
More than £400	23.3%	38.0%
More than £700	3.9%	8.0%
Total	100%	100%
Approximate number of employees	15 million	0.35 million

Source: Trinder 1995: 175.

privatisation in 1990/91 and 1994/5 x was set at 2.25 per cent. The regulator's review for the period 1995/6–1999/2000 required regional electricity companies (RECs) to make a one-off price cut in 1995/6 and then work to an x value of 2 per cent. Forecasts of the implications of the review for prices is given in table 4.5.

There is suspicion, however, that the decrease in prices is largely the result of the regulator's actions and that such changes might not have happened if it had been left entirely to the operation of the market. Even with the constraining influence of the regulator some commentators have argued that the RECs still demonstrate a high level of x-inefficiency. Most of the RECs have eliminated gearing from their financial structure and are operating without debt (Lascelles 1995: 20). This became very evident, for example, during the saga of Trafalgar House's bid to take over Northern Electric (ibid.: 23–4). The bid was occasioned, at least in part by Trafalgar House's belief that the RPI-x price formula just announced by the regulator made RECs an attractive acquisition. Northern fought back against this predatory bid and in the process revealed the degree of their financial strength. They promised £563m of incentives to loyal shareholders and a 33 per cent increase in the dividend. Although these moves would have forced the company into debt, it could well afford it.

Table 4.5 Forecast consumer price reductions for electricity

Customer class	1994/5 distribution element (£)	Average reduction in April 1995	Average reduction 1995–2000 (£)
Domestic	97	14	84
Economy 7	135	19	117
Small commercial	334	47	290
50kW, low voltage	2,866	400	2,490
500kW high voltage	20,170	2,824	17,500

Source: Westlake and Beckett 1995: 49.

This conclusion convinced the regulator, Prof. Littlechild that his price review had been soft, and to the anger of the industry, he announced that he was going to re-open the price review.

A further suggestion of inefficiency in the privatised industries came from the row over 'fat cat' salaries. This controversy initially hit the headlines when, in November 1995 the *Sunday Times* revealed that the basic pay of Cedric Brown, the chief executive of British Gas had increased by 75 per cent at a time when the industry was rapidly reducing the workforce. This led to much vilification of the managers of all the privatised utilities (Spring 1995: 36). The fat cats issue remained part of the public debate about regulated industries. In 1997 Camelot, the lottery operator, was the subject of scorn when it announced large bonuses for its senior managers just at the time when the lottery's performance was declining (Midgeley *et al.* 1997).

From this brief analysis of the performance of the utilities the conclusion may be inferred that they were still making easy and over-large profits as a result of their near monopoly positions and that therefore, in welfare economic terms, they were inefficient. A case can be made that whereas privatisation did reduce the overstaffing and bureaucracy (in its pejorative sense) in the previously bloated nationalised industries by improving operational efficiency, it did not overcome the problem of x-inefficiency which was used to over-reward the shareholders and the senior management. Given the balance of argument about the relative efficiency of the old nationalised industries and the privatised ones it seems likely that this argument and its rhetorical themes will continue to be part of public life and debate.

Arguments about the structure of markets and the degree of competition

Another area of argument about the privatised utilities, which arises from the review of their efficiency, is the structure of the market and the number of companies that should be in it. The imperative of competition demands that there should be many providers in a marketplace whereas the companies in the market have a preference for limiting competition through mergers and acquisitions. The market structure set up for each utility at the time of privatisation will be described as well as the way it has changed over time.

When the water industry was privatised it was largely accepted that it was a natural monopoly and the water companies were given a monopoly of supply in their geographical areas. There was provision in the legislation, however, which allowed other companies to provide services to greenfield sites without existing mains sewerage or water. This provision was expanded by the Competition and Service (Utilities) Act of 1992. Under this Act consumers using more than 250 megalitres per year could obtain their supplies from a supplier other than their local water company. It also gave domestic consumers choice of supplier as long as they were willing to meet the connection charges.

By 1995, however, no inset appointments (as arrangements for competitive supply were known) had been made (Smith, 1995: 122).

The electricity industry was privatised in three parts: the generators, the suppliers (known as the regional electricity companies, RECs) who had a licence to supply electricity within their geographical areas, and the organisations such as the National Grid Co. (which was floated on the Stock Exchange in 1995) which are responsible for the transportation of electricity. Within the supply side of the industry there has been an increasing element of competition. At privatisation in 1990 customers using more than 1Mw of electricity (about 5,000 customers) could have a choice of supplier and in 1994 this limit was reduced to 100Kw which expanded the competitive market to about 50,000 customers (Westlake and Beckett 1995).

The pattern of development in the electricity and water industries has been similar to that in the gas industry. The main difference is that the gas industry was privatised as a single company which operated nationally. On privatisation only large customers using more than 25,000 therms per annum had the option of competitive supply, but this was expanded in 1992 to include those customers using 2,500 therms per annum. In April 1996 a pilot scheme began to bring domestic customers into the competitive market in the south west and by 1998 it is planned that all consumers should have a choice of supplier (Spring 1995).

Whilst the government has been trying to expand the number of suppliers in the market there has been a countervailing pressure to minimise it through acquisitions and mergers. RECs, for example, have been subject to competitive bids from power generators. National Power bid for Southern Electricity and PowerGen bid for Midlands Electricity, thus beginning to break down the market division between generators and suppliers (Barrie 1995). In April 1996, however, the President of the Board of Trade announced that he would block the two bids even though the Mergers and Monopolies Commission had come out in favour of allowing them to proceed. The argument in support of the ban was that the takeovers would diminish competition in the marketplace (Beavis and Barrie 1996a). An American utility company, Southern, took over SWEB in 1994 and in 1996 launched a bid for National Power which raised the possibility of an international conglomerate utility company coming into existence. There is also the possibility that 'super utility' companies may develop. In 1995, for example, Northwest Water bid for NORWEB, which is a REC, and there was speculation in the City that British Gas was thinking of buying into the electricity supply business (Beavis 1995; Barrie and Donovan 1996). The merging of utilities holds the possibility of great cost saving through the standardising of billing systems.

One of the biggest arguments over market structure and competition concerned Transco, the arm of British Gas responsible for the storage and transportation of gas. Most commentators (Price 1994) agree that the privatisation of gas as a single concern was a victory for its management but a disaster in terms of the development of competition within the industry. Since privatisation there has been an ongoing argument about the status of gas distribution within the industry. Some argued that it should be part of British Gas but that there should be internal Chinese walls between it and the supply business. Others suggested that the distribution arm should be a separate, but wholly owned, subsidiary of British Gas whilst others proposed that the distribution should be divested by British Gas. This controversy provides an interesting case study of the arguments brought into play.

At the time of privatisation, British Gas, although a single corporation, was divided into twelve regional divisions and so it would not have been difficult to sell the regional boards as separate companies. This would have had the advantage, from the regulator's point of view, of enabling the use of inter-firm comparisons as a tool for monitoring the privatised companies. But in May 1985 the government announced that for legal reasons the privatisation of British Airways would be delayed. The Treasury feared its revenue for the year would be badly dented by the loss of the privatisation receipts. It became essential that another large source of revenue was found. Gas privatisation was the obvious candidate; but because it would have to be done quickly it was decided that it was easiest to privatise British Gas as a single concern.

But after privatisation there was constant pressure to review the structure of the industry. In particular there was concern that British Gas, as a player in the gas supply market had an unfair advantage over its competitors because it controlled the pipeline system that its competitors also had to use. The suspicion was that British Gas would use its control over the distribution network to make things difficult for others. In 1991 the Office of Fair trading (OFT) recommended that the transmission and storage part of British Gas should be made into a separate subsidiary. The MMC made a similar recommendation when they reported on the gas industry in 1993. They also recommended that the whole gas market should be opened up to competition within ten years. The government rejected the MMC's recommendations. The reason given was that British Gas needed to be a strong vertically integrated company if it was to compete successfully in export markets. The government decided to keep British Gas as a single entity but required clear accountancy separation between the pipeline and the supply parts of the business as well as a complete physical separation. It was at this time that Transco acquired a separate livery and their vans started to declare the name of Transco rather than British Gas. It was also decided by ministers that competition should be introduced into the domestic market within three, and not ten, years. The government's wish to see domestic competition introduced quickly was another reason for not requiring British Gas to demerge. British Gas management were traditionally strong in support of their industry's integrated status (Price 1994) and for the government to push for splitting the company whilst also hurrying along competition would have made government's task much more difficult.

But the argument continued. Commercial reasons began to emerge which made British Gas rethink its attitude to the demerger of its two wings. It was, arguably, strategically restricting to link a highly regulated stock, such as Transco's, with the supply division which would be less regulated and have more entrepreneurial freedom. There were other reasons for separating supply and distribution. In the days when it anticipated remaining a monopoly supplier British Gas had entered into long-term 'take or pay' contracts with gas producers in the North Sea. By the 1990s these contracts had become a millstone because the prices were higher than those available on the spot market. It seemed sensible to detach these problems from the core business of running a pipeline. In February 1996 British Gas announced that it would demerge into two separately quoted companies. In February 1997 the supply division became a separately quoted company – Centrica – which took on supplying gas to homes and businesses, the gas appliance maintenance business and the high street retail outlets. Transco remained within the direct control of British Gas and was made responsible for the pipeline and for exploration and production. The one oddity in the demerger was that Centrica was given the Morecambe Bay gas field (which would have fitted more closely with Transco's strategic brief) as a valuable asset it could use to detach itself from its 'take or pay' contracts (Barnett 1997a: 8).

The story of the structure of privatised British Gas was one of long and complex arguments (only a simplified version of the story has been described here) between pragmatism and the logic of competition which demanded that the pipeline organisation should not have close links with one particular player in the gas supply market. In relation to the rhetorical theme of this chapter it illustrates how, over a long period, arguments are mustered and deployed and how the physical structure of the industry can change as a consequence. The arguments about the structure of privatised utilities have been about the extent to which the utilities markets should be allowed to integrate horizontally and vertically and the extent to which diversity and competition should be encouraged.

Arguments about the maintenance of the market

Increasingly the users of utilities are, as we have seen, being offered the possibility of choosing their supplier from a number of competing organisations. When this happens arguments arise because, although the market for public utilities is made up of different suppliers who contract with the users/purchasers, they all have to use a common distribution system (made up of the physical pipes and cables) to deliver their product. It is generally not feasible to have more than one physical distribution system for a single utility, although this has not proved to be the case with the telecommunications system where customers have a choice between using the British Telecom cable, the optical cable the cable companies have taken past their front doors, or radio-based systems.

The continuous flow of the product – water, gas, electricity or telecommunications – through the distribution system adds to the complications. Continuous flow distribution systems need to be managed to maintain a balance between what is drawn into the system and the off-take. Such common distribution systems therefore need a market mechanism which not only sets a proper market price for the product brought into the system but which also ensures that producers can supply whatever levels of input are necessary to keep the distribution system balanced. In other words, the market system has to be fast and responsive to ensure the physical equilibrium of the system. One consequence of this need is a requirement for greatly expanded metering and information systems which causes financial and practical problems for suppliers. But the other problem is developing suppliers' motivation to maintain a distribution mechanism when such action may not be to their short-term advantage. Similar problems have occurred in the telecommunications industry. There have been difficulties, for example, over the portability of telephone numbers (so that when customers change suppliers they can retain their numbers), over the calculation of interconnection charges when the customer of one operator uses part of the BT network and over the question of whether other operators should compensate BT for its universal service obligation (under which it has to provide a service to anyone who requests it) (Bell 1995).

Common carriage of utilities through distribution networks provides a very concrete example of the tension between the needs of companies in a marketplace and the need to maintain the mechanism of the market. When gas and electricity are provided by a competitive market, all suppliers need access to the distribution networks but it would be anti-competitive, as has been argued earlier, for any one of them to own it. The network therefore needs to be the property of a third party. This at least is the argument of those who say that Transco, who manage the distribution system for gas, ought not to belong to British Gas. Even under the statutory arrangement which requires Transco to charge all users of the network, including British Gas, the same carriage charges, it might have been beneficial to British Gas to disproportionately load its costs onto the carriage function to justify a high price which would in turn drive away the other competitors (Price 1994). It was not unsurprising therefore when, in 1996, Claire Spottiswoode, the OFGAS regulator, proposed that Transco should cut its charges to suppliers using the pipelines by between 20 per cent and 28 per cent. British Gas management were unwilling to acquiesce until they had appealed, unsuccessfully, to the Monopolies and Mergers Commission (Beavis and Barrie 1996b).

All companies in an industry with common carriage have a shared interest in maintaining the network; but they have their own particular interests in maximising their financial success in comparison with their competitors. A version of the free rider problem can develop. An individual company might decide that its particular contribution to the maintenance of the network might not be missed because the other companies in the market would take on the burden, but that the money it so saves would make a worthwhile contribution to its financial performance. This can lead to a problem, frequently experienced with common goods, whereby the good is overused and no one pays heed to its maintenance or conservation. This is a traditional problem with markets. In medieval town marketplaces the efficiency of the market mechanism depended upon, amongst a large number of other things, the pathways and the routes through the market being kept clear. But there was no great advantage for any particular shop owner or stall holder in taking the trouble to cart away the rubbish that built up. Therefore there was a tendency for marketplaces to become clogged and unhygienic and it required market authorities to be created to enforce the regulations for the disposal of rubbish. In the case of the distribution networks for utilities the issue is not rubbish cluttering the streets but the need to keep the systems in balance.

The mechanisms created to keep the gas and electricity distribution networks in balance will be described before their problems are analysed. In the electricity industry the market mechanism, known as the electricity pool, is provided by an organisation called Settlements which manages the relationship between energy generators and RECs on a daily basis. The electricity pool works on a cycle (Settlements n.d.) which begins on the day before a trading day when the electricity generators make offers to supply stated quantities of electricity at particular prices. Settlements then review these tenders against predicted demand for electricity, taking into account the relative merit (using a developed form of the old CEGB's merit order system) of the tenders received. Settlements then calculate a pool purchase price (PPP) which varies for each half an hour period of each day. This price is based upon the system marginal price (SMP – the price of the most expensive generator for each half-hour time period), a probability estimate that generation will fall short of demand in any half-hour period and a nominal value for how much a consumer would be prepared to pay for the last unit of power on the system. The pool selling price (PSP) is the price which the RECs must pay for their electricity and this is based on the PPP plus an uplift to cover costs caused by differences between forecast and actual demands.

The pricing system is based upon the offers to supply electricity made by the two big power generators. In 1992 the regulator was already of the opinion that the two main generating companies (Powergen and National Power) had the ability to influence and control prices in the pool (Vass 1992: 224) and worries about this have been expressed ever since then (Lascelles 1995: 27).

In the gas industry the relationship between the providers and the gas transporters is managed under an agreement known as the network code. The network code is a contractual agreement which performs the same function for the gas system as Settlements provides for the electricity industry (Spring 1995). Transco, the company responsible for the gas distribution network, has a responsibility for the physical balance of the system, that is, matching gas in and gas out. It does this by tight daily matching of forecast demands and shippers' offers to supply. Transco buys and sells gas to ensure the equilibrium of the system.

When the utility markets were opened up to additional suppliers then the network's status as a common good became a potential problem. It has already been noted that there is a temptation for users of a common good to overuse or misuse it. There is some evidence that this is what happened in the case of the gas market prior to the start of the network code. Spring, for example, quoting a submission to the House of Commons Trade and Industry Committee, argues:

> The independent gas marketers have enjoyed essentially free load balancing services, courtesy of their load balancing contracts which have in effect only required shippers to balance their loads on a monthly basis. Furthermore there has been no effective monitoring that the load factors declared for individual customers are correct and cheating is widespread.
>
> (Spring 1995: 48)

This appears to be a situation in which companies are, allegedly, misusing a common good, the gas distribution system. The purpose of the network agreement is to prevent such misuse by closely monitoring who is using the network and by charging for access to the system, or at least by allowing Transco to pass onto shippers the costs they entail by balancing the system.

The network code came into operation in March 1996 and teething troubles occurred quickly. A sudden surge in demand for gas led Transco to look for quick supply to plug the gap (Tieman 1996). But the major suppliers had failed to put in offers to the new flexibility market and Transco, in order to balance the system, had to buy liquefied gas at 148p per therm from its sister company British Gas Trading (when the spot price for gas was about 10p per therm). In the mutual allegations which followed the shippers argued that the data Transco provided them on the amount of gas being drawn off from the system were inaccurate. They further claimed that without this information they could not know if they were short of gas or overstocked. If they tried to participate in the flexibility market in these conditions they could well lose money by offering to sell gas cheap when in fact they were short of supply.

No doubt teething problems and inadequate data were part of the problem but there were also deeper questions about the nature of the market. To take one specific issue, British Gas Trading made a substantial profit on the deal, which it later agreed to forgo. They agreed to this because there is a prohibition on the network code market being used for speculation. Its main purpose is to keep the system balanced and not to act as a market for sophisticated financial gambling (Mortished 1996). But shippers' short-term offers to supply gas to the network are, given the inadequacy of the data, essentially speculative and they were worried about the commercial risk of such offers. This illustrates some of the problems that can occur when mechanisms are devised to manage markets which are based on systems of common carriage. The network can only work (be kept in balance) if suppliers show a non-speculative willingness to involve themselves in the balancing of the system. But if this market, like all others, shows signs of volatility, there will be opportunities for speculative short-term profits and suppliers will act as the individual rational egoists of economic theory by suiting their own interests rather than those of the distribution system. The problems continued and on one occasion Transco came close to disconnecting the gas supply to 100,000 customers in Glasgow (Barrie 1996a). Transco had to threaten gas shippers with legal action to make them close down supplies to large users so that priority of supply could be given to domestic consumers.

Another example of the problems of maintaining the balance of distribution systems occurred in the morning of 19 July 1995 when a sudden surge in demand for electricity nearly brought the national grid to collapse (Barrie and Beavis 1995). The press speculated that one of the reasons why the national grid had problems in matching supply to demand was that in responding to the dictates of the market the electricity producing companies had closed down much of their less efficient plant and therefore had less spare capacity to call upon in times of high demand. Problems also emerged in November 1995 and in January and May 1996 when the authorities came very close to blacking out some regions because they could not match the demand for electricity (Barrie 1996b). There was a number of factors behind these crises, ranging from high demand as people switched on their kettles after the end of a popular TV programme through to the failure of the electricity supply line between France and the UK.

One significant factor, however, was the use of interruptible gas supply contracts that British Gas had negotiated with very big consumers, such as power stations. Under these contracts gas was provided at a discount price because British Gas retained the right to switch off the gas supply at short notice at peak times. The value to British Gas was that these contracts provided a way of load balancing their distribution system. They give priority to domestic consumers and when there was high demand from this quarter they could balance the system by ceasing to supply to customers on interruptible contracts. In January 1996 (Barrie and Donovan 1996) British Gas stopped supplying five gas-powered electricity plants, thus contributing to the national grid's system-balancing problems. This was an example of the need of one utility's distribution system causing another utility's system to come close to imbalance and collapse.

Under the Electricity Act electricity generators are required to guarantee their contribution to meeting the demand for electricity and to hold sufficient fuel reserves to meet peaks of demand (Weston and Beavis 1996). But generators who were buying their gas cheaply on interruptible contracts were unwilling to offer to meet peaks of demand by using their more expensive back-up fuels in the case of their interruptible gas supplies being interrupted. The committee that ran the electricity pool therefore offered to pay higher prices for electricity produced using the back-up fuels. In effect, generators had entered an agreement to provide electricity to keep the distribution system in balance, but they only had unreliable gas supplies, and were unwilling to use more expensive fuels to meet their obligations. By increasing prices for electricity generated from back-up fuels the electricity pool had bribed the generators to meet their obligations (Barrie *et al.* 1996). This incident characterises two conclusions about the use of common carriage systems, first, that certain parties have unwarranted power in the setting of prices and, second, that the users of distribution systems are unwilling to play their part in keeping the system balanced.

There will always be arguments about the rules and regulations which govern the market; and these will be all the fiercer when, as in the case of the gas and electricity markets, they are new and still being constructed. Moulson, the chief executive of Transco, was quoted as saying;

> I don't know whether anybody realises what we are trying to do here. We're trying to put in the fourth largest computer system in Europe, backing up, and supporting the network code.
>
> (Spring 1995: 49)

Westlake and Beckett (1995: 47) have pointed to similar difficulties in the electricity supply industry where it has proved difficult to install new half-hourly metering fast enough to cope with the opening up of the market to new suppliers. It is doubtful if the installation of all the new metering and monitoring equipment will stop the arguments about the mechanics of the market because the lack of information is only part of the problem. Whether it is medieval merchants trying to extend their shop frontage onto the public space of the market square or modern executives trying to minimise the expense of using a common carriage network, such arguments are the lifeblood of markets.

Markets are about argument as much as they are about exchange. These arguments have one feature in common. The essence of a market is that everyone is seeking to maximise their individual or corporate advantage; and what we have seen in all the examples is people attempting to use, structure or alter the mechanism of the market in a way that benefits them. Markets are designed to allow competition but they also need collaboration in order to maintain their fabric and structure.

Summary

The workings of markets for public utilities is a potent source of argument. These arguments are intended to persuade. The organisations within the utility markets wish to persuade the public that they are more efficient and customer-responsive than the old nationalised industries, that it would be to everyone's benefit if they were allowed to integrate horizontally and vertically, and that the problems with the common carriage systems are not their fault. The regulators, and the media, however, are concerned to convince the public that the utility companies are in need of careful monitoring and control.

Conclusion

This chapter is a pivotal one in the story being told in this book. It links the two main discourses concerning the allocation of public services that have developed historically. There is the discourse of public service which was predominant from the time of the postwar Labour government through to the early 1980s. Since then, during the Thatcher years, the discourse of markets became more powerful in relation to the question of public services. It remains to be seen whether the election of the Labour government in 1997 means a return to the public service discourse or the creation of a new discourse which incorporates elements of both predecessors. In this chapter the arguments within each of the discourses, as well as the arguments between them, have been laid out for review. On inspection of these arguments their rhetorical characteristics have become clear. Resource allocation and public services are matters of argument and not matters which can be definitively resolved.

ADDENDUM
RESOURCE ALLOCATION
PREFERENCES SURVEY
(RAPS)

RAPS is an instrument designed to identify your personal values
about the ways in which public services should be allocated.

Instructions

Please read each of the following statements and rate them according to its
relevance to your values, beliefs and actions in your job. Use the following
rating scale:

1 = this statement expresses my preferences very well
5 = this statement does not express my preferences at all

The numbers 2, 3 and 4 can be used to show intermediate points between the
two extremes of 1 and 5.

Statements   *Rating score*

1 Resources and services should be allocated according to
   careful, expert and objective assessment of individuals'
   needs.

2 If people have to be made redundant the fairest way of
   choosing who is to go is by drawing lots.

3 The reality of resource allocation means treating interest
   groups, pressure groups and lobbies as an important part of
   the process and not as an irritation and distraction.

4 The willingness of clients to co-operate in the provision of
   services should affect the services they receive. The uncooperative should receive less than the co-operative.

5 Resource allocation should involve measurement of output and the economic evaluation of professional activities and services.

6 Interest groups who take the trouble to inform themselves about the organisation's services should have an important contribution to the planning and delivery of services.

7 If budgets must be cut, then all budgets should be cut by the same percentage.

8 The provision of services should be standardised and allocated by formal rules applied equally to all clients.

9 If we have to make people redundant we should retain those whose lives would be most disrupted by redundancy.

10 If budget cuts have to be made, then those departments and services which make the least contribution to the organisation's objectives should bear the brunt of the cuts.

11 People are morally responsible for their actions and so moral judgements about clients are an important factor in allocating services.

12 When resources are limited, staff should be constantly vigilant for people trying to cheat the system and abuse services.

13 Sometimes we have to provide services to meet individual needs even if it is not cost effective to do so.

14 When making people redundant, criteria must be used which are acceptable to management, unions and any other powerful interest group involved.

15 The goal of resource allocation should be equality of access and opportunity.

16 Resource allocation is deeply involved with the mobilisation of support in an area and with satisfying particular interest groups.

17 In hard times public sector organisations should concentrate on responding positively to groups in the community who are trying to help themselves.

18 It makes good sense to put resources where they can do the most good, and not necessarily where they are most needed, as long as nobody is made worse off than they already are.

19 When redundancies are inevitable it should be those who make least contribution to the organisation's objectives who go.

20 The focus in service provision should be on the individual client and the need to do everything possible to help her or him. All services that have some chance of doing some good should be provided.

Scoring sheet for espoused values

1 Transfer your scores to the appropriate box and enter totals in the *Total* boxes.

Individual need

Q1	
Q13	
Total	

Fairness

Q8	
Q15	
Total	

Utility

Q5	
Q18	
Total	

Ecology

Q6	
Q16	
Total	

Deservingness

Q4	
Q11	
Total	

2 Now transfer your scores into the score column below. Then put the values into rank order. The lowest scoring value is your most preferred and should be ranked 'A'. The highest scoring value is your least preferred and should be ranked 'E'.

	Score	Rank
Individual need		
Fairness		
Utility		
Ecology		
Deservingness		

A = lowest scoring = most preferred
E = highest scoring = least preferred

Scoring sheet for preferred values in 'hard' cases

1 Transfer your scores to the appropriate box and enter totals in the *Total* boxes.

Individual need

Q9	
Q20	
Total	

Fairness

Q2	
Q7	
Total	

Utility

Q10	
Q19	
Total	

Ecology

Q3	
Q14	
Total	

Deservingness

Q12	
Q17	
Total	

2 Now transfer your scores into the score column below. Then put the values into rank order. The lowest scoring value is your most preferred and should be ranked 'A'. The highest scoring value is your least preferred and should be ranked 'E'.

	Score	Rank
Individual need		
Fairness		
Utility		
Ecology		
Deservingness		

A = lowest scoring = most preferred
E = highest scoring = least preferred

5

THE MECHANICS OF MAKING MARKETS

An overview of the mechanisms

Once policy makers have come to the conclusion that public services are better allocated by markets than by public sector decision making they are faced with the practical problem of how to create markets where there were none before. This chapter is about the devices and mechanisms that are available to them. It has been argued earlier that decision makers in the public sector refer to a fixed stock of heuristics when making resource allocations; and in a similar vein people charged with marketising public services draw upon a number of specific mechanisms when carrying out the task. The mechanisms are briefly listed in the first section and considered in more detail later in the chapter.

Making public organisations open to consequences

Government in the United Kingdom was traditionally protected from all but the political consequences of its policies and actions. The Crown could not be sued because of the legal maxim 'the king can do no wrong' and it was safe from financial insolvency because it had the power to raise whatever taxes it needed. Public bodies have not had total protection from litigation for many years but, until 1986 for example, hospitals, as part of central government and so under the prerogative of the crown, were exempt from the provisions of the health and safety acts. One of the mechanisms for making public organisations responsive to market discipline therefore is to open them up to litigation and to make it possible for them to become insolvent. Many bodies created in the last decade to provide public services have had to earn their revenue by winning contracts to provide services, rather than by levying taxes. If they were unable to do so they were dissolved. Many public bodies have also been made directly liable for negligent actions taken in their name. Until the late 1980s negligence claims against hospitals were dealt with by regional solicitors who worked for the regional health authorities; when hospital and community trusts were set up they became responsible for the legal claims made against them.

Making public service providers open to the legal and financial consequences of their actions is the bedrock mechanism for marketising the public sector. Without such changes there are no strong reasons why the managers of public service organisations should pay attention to the messages sent to them by their customers.

Purchaser–provider distinctions

A market is, partly, defined by the presence of customers and sellers. Once public service organisations have been made accountable, the next necessary mechanism is to make sure that there are buyers and sellers in the market and, ideally, plenty of both. This is done by creating a split between buyers and sellers of public services in the market, and by creating the mechanism through which buyers and sellers can negotiate and make deals.

Creating a purchaser–provider split can be done in a number of ways. The simplest method, which does not involve anyone beyond the organisation, is the use of service level agreements (SLA). Under this regime an organisation is divided into providing and purchasing units which enter into agreements with each other. These agreements specify the type, quantity and quality of the service to be provided as well as the fees to be paid. Competitive tendering takes this principle a stage further because the contract for providing a service is put out to tender and external private and public organisations, as well as in-house units, can bid for the work. The 1988 Local Government Act, which reinforced the practice of competitive tendering in local authorities, had a large impact. By 1994 the annual value of work under contract was £2.4 billion. Of this total the biggest expenditure was for refuse collection, the other services commonly contracted out were catering, education and welfare, cleaning, ground maintenance, vehicle maintenance and sport and leisure management. In the case of refuse collection, between 1980/81 and 1994, the net cost fell by 40 per cent, two-thirds of the saving, however, had been made before the introduction of the 1988 Act. The Audit Commission (1995: 2) attributed the savings to:

- changes in specification, i.e. front door rather than back door collection;
- larger capacity bin vans;
- improved productivity;
- changes to the net cost of commercial waste collection;
- and, possibly, lower wage rates.

CCT is based on block contracts, in which a supplier agrees to provide all the services needed in a particular time period, often several years. In an internal market, which is an extension of CCT, purchasers often use spot contracts to buy one-off services from a range of suppliers. CCT has always been a contentious issue, however, and some local authorities implemented it with greater energy and excitement than others (Colling 1993).

Quasi-markets

In internal markets the decisions about what services to provide, and to whom, are still made by public officials. These bureaucrats buy the services on behalf of the service users. It is a common right-wing criticism of internal markets that the purchasing decisions of administrators are not necessarily those that the consumers of the services would have made if they had had the choice. Quasi-markets are the next logical step in creating markets because they involve taking the purchasing power away from high level bureaucrats and giving it to groups who are in closer contact with the consumers, but not actually to the consumers themselves. Two of the main examples of quasi-markets stem from the NHS and Community Care Act of 1990. They are the GP fundholding system and the market for residential and community care services which are purchased by social services care managers on behalf of their clients. In both of these cases devolution of decision making is a strong theme. The power to decide what services are needed is removed from centralised planners and given to many local service assessors, in these cases either GPs or social workers operating as care managers.

In defining quasi-markets in this way I have taken a small liberty with the normal definition. LeGrand and Bartlett's (1993: 10) definition includes the structural characteristics of the internal market as well as the use of third parties, such as fundholding GPs, to act as proxy purchasers for their patients. In the definition used here, although the internal market is a necessary condition for a quasi-market, its key element is the use of purchasing proxies. The exchange mechanisms used in these quasi-markets are provided by the budget systems of health and local authorities. Proxy purchasers can buy services without there being a cash transaction; all that is required is that proxy purchasers have an allocated budget against which they can code the expenditure. Popular myth suggests that early members of the fundholding scheme did not understand this system and were surprised when they didn't receive a cheque for the whole of the fund which they might bank in the practice account.

Vouchers

The obvious shortfall of quasi-markets, when they are compared with normal markets, is that although purchasing decisions have been moved closer to the consumers of service, it is still not the users who make the choices. The next logical mechanism therefore for making the provision of public service more market based is to provide the users with funds that they can spend as they wish on the open market. The main examples of this technique are the open enrolment scheme for primary and secondary education, the voucher scheme for nursery and play school services and the concessionary bus pass schemes. In all of these cases the user of the service is given a voucher, or an entitlement, which they can use to purchase a service from a provider of their choice. In practice there are constraints upon the users' choices. In open enrolment the choice is dependent on the school having the space to take a pupil, and, in some schools, on whether the potential pupil performs adequately on a selection test. In the concessionary bus pass scheme the holder of the card or voucher may only be able to use the voucher on services provided by a particular company or within a given geographical area. A further constraint on the use of a transport voucher is its lack of transportability; a bus pass cannot be used to buy a railway fare. The voucher scheme for nursery education, which was piloted by the Conservative government in 1996, came closest to the definition of a full voucher scheme. It was one of the first of the Tory projects closed down by the new Labour government in 1997. Voucher systems, in theory at least, make it possible for people to take an active part as purchasers in a marketplace.

Competitive bidding for funds

Decisions about how much money can be spent on publicly funded projects have remained an administrative cum political decision, even in those services, which in other respects, have been marketised. Competitive bidding mechanisms have been developed, however, to bring decisions about which projects to fund within the ambit of market disciplines.

The main feature in competitive bidding for project funds is that public organisations' bids are competitively judged and only the best are funded. This is not an entirely novel mechanism in the public sector but in the 1980s it became more common. Local authorities, for example, bid for money for the City Challenge inner city regeneration programmes. Under traditional funding mechanisms all authorities were funded to meet local needs; but the two rounds of the City Challenge competition introduced a 'winner takes all, loser takes nothing' culture (Stewart 1996). The Private Finance Initiative (PFI) (Bailey 1995: 136–42) gave a major boost to competitive funding in the 1990s by requiring that all public capital projects should be considered for eligibility for the PFI. Competitive bidding is not restricted to capital projects. University research funding, for example, involves competitive bidding for capital and revenue costs. None the less the PFI has focused attention on competitive bidding for large infrastructure projects.

Under the PFI, which was introduced in 1992, private organisations bid for the right to fund capital developments such as new hospitals or rail links. They gain their profit from the fees they charge for leasing the facilities to the public service provider(s) who will use it, as well as from providing associated services such as building maintenance. Whether a particular proposal is funded therefore will depend upon its financial viability as judged by the various organisations making bids. A form of this device, often found in developing countries, is the *build-operate-transfer* (BOT) system. In BOT projects a private organisation funds and builds a facility, a bridge for example, and is given a concession by government to operate the bridge and charge fees for a number of years. The time span is sufficient for the company to recoup its capital outlay and to earn an appropriate rate of profit. At the end of this period the ownership of the facility and the right to charge tolls is transferred to the government.

There are important differences between the two main examples of competitive bidding given. In the case of City Challenge there were many bidders but only one supplier of funds, the Department of the Environment. PFI is different, however, because there is only one bidder, the government department, NHS trust or other public body which has a project it wants to fund, but potentially many funders, the construction companies who want the opportunities to earn revenue by building hospitals, roads or whatever. In one sense therefore it is the construction companies who are bidding, competing against each other for the contract to build the road or hospital. But they are competing on the grounds of their cost efficiency. On the question of which projects are funded and which remain on the blocks (as opposed to the question who can build it cheapest and best), the key bidder is the public body which is concerned that its proposed building is built. PFI projects have to compete against the other investment opportunities open to the private sector companies. They have to be competitive in terms of their level of risk and return, otherwise private sector companies will not tender for them. In practice the boot has been on the private sector's foot. The competition to take on PFI projects is not heavy; and the new Labour government has had to change the PFI system to make the projects more attractive to the construction companies. The focus on financial viability was a major change caused by competitive bidding. In the City Challenge projects the funding mechanism had a competitive element but the criteria of success were related to the bids' merits and not their profitability. Within the PFI scheme public bodies may choose the projects they put forward for tendering on their merit but their attractiveness to the private sector will be judged on commercial grounds alone.

Privatisation and regulation

Privatisation is the ultimate mechanism for placing the provision of public services onto a market basis. Under privatisation, shares in public organisations are sold and their ownership moves from public to private bodies. The privatised organisations have commonly been public trading organisations who already had customers to whom they provided services. The effect of privatisation therefore was to transfer the risk and rewards of providing the service from government to the private sector. Typically, however, especially in the case of the privatised utilities, the government did not lose all of its responsibilities for the service provided by the private companies. The Acts of Parliament which privatised the utilities imposed obligations on the new companies and created regulatory regimes to oversee them.

Combining the mechanisms: the mechanisms for marketising
public services as recipe ingredients

The mechanisms for installing market characteristics in systems for allocating and delivering public services may be seen as ingredients which can be combined in different proportions and styles in different recipes for marketisation. The examples of water and rail privatisation, as well as the GP fundholding scheme and compulsory competitive tendering, show how this can be done.

When the water boards were privatised the main mechanism used was the creation of privately owned corporate bodies which had monopolies in their own geographical areas. The water companies took over government's taxation prerogative and water services were charged for on the basis of the old rating system. It is only with the increasing use of water meters as the basis of billing that consumers can be said to be customers rather than rate payers. Water privatisation involved only one of the mechanisms listed above and it can be contrasted with rail privatisation in which most of the mechanisms were used. In this case not one, but many, new corporate and private bodies were formed. An internal market was created in which some of the new companies were purchasers, responsible for marketing and operating services; whilst others were provider companies, charged with providing rolling stock, the permanent way, stations, signalling and so on to the service operators. There was also an element of competitive funding. The companies who sought franchises to run services had to bid for a share of the public subsidy that was available to fund rail services. In general those who claimed they could provide services with the least subsidy were the most successful. It appeared that in some cases the degree of public subsidy was higher than was first thought. Some rail companies were allegedly sold at a price far below market value. The National Audit Office, for example, was investigating the case of Porterbrook Leasing, a rail rolling stock company which was sold to its management in January 1996 for £527m and was resold seven months later to Stagecoach for £825m (Harrison 1997). If franchises were sold at much below their value it would suggest that the element of competition in the bidding process was more apparent than real. It is also just possible to argue that the director of franchising for rail services is a proxy purchaser in a quasi-market inasmuch as he determines the minimum services that rail companies are obliged to provide and has the power to fine companies who fail to meet their contractual obligations. Rail privatisation provides an illustration of the use of many marketisation mechanisms in the shifting of public services into a market-based system.

Similar contrasts can be found in other major reforms of the public services. It is useful to contrast the GP fundholding scheme with competitive tendering for local government services. Fundholding involved many of the mechanisms discussed above whereas competitive tendering involved only one. GPs have never been state employees, they have always been independent practitioners contracted to the NHS. They have always been small businesses and as such they are open to the legal and financial consequences of their actions, although their relationship with the NHS puts them in a more secure position than that experienced by most small businesses. The fundholding scheme involves an internal and quasi-market in which GPs are given a budget to buy specified medical services (excluding emergency hospital admissions, medical and mental health inpatient services, accident & emergency and maternity services) for their patients. There is also an element of a voucher scheme in fundholding. Patients are not given a voucher but they do have an entitlement to be registered with a GP and so they have a degree of choice between being registered with a fundholding or a non-fundholding practice and indeed, subject to availability, some choice between fundholding practices. This choice is circumscribed by a number of constraints such as geographical location, the willingness of the GPs to accept patients onto their lists and the preparedness of the health authority to accept a GP's list size. Competitive tendering in contrast utilises a smaller range of devices. It is not necessary for the body that is putting its services out to tender, or indeed for bodies who are bidding for the contract, to be technically capable of insolvency; although they do have to keep proper trading accounts. The main requirement of competitive tendering is that the market should be structured into purchasers and providers. There is no element of quasi-markets or voucher funding of ultimate consumers within competitive tendering.

The techniques listed in this overview section occupy positions on a spectrum which ranges from making organisations legally and financially accountable, at one end, to full-blown privatisation, at the other. The positions have been listed in this section in an ascending order of market sophistication. The earlier mechanisms in the sequence are used only for the purpose of cost efficiency and economy. The latter techniques in the sequence are also concerned with the effectiveness of the resource allocation. The point of competitive tendering therefore is not to change the range of services provided to users, nor to change the balance of provision between different types of users. It is simply to deliver the services as cheaply as may be. This is not an insignificant ambition. If it is achieved, it means that more resources are available to provide more services or that less money is spent overall and pressure on the public sector borrowing requirement is reduced. Within fundholding, as an example of a quasi-market, there is a similar concern over cost (keeping the drugs budget under control, for example, by using generic rather than branded products) but there is also an intention to improve the effectiveness of the health service by changing the priorities and the allocation of services. The scheme had the objective of changing the balance and nature of services. According to the Audit Commission (1996: 38–9) fundholding was set up to, *inter alia*:

- increase the focus given to the individual needs of patients;
- improve the quality of services;
- provide more effective healthcare by changing clinical practice, e.g. reducing surgical intervention and increasing the use of watchful waiting in the treatment of glue ear;

- providing a wider choice for patients;
- developing services nearer to the patient, e.g. by consultants holding out-patient clinics at the GPs' surgeries.

It is clear from this list that the aim was effectiveness as well as efficiency. The scheme was designed to change the services provided so that money was better spent. Whether this was achieved will be discussed later. At this stage of the argument it is sufficient to note that the various devices available to the makers of markets have markedly different impacts.

The mechanisms in detail

The rest of this chapter is concerned with the operation and impact of the market-making mechanisms. Each will be evaluated in detail and the analysis will be used to identify their limitations and advantages.

Making public organisations open to consequences

The essential ingredient in any recipe for the creation of markets (to replace public sector organisations) is corporate bodies that are responsive to the wishes and criticisms of their customers. Without this element the effort of creating market structures or funding users to buy services would be wasted. A customer can influence a supplier in two ways, by withdrawal of their custom, which threatens the solvency of the provider, or by legal action to seek redress for a wrong done or to force the provider to conform with their contract with the customer. The legal aspects will be discussed first.

There was always a distinction in law between public bodies who were agents and servants of the Crown and those who were not. Until the Crown Proceedings Act of 1947 the former could not be sued in court whereas the latter could. Ironically, but perhaps typical of the British constitution, the one body that was called the Crown Agents did not have Crown immunity. There are a number of exceptions in the Crown Proceedings Act which allows certain public bodies (e.g. the armed forces) to retain legal immunity. But generally the Act gave people the right to redress for the wrongs done to them by public organisations. The legal position concerning acts of omission rather than acts of commission has been different, however. People could sue public bodies if they had been wrongly treated but they could not easily sue to force public corporations to fulfil their statutory duty. Most Acts of Parliament which author-ise public services (such as the Library Act 1964) require the appropriate organisations to provide a reasonable service. But whereas in the nineteenth century the courts were willing to enforce these obligations by damages or injunctions, in the twentieth century the courts have been unwilling to do so. There have been some returns to the older practice, however. In 1979, for example, in *Meade* v. *The London Borough of Haringey* (Bradley *et al.* 1993:

181

738) parents were allowed to sue the LEA because it had closed a school for five weeks in sympathy with a trade union's wage claim on behalf of school caretakers. The parents already had the right under the Education Acts to complain to the Secretary of State but this judgment also enabled them to use legal remedies. In 1996 a group of twenty-four parents sued their local education authority for negligence in failing to identify and meet the special educational needs of their children (Bale 1996).

A major change in the position of suppliers of public services, in summary, has been their increased responsiveness to consumer rights. Channels, such as ombudsmen, community health councils and charters, have been developed to enable customers to complain and receive an explanation (and sometimes compensation) when public services go wrong. But generally consumers have limited rights to use the law to insist that public corporations provide proper services. One exception to this argument is where the consumer is a public body carrying out a purchasing role. Health authorities, for example, commonly place quality standards, as well as detailed specifications of the services to be provided, in their contracts with hospitals and these could form the basis of an action for breach of contract if the hospital failed to deliver. These examples suggest that public accountability through politicians has been replaced by contractual and consumer rights. Contracts for service, customer charters, the right to sue for services negligently delivered, or not delivered at all, have emphasised the consumer rights of individuals at the expense of political accountability to communities. In response, organisations supplying public services have come to see their clients as customers.

Developments in the financial responsiveness of public bodies have been more dramatic. Until the late 1980s most public bodies were either part of central government or were statutory bodies with revenue-raising powers. Insolvency therefore was not a threat. Two types of changes have altered this picture. The first was the capping of local authority expenditure (Flynn 1993: 45–8) which gave central government control over local authorities' levels of expenditure. Any council that spent more than allowed faced severe financial consequences which would not quite amount to insolvency but would be just as painful. The second change was the creation of a new type of body which the Nolan committee (Committee on Standards in Public Life 1995b) refers to as local public spending bodies (LPSB). These are defined as not-for-profit organisations which are neither fully elected nor appointed by ministers but which provide public services, often at a local level, which are wholly or largely funded by public money. Nolan included in this category higher and further education bodies, grant maintained schools, training and enterprise councils (TECs, but LECs in Scotland) and housing associations. These bodies have no taxation powers, they are dependent upon earned income and they can become bankrupt. To these bodies ought to be added NHS trusts. They are not included in the Nolan LPS category because they are appointed by ministers and they have to make a return of 6 per cent on their average net assets. This return is calculated gross before interest payments on the loans granted to the Trusts by the government are taken into consideration. In practice the requirement for a financial return is a complicated way of accounting for capital charges. The rules were set up in this manner to make a NHS trust's balance sheet look as close to that of a private company as possible. The financial position of NHS trusts, however, is similar to that of LPSBs in that both are dependent on income and they are liable to go bankrupt or out of business. One notable example was Harlow Wood Hospital which was a national specialist institution providing orthopaedic treatment. Because it drew its patients from a national catchment area it was very dependent on extra contractual referrals (ECRs). Under the rules of the NHS internal market, health authorities and GP fundholders purchased most of their hospital services from local hospitals and special arrangements had to be made if doctors wished to send their patients to out-of-area specialist hospitals such as Harlow Wood. The hospital could not attract enough patients. It was closed down and most of its staff and services were transferred to other trusts.

TECs have also proved vulnerable and South Thames TEC went into receivership in 1995. The eighty-one TECs and twenty-two LECs were formed in the period 1990/2 by groups of business people and others in response to a prospectus issued by government. They are private limited companies (usually limited by guarantee) and they are governed by their Memorandum and Articles of Association. Several TECs have taken advantage of their legal status to merge with their local chambers of commerce. But entrepreneurial freedom has its drawbacks, and Oldham TEC and the Inland Revenue went to court (Barrie and Beavis 1996) over the question of whether a TEC is a charity. Oldham TEC claimed it was a charity because of the tax advantages such status brings. But a charity that acted beyond the remit of its Memorandum and Articles of Association would be acting illegally. This created a problem for the TECs/Chambers of Commerce because their range of activities was much wider than that of pure TECs. If TECs were declared to be charitable bodies then the mergers of TECs and Chambers of Commerce might have to be dissolved. The development of TECs provides an example of the increasing use of private bodies to deliver public services and it shows how tensions can develop between their legal status, their entrepreneurial approach and their public service obligations.

The creation of markets requires that organisations decrease their political accountability and increase their commercial accountability. The universities that were created from the old polytechnics provide an example of this move. Originally polytechnics were part of local government. As such, they were responsible through the education committee (albeit at a fairly long arm's length) to the electorate. In higher education corporations (the legal form of the polytechnics that were transformed into universities) the governing bodies are responsible for making or renewing appointments to their own number. No democratic mandate is needed to become a board member. There is no requirement for boards to hold any public meeting and practice in making papers public is variable (Committee on Standards in Public Life 1995b). When they were polytechnics many of these institutions were probably running foul of the law in undertaking commercial activities, such as consultancy and training, which were possibly *ultra vires*. Their new legal status has made such activities much easier to pursue and universities now set up wholly owned private companies through which they can account for their purely commercial work. Commercial accountability has become more important; public accountability less important.

Creating purchaser–provider divisions

Markets are not natural organisms, they have to be built. When the provision of public services is put on a market basis it is necessary to ensure that there are buyers and sellers in the marketplace. In the early days of compulsory competitive tendering in local authorities this task was achieved by vesting the roles of purchaser and provider in one person or unit. This was the so-called two-hatted approach in which people, typically, county surveyors, acted as contractor and customer for road maintenance work. As contractor they would keep trading accounts for their activities and as customer they would write letters to themselves complaining about the quality of the work they had done (Flynn 1993: 128, 144). More commonly, however, works departments divided themselves into contractor and client units and attempted to create Chinese walls between the two functions.

The Conservative government's view, however, was that providers should be completely separate from the commissioning organisations and should preferably be located in the private sector. This end was not always easy to achieve. The building of the community care market was phased by government. Residential care services were marketised first because private providers already existed. The spread of the market into non-residential care was going to be more difficult until private suppliers could be encouraged into the market. In their review of the creation of the market for the provision of community care services, Wistow et al. (1996) found that 68 per cent of the social services departments they surveyed were encouraging the setting up of new voluntary organisations to provide services in the new market. By 1997 the Conservative government's policy seemed to be moving towards wholesale privatisation of social service provision; and Kent County Council social services department, for example, recommended to the councillors that it privatise all its home care services to save £24m (Brindle 1997) and to create private sector providers.

There were similar problems of ensuring there were enough sellers in the market during the preparations for the nursery voucher scheme that was planned to come into effect in April 1997. Nursery schools which wished to take part in the scheme had to be inspected before they could be accredited. According to Bright (1997) inspectors of pilot schemes in four local authority areas found that nursery schools were being accredited to the scheme even though they were failing pupils in some curriculum areas. The Labour Party claimed that standards in the inspection of schools were being lowered to ensure that there would be enough providers in the scheme to make it viable.

In addition to ensuring the presence of sellers, market building also requires the development of a channel through which sellers and buyers can communicate and negotiate. These forums or, as they are sometimes termed, commissioning systems, cannot be allowed to develop by happenstance because of the requirement that a public sector purchaser should choose its contractors in a transparent and fair manner. There are direct costs involved in setting up and maintaining channels of communication and if there are imperfections in the mechanism there will also be opportunity costs arising from the inadequacies of the system. These are defined by Williamson as transaction costs and they are the main focus of this section.

What follows is closely based on the analysis presented in Wistow et al. (1996). There are five kinds of transaction costs. The first type is structural costs. These are caused by structural inadequacies in the market, such as the under-provision of suppliers in the market for home-based social care, and they manifest in over-pricing and excessive profits. The second type of costs arise from inadequate information in the markets. Poverty of information potentially enables suppliers, for example, to state that their clients are more costly to deal with than they are (this is a moral hazard of hidden information) and to charge a higher than justified price; or to provide fewer services than they contracted for (the moral hazard of action) or to reject clients who would not be cost effective (biased selection). Bargaining costs, the third type of transaction costs, arise because both buyer and seller in a market have to do their homework before signing a contract (whereas in a bureaucracy there is only one person involved and so the process is cheaper) and because, when a problem occurs, which had not been anticipated in the contract, both sides have to give time to resolving the difficulty. The costs of selective intervention, the fourth type of transaction cost, are caused by the meddling of the purchaser. It is in the nature of public service managers that they cannot help interfering, even when there is no need. The costs to the provider of dealing with this intrusion are a transaction cost. Lastly, there are the costs, to the seller and the purchaser, of monitoring performance against the terms of the contract. In total therefore transaction costs can be seen as all the costs involved in making a contract (Lane 1995: 229).

The central question to ask when analysing the operation of a purchaser–provider split is whether it minimises the transaction costs of providing a service when compared with other company- or bureau-based options. Flynn (1993) in his summary of Williamson's argument presented the issue as follows. At one extreme, in a situation where the contracts between buyers and sellers are simple, and there are many sellers to choose between, transaction costs are likely to be minimised by the use of spot contracts in a market. At the other extreme, where the contracts are hugely complex and there is a monopoly provider, transaction costs may be high if a spot contract system is used. In such a situation the transaction costs could be lowered by replacing contracts for a particular service with employment contracts which oblige employees to do as their employer tells them rather than complete a contractually defined task. In other words, in such a situation a market is not necessarily the optimum solution and it would be better to replace expensive contracting procedures with the cheaper process of providing the service through a directly funded public agency. There is a mid-position in Flynn's analysis which involves long-term contracts between buyers and sellers in the market and this is typically what happens in the market for community care.

Contracts in the markets for public services tend to be complex; certainly more complex than government wishes and there are often fewer providers than would be ideal. There is consequently a possibility that transaction costs might be higher than they would be if the services were planned and provided by a single institution. Great care therefore needs to be taken to ensure that the commissioning system minimises transaction costs.

Wistow *et al.*'s study of the commissioning arrangements for the social care market is interesting because it uses a transaction cost analysis to review the commissioning arrangement for the social care market. I will summarise their discussion by considering the different elements of a commissioning system. One issue is the organisational level within the commissioning organisation at which responsibility for purchasing community care should be placed. This can either be high in the structure, in which case there would be a system of centralised strategic purchasing, or low in the hierarchy, in which case there would be decentralised and local purchasing arrangements. The main advantage of centralised purchasing is that the risks of bargaining can be spread, the costs of a poor deal can be offset by the benefits of more successful negotiations. An effective, risk-taking, purchasing strategy can be more easily achieved under centralised buying. But centralised purchasers are, by definition, at a distance from the users and the contractors and the transactional cost of informational losses may be higher when compared with a local system. The benefits of localised purchasing are the opposite of the benefits of a centralised system. Informational losses should be smaller because the purchasers know the contractors and the users better; but the risk of overspends on purchasers' budgets is greater when a single large budget is replaced by many small budgets. The costs of training and reorganisation and of developing information and control systems are also likely to be higher in the case of local purchasing. The auditors of contracting systems in local government (Audit Commission 1995: 15) found that responsibility for purchasing was in varied locations. Most contracts were handled by a departmental client (e.g. an education department), and whilst some authorities had centralised CCT purchasing teams, in other cases, these had been disbanded and the purchasing role devolved. The costs did not differ according to the commissioning structure used.

Another important question about commissioning arrangements is whether there should be a select list of contractors/tenderers or whether there should be open purchasing. A select list has the advantages of better working relationships between purchasers and contractors and the likelihood of reduced informational losses and moral hazards. Such systems also make it worthwhile for suppliers to develop a reputation for quality. Many companies in the training and education fields find it useful to gain accreditation under such schemes as BS5750 or Investors in People because the people they contract within the TECs and the DfEE either require or prefer them to have these kitemarks. The disadvantage of select lists is that contractors may feel protected from competition and become lazy and sloppy. In contrast, an open purchasing system means that the chances of making a good match between users' needs and contractors' services is enhanced because there is a wider range of providers to choose between. Where there is open purchasing, and thus more suppliers, the danger of selective intervention by the purchasers is also lessened. The logic of the analysis is that transaction costs are likely to be lower in an open system but twenty-one out of the twenty-five social services departments in Wistow's survey opted for a select list system. Even in a supposedly open purchasing system the breadth of tenderers can be limited by a range of factors. Many of the firms that could undertake work for local authorities, for example, are small and they regard the contracts that local authorities put out to tender as too large and risky. Consequently, according to research funded by the Department of the Environment, only a small proportion of firms who could have worked for local authorities did so (Audit Commission 1995: 8). Competition for contracts in the local authority field is not well developed. In one survey, conducted in 1994, around 50 per cent of contracts for catering and sport and leisure management had been awarded without competition, although in the cases of other services, such as refuse collection, this figure dropped to about 10 per cent.

The next issue requiring discussion is pricing arrangements. One option is spot purchasing where the purchaser contracts at whatever price is prevailing in the market, the other option is for the purchaser to publish a price list. In the case of the community care market price lists are normally very close to the rates for care set by the Department of Social Security. Spot purchasing is costly because it involves more time and effort in negotiation but the disadvantages of price lists is that they may be wrong. If they are set too low no one may come forward to bid for the work, if set too high then money is wasted. There is also the question of whether contracts should be fixed price or cost plus. Both systems have disadvantages. Providers under a fixed price system might cut costs by not providing all the services contracted for at the specified standard and providers under a cost plus regime may use their better information to manipulate their costs upwards,

One of the big questions in commissioning arrangements is the choice between block, cost and volume and cost per case contracting (Audit Commission 1996: 124–5). In the early stages of GP fundholding most GPs opted for block contracts under which they paid a hospital a lump sum to carry out all activity in defined medical specialities. By 1995 only a minority were using these contracts. The predominant form of contract had become the cost per case in which each individual treatment was paid for separately with no commitment to any annual activity rates. In 1994, 31 per cent of fundholders were using cost and volume contracts with their main supplier. Under these contracts GPs pay a lump sum for activity up to a set level (say 80 per cent of anticipated annual activity) and once that level has been reached they pay the hospital on a per case basis. Block contracts have some transactional cost advantages. They represent security to suppliers who might therefore be inclined to give a price discount. But there is an increased risk of moral hazard with these contracts as suppliers are tempted to shirk their contractual obligations. Cost per case (or spot) contracts increase the purchasers' choices but they increase the bargaining and administration costs. In many fundholding practices the clerical staff are overwhelmed by hundreds of invoices from hospital for amounts smaller than £100. But the use of spot contracts also means that downturns in the market price can be taken advantage of whilst those on block contracts can only regret their misfortune.

The final issue in commissioning arrangements concerns the processes of specifying and monitoring contracts. The Audit Commission (1995) argued that in local authorities these costs are too high. They recommended that contracts should only specify the desired results and not the methods to be used. They also proposed that monitoring costs could be cut by placing more reliance on the contractors' own quality assurance and control systems. Wistow et al. (1996) supported this argument by arguing that social service purchasers should develop a system of obligational contracting (or as it is more commonly known in the private sector, partnership sourcing) under which trust is built between buyers and sellers which allows problems in the contract to be resolved mutually rather than settled by expensive formal arbitration.

The purpose of this review was not to find the balance of the arguments, or to define the best commissioning system, but to show how options in the design of commissioning systems have different effects on transaction costs and hence different consequences in terms of the utility of the marketplace. If the commissioning system is well designed and compensates for the imperfections of the marketplace, then transaction costs will be low and the market will provide optimum benefit as a means of allocating services. But if the commissioning system cannot minimise transaction costs then it may be that alternative methods (forms of governance) may be better suited to the provision of services. Bourn and Ezzamel (1986) used a transaction cost analysis to review the introduction of general management into the NHS in the early 1980s. They argued that the mode of organisational control appropriate to the delivery of particular services was related to two factors. The first was the degree of ambiguity in performance management. This concerned the ease or difficulty involved in deciding whether an organisation had done its work well. The second factor was the degree of goal incongruence between the parties involved in the supply of a service. If all parties saw the purpose of the service in the same way then this factor was rated low, but if they disagreed on the service's objectives then this factor would be rated high. Bourn and Ezzamel suggested the forms of organisational control appropriate to various combinations of these two factors. Appropriateness was judged in terms minimising transaction costs by choosing the cheapest mode of control for each combination of these variables (Bourn and Ezzamel 1986: 206).

They argued that clans, as represented by doctors as a profession, with their concern with clinical freedom, had been the appropriate form of organisational control in the health service.

> Clinical freedom is interpreted here as a form of clan control ... it minimises both internal and external transaction costs for an organisation such as the NHS which is characterised by a high ambiguity of performance measures and relatively high agreement about operational objectives.
>
> (ibid.: 213)

The introduction of general management, as a consequence of the Griffiths report (Department of Health and Social Security 1983), they saw as an attempt to move the NHS towards a hierarchical (or bureaucratic) form of control. Such a development would only work, they argued, if performance management could be introduced into the NHS. The subsequent introduction of markets would, according to this model, require even tighter performance management systems. The introduction of general management, however, subverted the clan-based agreement about the purposes of the NHS which, Bourn and Ezzamel argued, was an ideal circumstance for the adoption of market systems.

Quasi-markets

The belief that local proxy purchasers can make better decisions on behalf of their clients than centralised planners is the key idea incorporated in quasi-markets. The example of GP fundholding will be used to review whether there is evidence for this belief. The first wave of fundholders began working under the scheme in April 1991 and there have been subsequent waves every year since. There have been two major research reports on the working of fundholding: one by Glennerster et al., published in 1994; and one by the Audit Commission that was published in 1996. Both of these will be used to provide an answer to the question whether quasi-markets can lead to improvement in the allocation of public services.

One of the early worries about fundholding, which derived from the American experience of healthcare provision (Weiner and Ferriss 1990), was biased selection, or as it is more colloquially known, cream skimming. This is the practice of excluding patients who were likely to be very expensive and so put a strain upon the proxy purchaser's budget. Glennerster found in his analysis of one practice's records that most patients caused no expenditure in terms of hospital costs but a single patient could account for nearly 10 per cent of the practice's hospital costs. There is anecdotal, but not widespread, evidence of cream skimming. It was reported (Pilkington 1994) that in 1993, 82,000 patients had been excluded from their GPs' lists compared with an estimated 30,000 the previous year. Many pundits were tempted to make a connection between this increase and the advent of fundholding; a view that was enhanced by the opinion of one Arthur Bills, aged 68, when he and his wife were removed from their GP's list. He said:

> Since practices have turned to fundholding they have been trying to save money and get rid of old people like me.
>
> (Pilkington 1994)

Nevertheless Glennerster (1994: chapter 11) and his team pointed out that there was no systematic or rigorous evidence that cream skimming was taking place. But a statistical simulation they conducted suggested that there could be a temptation for GPs to pick and choose whom they wanted on their lists. When this analysis was prepared it was anticipated that regional health authorities would quickly move to a capitation-based formula, focused on age and gender, to calculate the size of the funds particular practices should receive. In the simulation two models were used to calculate forecasts of likely expenditure on hospital treatments for a particular practice to which the researchers had access. One was an age- and gender-based model, such as the RHA might come to use, the other was a forecast based on indicators of clinical need which could be developed from the information available to GPs in their patients' medical records. On average the two models gave very similar estimates but there was a great deal of variability between the predicted costs for different treatments. For example, the age and gender model predicted an average cost of £74 for a patient with diabetes when the model based on patients' records more accurately (the out-turn expenditure was £163) forecast an average cost of £154. The conclusion was that GPs in principle had access to better information and could be able to make better cost predictions than the regional health authority who worked out their budgets. Armed with such information GPs would know what sorts of patients would cost them more than the RHA had estimated and therefore could begin to cream skim their patients.

The question of whether GPs did cream skim of course was still an open one. There were two main considerations which suggested that it was not a major problem. The first was that the costs of very expensive patients (initially defined as those costing £5,000 a year, later increased to £6,000 a year) were not charged to the funds. The second was whether GPs or their fund managers would have the knowledge and the inclination to produce elaborate statistical models. The BMA had in any case ruled that it was improper for doctors to exclude patients from their lists on the grounds of the costs or the workloads they generated. Other research, however, such as Baines and Whymes' (1996) study of fundholding in Lincolnshire, did find evidence of selection bias. In the Audit Commission's (1995) report there is little direct reference to biased selection or cream skimming. The issue is dealt with in an appendix (Audit Commission 1996: 106) where it was concluded that there was no evidence of cream skimming and that the scheme offered little incentive to do it.

Another important issue in the evaluation of fundholding is the control of the costs of the drugs that doctors prescribe. Glennerster's conclusion (1994: 169) was that fundholding doctors were paying more attention to the cost of their prescribing and it seemed as if fundholders' overspends on drugs were increasing at a slower rate than those of non-fundholders. The Audit Commission came to a similar conclusion. They argued that fundholders were making savings by a greater use of generic, rather than branded, drugs and by agreeing practice formularies which specified the drug regimes appropriate to different conditions. But whilst fundholding GPs generally spent less than non-fundholders there was much variability between fundholders. It was also notable that most of the savings on drug expenditure were achieved in the first year of being a fundholder. Fundholding therefore had an initially strong, but subsequently diminished, impact on prescribing practices.

A third area in which the government hoped fundholding would have an impact was the volume of referrals from GPs to hospitals. It was hoped it would fall although this might seem an unrealistic ambition when the budgets for fundholders were based on their historical referral patterns. By the time of the Audit Commission's (1996) investigation this hope had become restricted and was focused on the ratio of follow-up to initial visits. The common pattern of a hospital referral is an initial appointment for assessment and follow-up appointments for treatment and check-ups. It was thought that GPs would have an incentive to reduce the ratio of follow-up to initial visits as a way of saving costs. And some fundholders did, in their contracts, specify a maximum number of follow-ups they would pay for. Any appointments beyond this number had to be justified by the consultant. Fundholders' practice of arranging for consultants to hold clinics at the practice rather than at the hospital also affected the follow-up ratio. This was because contracts often specified the presence of the consultant whereas in a hospital clinic patients were more likely to see a junior doctor. Consultants were quicker than their junior colleagues to discharge patients. Overall, however, no difference was found (Audit Commission 1996: §26-7) between the average number of repeat attendances for fundholder patients and for all patients attending at NHS hospitals. So, whilst there were examples of fundholders trying to deal with this issue, the general impact had been negligible.

Another early concern about fundholding was that patients would be denied hospital services because their doctors had managed their fund badly and had run out of money before the end of the financial year. This has not turned out to be a significant problem. Although it is not uncommon for fundholders to overshoot their budget – in the year 1994/5, 22 per cent of first wave fundholders overspent as did 18 per cent of fourth wave practices. This has not resulted in people being denied treatment. What was more likely to happen, and it was the practice in one fundholding partnership in which I interviewed the practice manager and the lead partner, was that the posting of the referral letter to the hospital would be delayed. The speed of referral becomes the main controlling mechanism fundholders have for increasing or decreasing the rate of expenditure.

There was evidence, however, that fundholding has had an effect on doctors' responsiveness to the expressed wishes of their patients. The main area in which this can be seen is physiotherapy. The view of the planners in purchasing health authorities (and of some practitioners) was that the therapeutic value of much physiotherapy treatment was suspect (Glennerster et al. 1994: 172; Clifton 1984). But patients like physiotherapy treatment and asked for it and GPs, in response, set up physiotherapy clinics in their surgeries. As the Audit Commission reported:

> fundholders are increasingly purchasing physiotherapy, counselling and complementary therapies, services where effectiveness is not proven but which are popular with patients and may have benefits other than those demanded by a strict adherence to currently available scientific measurement.
>
> (Audit Commission 1996: §26)

In other words, fundholding may be changing the balance of priorities between need and demand, giving more importance to the latter. Markets of course are predicated on the idea that demand is more important than need.

The remaining, and probably the most significant, controversy about fundholding is whether it leads to a two-tier health service in which the patients of fundholding practices receive a better level of service than the patients of non-fundholding practices. Various aspects of this question need to be discussed. The first is the level of resourcing. There was a popular suspicion when fundholding began that fundholders were being better resourced than the health authorities who were purchasing services on behalf of non-fundholders' patients. The evidence according to Glennerster et al. (1994: 175) did not support this view and what studies there were pointed to different conclusions. A similar situation was discovered by the Audit Commission (1996: 69). They found that in the NW Thames region fundholders were receiving a higher share of per capita funding whereas a study in the Oxford region found that in four out of the five districts fundholders would have received bigger funds if the budgets had been calculated on a capitation basis. Fundholders do have the ability to vire between heads of expenditure. They can decide how to divide their budget between staff and training costs, drug expenditure and the costs of hospital treatment and this gives them more flexibility in the use of the budget even if it is uncertain whether they are better funded.

There are two areas in which it is agreed that fundholders receive a better service than non-fundholders and that is in the area of communication between GPs and hospital consultants and in direct services such as pathology. Consultants have slowly learnt to be more responsive to the needs and wishes of their general practice colleagues. An important manifestation of this is discharge letters. When a patient finishes a course of treatment at a hospital the consultant writes to the patient's GP specifying the outcome and any further actions which need to be taken. Traditionally these letters were only sent late and erratically. Most fundholders have improved the speed and reliability of these letters. GPs can easily change the provider they use for pathology and other direct services and it is probably for this reason that fundholders have been able to negotiate improvements in the service they receive. These commonly include changes to the times at which pathology specimens are collected to make the service more convenient for surgeries.

On the big issues of clinical decision making, waiting times and changes in referral patterns the Audit Commission found that, although there were local examples of valuable changes, the overall picture was of little change. They studied how fundholding doctors made decisions on a number of tracer medical conditions and they concluded that there was no clear proof that medical decision making was more evidence-based than it was under non-fundholding conditions. When waiting lists were considered, there were examples of fundholders negotiating with providers to manage and reduce the waiting lists for their patients. There were also examples of hospitals fast-tracking fundholders' patients. In three Essex hospitals in 1993 (Brindle 1993), for example, the contracts manager wrote to consultants saying that preference should be given to the patients of fundholders to make up for the limited income being earned from the health authorities. This involved secretaries identifying referrals from fundholding GPs and placing a red marker on them. The consultants were then asked to consider bringing forward the treatment of those flagged up patients who were not due to be seen until later in the year. But, in aggregate, the waiting times for fundholding and health authority-funded patients were similar. Likewise, whereas 55 per cent of fundholders had changed their providers for some services (most frequently pathology and physiotherapy), referral patterns were largely as they had been before the practices had become fundholding.

The conclusion of this review of fundholding, as an example of quasi-markets, is that although the proxy purchasers have in some cases changed and improved the services they obtain for their patients, for example some providers have fast tracked fundholders' patients in return for extra income or the provision of extra clinical equipment (Smith 1993), in general quasi-markets do not provide a markedly different service from that provided by traditional non-market mechanisms. The Audit Commission attributed this to the failure of fundholders to take full advantage of the market. They argued that this was because fundholders lacked the managerial vision and purchasing competence to utilise the scheme fully. Some of the Audit Commission's criticisms of fundholders, however, stemmed from an implied criticism of market mechanisms. They still saw a need for comprehensive planning of healthcare, the identification of healthcare needs and the setting of national, regional and local priorities. They criticised the majority of fundholders who did not mention in their purchasing plans the priorities of the health authority (Audit Commission 1996: 67). As their own research suggested, proxy purchasers in a quasi-market are more interested in responding to their customers' demands than responding to the assessment of needs promulgated by a planning body.

Although there was no convincing evidence that fundholding led to the creation of a two-tier system for healthcare there was still an impression of inequity in the minds of many. A typical illustration is the woman who complained to the press because she could not get a hip operation from the NHS and had decided to pay for a private operation. It does not matter whether there were good clinical reasons for withholding the operation; she was, for example, a young woman and, because hip prostheses have to be replaced, there is an argument for not doing them too early. The important point is her belief that had she been registered with a fundholding practice she would have received the operation.

> If I'd had a fundholding GP things might have been very different.
> He could have referred me directly to a consultant of my choice.
>
> (Cohen and Illman 1995)

This was one patient who had clearly absorbed the consumerist import of the government's reforms of the health service. This view, when seen in the context of the evidence for GPs' increased responsiveness to the wishes of patients under fundholding, leads to some interesting speculations about the nature of public services under a quasi-market system.

The investigation of the impact of a consumerist perspective on quasi-markets begins with an analysis of the nature of collective goods. Economists (Bailey 1995: 28–9) often analyse the nature of goods by reference to two dimensions. The first is whether people can be excluded from the enjoyment of a good. Street lighting, for example, is a non-excludable good because, once installed, you cannot prevent people seeing by its light. The second dimension is whether a good is rivalrous in the sense that if one person consumes the good it becomes less probable that other people can benefit from it. Except in conditions of extreme congestion roads are non-rivalrous because one person driving on a road does not prevent others doing the same. If another two by two matrix can be allowed, these distinctions can be used to classify goods into four groups (table 5.1).

Table 5.1 Private, common, public and toll goods

	Rivalry in consumption	*Non-rivalry in consumption*
Excludable	Private goods e.g. food, houses	Toll goods e.g. golf courses and toll bridges
Non-excludable	Common goods e.g. fisheries	Public goods e.g. defence and public health

Source: Levacic 1991: 39.

Private goods are normally reckoned to be properly provided by the market, although there are many private goods, such as local authority housing, which are also publicly provided and allocated. The other three classifications are all, in different ways, collective goods in that they have a significant externality element in their costs and benefits. An externality is a cost or benefit which extends beyond the private costs or benefits of the person buying the service and is external to the marketplace. Public goods are things which have to be provided publicly because, as in the case of public health services (as opposed to general medical services), everybody benefits from them and, if they were provided by a market, people would be able to benefit from the service even if they did not pay their share of the costs. This difficulty is labelled the free rider problem by economists. The fact that government may be involved with the allocation of public goods, however, does not necessarily imply that they should be involved in the production of them. Common goods are interesting because, if left in a natural state, too much of them would be consumed. Fisheries, as has been seen in European waters in recent years, are over-fished because there is no incentive for an individual to desist. The effect of their individual action would be so small as to have a negligible impact, but others, who were still fishing would benefit. The normal methods for preventing over-consumption are the granting of property rights and regulation. If we take broadcasting as an example of a common good, then the number of broad-casters using the frequencies is limited by granting property rights in particular bandwidths and by regulations to enforce those rights. Toll goods are those from which people can be excluded and for which therefore a toll charge can be made before people are given access. The classical examples are toll roads and bridges. The problem is that tolls can lead to too little of a good being consumed. Sometimes this is because of the high costs of enforcing excludability. In these cases toll goods, such as roads and motorways are provided by the state who charge a zero toll and finance provision from the general revenue.

I do not want to use the analysis just discussed to make an argument about the proper demarcation between public and private domains. As Lane pointed out (1995: 164), only 10 per cent of the items in the state budget of OECD countries can be properly defined as public goods. Instead I want to use the

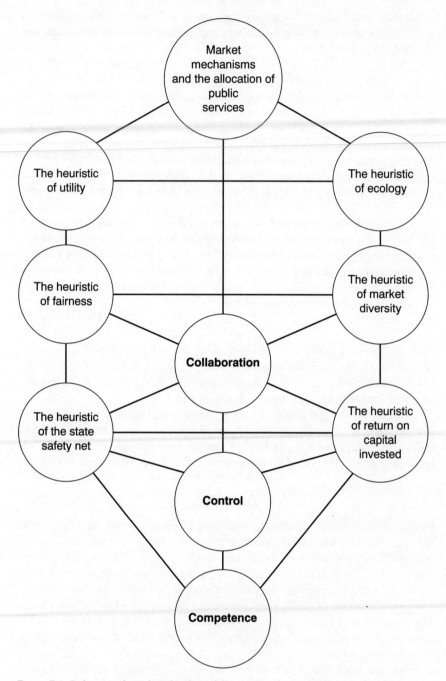

Figure 7.1 Balancing formal and informal heuristics when markets are used to provide public services

framework to suggest how quasi-markets may affect the nature of the services they allocate and deliver.

A particular effect of the development of quasi-markets was to transform many goods, that had been common goods, into private goods by making access to them excludable. Services such as education and health under the traditional post-Beveridge welfare state were not excludable. All people had a statutory right to them. They were also rivalrous to a limited extent. The use of the service by one person could diminish its availability to others. It is for this reason that the waiting list was such a common feature of the NHS and why the quality of education could be threatened by increasing class sizes. These services therefore could be defined as common goods, and as such they tended to suffer the problem of over-consumption.

The transformation of the services into private goods was achieved by the creation of quasi-markets, in which the consumers of a service were given a choice between suppliers, and by focusing clients' attention on the range of different and discrete services available rather than on a standard universal service. The development of quasi-markets for public services meant that the public sector was restructured so that they were many different providers of services. At the same time these new bodies were encouraged to differentiate themselves from each other so that the purchasers in the quasi-market could exercise choice. In the case of GP medical services, for example, a person could choose between different sorts of practices. Some offered homeopathic treatment (in addition to normal medical care), others claimed to offer care within a Christian framework, or stressed the number of women partners. The government had always hoped that GPs would compete for patients. In practice, however, the Audit Commission (1996: 35) reported that this had not happened. There was no evidence that patients were changing practices for any other reason than a change of address.

Even though, in the case of fundholding, there was no evidence of patients shopping around between GPs, the differentiation between suppliers of primary healthcare began to change the users' perceptions of services. Their concern was no longer access to a (at least nominally) standard, comprehensive national service, but whether they could obtain access to a particular, privileged, service at a particular place and time of their choosing. In plainer terms, and to take some specific examples, the question was no longer, would you receive schooling for your child, but whether you would obtain it at a particular school which met your requirements: no longer whether you could obtain healthcare, but whether you could register with a fundholding GP who was willing to fund grommets or physiotherapy when, maybe, the local health commission was not. The important issue, when there was a diversity of providers to choose from, was access to the provider of choice.

In the cases of education and health the result of public sector reforms has been to make these services more rivalrous than they were. If a school or a GP's practice was becoming congested and they found it difficult to expand, then one person being enrolled with them was at the cost of someone else's rejection. But the main difference caused by the changes was that people could be excluded (from access to a particular provider if not from a right to service from some supplier). Schools could always refuse to take someone who was not from their catchment area and GPs could always refuse to register a new patient. In a system which offered uniform services this was of no great importance to the users, it was the general right to services that mattered; but in a market of diverse providers it became crucial. Popular schools and practices in this situation came under pressure of demand.

In a free market, access to such popular services becomes a commodity in itself and the option to have access to a popular facility becomes a kind of derivative property right for which a price could be charged. Such charges would be similar to the eighteenth-century practice of buying commissions in the navy and the army. They are fees paid to gain access to a particular benefit from which people could otherwise be excluded. Now, clearly, a formal market, or property rights, in these options on access have not developed; you cannot yet buy the right to be registered with a fundholding GP or send your child to a particular state school but there are signs that something analogous to it may be developing.

Let me give some examples of these indications. The most widespread example is families moving home in order to live in the catchment area of a particular school. House purchasers are prepared to pay premium house prices in an area served by a popular school. Other people resort to dirty tricks. According to a *Today* radio news report in May 1996 a school secretary of a popular school in Derbyshire had, as one of her duties, the task of keeping watch on the addresses within the school's catchment area, given by pupils' parents as their home address, to see if the children actually left from there in the mornings to go to school. There were instances of parents giving their business addresses, the addresses of friends or relations and the addresses of houses they rented, but did not occupy, in order to get their children a place in this school. According to some newspaper reports, people have been buying *poste restante* addresses in the chosen catchment area while continuing to live elsewhere. In an indirect form these actions represent people purchasing a privileged access to a particular public service.

In a similar vein it has sometimes been the custom for people who need medical treatment to pay for a private consultation with the consultant of their choice, but then to have the treatment or operation they required from the same consultant but under the NHS. The advantage is that the patient may be treated more quickly than would have been the case if they had entered the waiting list in the normal way. At the least, they would have avoided the wait for the initial consultation with the doctor. A more unusual example was privately reported to me while I was planning this chapter. It was believed by the parents of pupils of one school that, under the procedures of some public examination boards, it was possible if you were unwell at the time of the exams to submit to the board a medical certificate which described your illness. If the exam results were not as expected, this certificate could be used to seek mitigation or a review of your marks. Now, I do not know whether this provision actually exists, but in at least one area the local GPs were besieged by requests from kids taking exams for medical certificates. Such was the demand that they thought it sensible to begin charging £7 for each certificate. This story could be interpreted as an example of people buying an option for special consideration, but again the purchase is indirect and certainly involves no direct payment between client and service provider. Nevertheless these stories represent the possibility that something like property rights, and a market in options on particular services, could develop. Such stories are the stuff of argument and debate about the role of quasi-markets. They represent debates about whether people should have the right to acquire improved public services by their ability to manipulate the opportunities provided by the system and about whether it is proper for there to be different tiers of service quality.

Vouchers and funding the user of services

Education has always been a fertile field for people with an interest in voucher schemes. The open enrolment system that applies to schools is close to the ideal of a voucher system, but it lacks portability. The legal entitlement to an education cannot be used to buy a private education. Student grants were also close in spirit to vouchers. They could be used to purchase an education in a private institution as long as it was of a recognised standing. But grants failed to meet the exacting demands of a voucher scheme in two respects: first, they were means tested, whereas vouchers are normally seen as a universal benefit, and, second, the value of the student grant was insufficient to pay for an education. As Jane Hands, Treasurer of Sommerville College Oxford wrote to potential students in 1995:

> The college would like to draw to your attention the finances needed by a student in Oxford ... Government assistance, whether in the form of a loan or a grant no longer provides sufficient funds to support an undergraduate in Oxford.
>
> (Hugill 1995)

In 1979 the student grant was £1,245 for students living away from home but not in London, in 1995 the grant was £2,040 and students had the option to take a maximum loan of £1,150. In this same period inflation had increased: £1 in 1980 would have the purchasing power of 40p in 1995 (Office for National Statistics n.d.). A proper voucher scheme would be one which provided people with sufficient resources to buy a service from any suitable provider and it would be available to all irrespective of their means.

The first proper voucher scheme, for nursery education for 4 year olds, was piloted in 1996/7 with full-scale implementation planned for spring 1997. Parents of all 4 year olds were given vouchers with a nominal value of £1,100 which was reckoned to be sufficient to buy a part-time place (up to 2.5 hours) for at least 33 weeks during a year. Parents could use the voucher at more than one institution but if the fees were greater than the worth of the voucher then parents would have to top up the fees. Possession of a voucher did not imply any entitlement to a place at a particular school or nursery. If a nursery was full then the voucher was of no use but the DfEE argued that the voucher scheme would lead to an expansion in the number of nursery places (DfEE 1996). This was necessary because in 1994 only 55 per cent of 3 and 4 year olds were attending nursery school (Office for National Statistics n.d.). A range of organisations could become providers in the scheme including LEA schools, grant maintained schools, independent schools registered with the DfEE, local authority day nurseries, play groups, non-maintained special schools and play bus schemes. The most significant exception was child minders who could not become providers in the scheme. Providers had to staff their schools or nurseries to prescribed adult:child and teacher:child ratios and had to be inspected by OFSTED registered inspectors to show that they were working towards 'desirable outcomes for children's' learning on entering compulsory education' as defined by the School Curriculum and Assessment Authority (SCAA) (DfEE 1996). The management of the inspection process was won at competitive tender by Group 4, the security company. The pilot scheme was run in the boroughs of Wandsworth, Westminster, Kensington and Chelsea and the shire county of Norfolk, presumably the only authorities that could be trusted by the government to give such an ideologically baggaged scheme a fair trial.

One of the major criticisms of the scheme was that it benefited holders of vouchers in such a way that the deserving (who by thrift and hard work could afford to pay for nursery education) were rewarded for taking their responsibilities seriously whereas the undeserving (who presumably were too feckless to take responsibility for their children's nursery education) would have to put up with a minimum level of service. One teacher who ran a private nursery in Putney said that she would not accept vouchers. She thought the scheme benefited most those who least needed it and jeopardised the local authority provision for 3 and 4 year olds which met the needs of the poorer section of the community. She said:

> Why give the money to people like those I cater for who can afford nursery education anyway?
>
> (Kingston 1996)

This theme was taken up by a leader writer in *The Guardian* who wrote:

> The comfortably off – already paying for their children, will welcome the subsidy – many of the poor who have been unable to find a free place or pay for a private one will still be cheated.
>
> (*The Guardian* 1996)

In the pilot studies not all of the comfortably off bothered to claim their vouchers. The overall take up of vouchers was 80 per cent of those eligible; the comparable figure for Kensington and Chelsea was only 55 per cent. It was 92 per cent in Norfolk (McLeod 1996a).

One of the recurrent themes in the debate over nursery vouchers concerned the impact of the scheme on the range and number of nursery places that would be provided. There were persistent worries during the pilot schemes about whether sufficient new providers were being drawn into the market by the lure of the vouchers. Only a limited amount of new money (£180m) was put into the nursery scheme, the balance of the expenditure (£570m) was clawed back from local authority budgets. This suggested that much of any growth in the private providers could come at the cost of local authority schools (Wintour 1996). But state primary schools realised that they could fight back. Some primary head teachers at popular schools began to indicate to parents of potential pupils that, when deciding whom the school could accept as pupils at the start of compulsory education, preference would be given to pupils who had entered the school in the nursery class. This led to the suspicion that parents would be disadvantaged, when trying to choose a school for their children, if they had sent them to a private nursery under the voucher scheme rather than to a state school. In a circular to teachers the National Union of Teachers (NUT) stated that where:

> teachers become aware that the voucher scheme is likely to encourage the transfer of any of their school's four year old pupils to other forms of provision they should inform their head teachers.
>
> (O'Leary 1997: 13)

The Pre-School Learning Alliance, which at first saw the voucher scheme as beneficial because it would help poor parents pay their play group fees (McLeod 1996b), later became alarmed that they might be squeezed out of the market. The worry was based on the ability of schools to expand their nursery provision and change their policies to allow more 4 year olds to enter their reception classes on the anticipation of future voucher income. In Norfolk during the pilot scheme it was reported that 800 new nursery places were created, largely through the setting up of sixteen new LEA nursery classes funded by an exceptional central government grant (Kingston 1996). Play groups, on the other hand, were seen as characteristically short of cash and unable to afford to expand their facilities to take advantage of the voucher scheme. There was a fear amongst the play group lobby that vouchers could lead to the closure of some play groups (Bawden 1996).

The general view amongst those involved in the scheme was that there was insufficient evidence to say whether the voucher scheme would lead to an expansion of nursery school places and an increase in the participation rate amongst 4 year olds. However, there was a suspicion amongst commentators that the nursery voucher scheme could lead to a lessening in the range of providers in the fields, as popular schools took advantage of their position to maximise their voucher income. In response to a parliamentary question it was reported that in Norfolk during the pilot phase of the programme there was a 70 per cent decrease (between the summer and autumn terms) in the number of vouchers spent in the private sector and an increase of one-third in the number of vouchers spent in state-provided nurseries (Smithers 1996). In summary, there was little expectation that the voucher scheme would cause many new providers to enter the market and there was concern that the range of providers would decrease. The voucher scheme appears to be discriminatory in its application; providing a useful subsidy for the relatively well off but not doing much to expand the range and extent of provision available to the less well off parents.

Putting funding on a market basis

Competitive tendering and quasi-markets are essentially mechanisms for putting the provision of revenue-funded services on a market basis. A further development is to place decisions on which projects and activities are to be funded on a market footing. Under this mechanism the government puts capital projects out to tender. The projects that are successful are those that are seen as commercially viable by a private company when compared with other projects in which they could invest. These devices therefore are not simply designed to gain the efficiency benefits of a market, though that is part of the case for them, they are also mechanisms for prioritising need. In an age where the demand for infrastructure projects outstrips the capacity of governments to fund them, these devices provide a way of prioritising the demands according to the willingness of the private sector to fund them. The corollary advantage claimed by proponents of these schemes is that the private sector are better at project management than the public sector and that under private project management the time and cost overruns experienced on projects such as the British Library at St Pancras can be avoided.

The build-operate-transfer approach is the generic name of the devices used to encourage private sector investment in public sector projects. In the UK they are wrapped up in a package known as the private finance initiative (PFI). The general principle is that the government takes responsibility for defining what projects are needed, in terms of the strategic planning of infrastructure and public services, and the private sector bids for the right to finance and manage the project and operate the facility. Obviously therefore the project must be one which generates future revenue streams to enable the contractor to recoup their financial outlay and earn a reasonable return. In the case of a road bridge or tunnel the revenue may come from the right to levy tolls. If the road is a public one on which tolls are not charged, the government may pay an imputed (or shadow) toll to the operator by paying the contractor a fee which is pro rata with the measured usage of the road. This form of BOT has become popular in the UK where it has been proposed for road schemes such as the A1–M1 link and is known as the DBFO (Design Build Finance Operate) approach (Walker and Smith 1995: 194). In the case of a company providing medical diagnostic services using high technology scanners the revenue would come from the fees they charged to both NHS and private clients for their services. Under a BOT scheme the contractors are given a concession to operate the facility for a specific period of time. At the end of that period the ownership of the facility would be transferred to the government. In the case of the Dartford Crossing of the River Thames the Dartford River Crossing Company has a concession to operate the bridge and the tunnels for a maximum of twenty years. However, the bridge and tunnels will be handed back to the government when the debt (including the remaining debt on the construction of the original tunnels) and costs have been recovered; it looks as if this may take fourteen years (ibid.: 229). The underlying concept in these schemes is a transfer of risk from the public sector to the private sector, that the construction of the project may be more difficult and costly than expected and that the revenues are not as great as expected, and that, in exchange, the contractors are free to maximise their revenue from the facilities they have provided.

The private sector had always been prevented from funding public projects by the Treasury's Ryrie rules which stated that any private/public joint venture should not result in investors having a degree of risk that was less than they would have in a purely private venture; and that they should yield returns commensurate with those arising from the use of risk capital from the financial markets. The rules were intended to prevent the creation of any publicly owned assets other than those funded by the Treasury and so prevent a loss of control over the PSBR (Terry 1996). The main PFI projects have been in the fields of transport, prisons, education and health services with one of the biggest projects being the rail link between the Channel Tunnel and London. In the health service, projects have ranged from the food court in Addenbrooke's Hospital, Cambridge, in which the staff and visitor canteen was replaced by a new food court offering snacks and meals from a range of well-known franchised brands, to the proposal to build new hospitals in Coventry and sixteen other towns. In these cases the contractor will fund, build and own the hospital and lease it to the hospital trust. The contractor will also provide a number of facilities or management services, after the new hospital has been built, for which it will charge in addition to charging the NHS trust for the use of the hospital. An interesting example of PFI in schools can be seen in the Garibaldi Comprehensive school in Nottinghamshire. The head teacher in the 1990s was transforming the school from an under-performing to a successful one. This involved an arrangement with private companies who funded improvements to the language centre, the science laboratories and home economics room in return for the opportunity to earn money from the facilities as a conference centre and as a showroom for demonstrating their products to customers (Brown 1995: 98–9; McCarthy 1995: 37).

Despite these local examples, however, the general assessment is that the PFI has not been successful in attracting private capital. In 1995 the value of projects identified was £21 billion but only small fraction of this amount had been taken on by the private sector. The proportion increased in 1996 but this was largely as a result of the contract for the Channel Tunnel rail link; and it was considered by the media that the private sector only took the project on because they were given much free real estate around St Pancras station as part of the deal. The problem was that the private sector was only interested in projects with low risks and high return and most of the PFI projects did not fall into this category. The risk of PFI proposals was increased by the inflexibility of many public sector buildings; it would be difficult to find an alternative and profitable use for a prison if it turned out to be less profitable than had been anticipated. As a result of the risk most PFI projects have been small, around £1m or £2m which would not cause the contractors big problems if they failed in some way. In the field of hospital building, Trafalgar House and W. S. Atkins pulled out of the competition to build a hospital for Central Sheffield University Hospital Trust (Woolf 1996) and Taylor Woodrow withdrew from the bidding to build a hospital in Dartford, Kent (Barnett 1996c), all citing the cost of bidding as their reason. At the time of writing no contracts for a hospital project have been signed. This was partly because trusts' legal powers to sign PFI contracts was being challenged in court. Private companies were also worried that, if they become involved in PFI projects, a future government might decide to change any subsidies or alter the regulatory framework during the concessionary period.

A broader criticism of BOT schemes is that they can distort public priority setting. Instead of projects being selected according to need, they would be selected according to their financial viability. The problem is clearly stated by Terry:

> Government is at risk of reducing its role in steering policy through the application of public resources, if it does not introduce new criteria for backing other, socially necessary, projects where PFI is inappropriate. Priority in many fields will now attach to schemes where private finance is available rather than schemes that may have a stronger case on grounds of need but can only be funded with public money. The logical implication is that needy areas will become needier; while the prosperous ones (i.e. those which are a good prospect for investors) will become more so.
>
> (Terry 1996: 4)

Boyfield (1992) from the Centre for Policy Studies argued, contrariwise, that the need for the project to pass a market test will make for a better allocation of scarce resources. Betts (1996) had a similar argument to Terry but from the standpoint of public accountability. If, he argued, the situation arose where major developments such as the building of hospitals became dependent on private investors, then effectively the private sector would decide which hospitals should be built through the veto which it could exercise by not choosing to put forward bids. The government in such cases might propose (by publishing a list of desirable projects) but it would be the private sector that disposes. Hulme (1996) extended the argument about distortion of need. He speculated that if a private investor were to build and operate a school, their financial success would depend on their ability to attract pupils to the school. As good managers they would want to change the curriculum and teaching methods to make it attractive to parents in the area. The question he raised was whether the curriculum was a matter for government (through the National Curriculum) or whether it was a matter to be decided by parents expressing their demands in a responsive and open market. BOT schemes therefore bring us to the core of the question concerning the role of need in setting priorities for public services.

Privatisation and regulation

The common criticism of privatisation, especially in the case of public utilities, was that it opened the door to greed. As Price has argued:

> The main difficulty is in the mind of the public. The privatised utilities are perceived to be indulging in corporate exploitation and their directors in corporate greed.
>
> (Price 1996: 170)

The charge was made that senior management in the privatised utilities have made easy and comfortable lives for themselves. The remedies normally prescribed for such a condition are competition and regulation. In the case of some utilities, which would always remain a monopoly, regulation was seen by policy makers as a perpetual activity, whereas in the case of other industries regulation was seen as a temporary phenomenon which would only persist until the market for their services became competitive. The development of competition in the market for utilities has already been discussed in chapter 4. In this section the role of public regulation as a means of preventing managerial ease in the utilities will be reviewed.

There are two main issues concerning regulation. The first is the problem of creating a system of regulation that the industries cannot manipulate to their own advantage; the second is the independence and accountability of the regulators. The regulatory mechanism developed in the UK is the RPI-x system. The regulators have to make periodic reviews of the industries they are responsible for and set a figure for x for a period of (normally) five years. The figure x means that in each year of the settlement the industry has to change its prices by the retail price index (RPI) plus or minus the x figure. So, for example, between 1987 and 1992, the x figure for the British Airways Authority was –1 per cent; for the water companies between 1990 and 1995 it was + 5 per cent and for British Gas (supply) between 1994 and 1997 it was –4 per cent (Vass 1996: 160–1; 1997). In some cases additional factors are included in the price calculation, in the case of airports S (95 per cent of the cost of security) is added into the equation.

The principle of the RPI-x system was to maximise the discipline acting upon the company by uncoupling regulated prices from the company's reported costs. If the level at which x was set was dependent upon a company's costs, then it would be sensible for the company to maximise the costs presented in the accounts to show that it was having a hard time making a decent return on its capital. It could then argue that it could not afford to survive if x were set high (Burns 1995: 183). But a RPI-x system makes it more difficult for a company to do this because its costs are not a direct part of the formula. The regulator can say in effect, 'whatever you may tell me about your costs I believe you can afford to increase your prices at a rate lower than inflation'. Vass (1996: 163) argued that the impact of such an incentive regulatory system should be to encourage companies to make good profits by being more efficient than the level of x requires. The system is claimed to be an incentive one because it makes it worthwhile for the companies to beat their x target. This regime is in contrast to the system of rate of return regulation applied to utilities in the United States. Under this system the rate of profit a company can make is capped and any excess profit has to be repaid to the customers. This system encourages companies to invest in fixed assets beyond a sensible level to make their rate of return look smaller; it discourages efficiency. But under the UK incentive system companies reveal their efficiency to the regulator when they beat their x target and make larger profits and so, in the next review period, the regulator will accept a lower cost base for the company and require that prices to the consumer be cut. Vass argued, however, that the public have come to see this 'jam tomorrow' argument as the purest sophistry.

In practice the regulator has to pay some regard to the company's costs when determining the level of x; and he or she also has to consider what constitutes a reasonable and fair rate of return on the industry's investment. As Price (1994: 150) argued, the system of regulation in the UK is one which is interested in an industry's rate of return and costs at the time of the quinquennial reviews and with price capping, through the RPI-x mechanism, in the period between reviews. On occasion of course regulators became interested in costs and rates of return during the inter-review period. Such was the case in 1994 when the Trafalgar House bid for Northern Electricity made it plain that the company was doing better than the regulator thought and the REC settlement was subsequently reviewed mid-term.

As regulators do take cost into consideration when setting x it is important that they have the fullest cost information from the companies. Most regulators put in place detailed procedures to ensure that they had all the information they needed and that it was checked and verified. It was in the companies' interest of course to maximise the costs in their accounts. An example can be taken from the behaviour of British Gas in 1986 when a joint cost allocation exercise was undertaken with the regulator (Price 1994: 151). British Gas's markets could be divided into three. These were the regulated domestic market for consumers using less than 2,500 therms per annum, the firm market for large industrial users and the interruptible market for very large users. It was advantageous to British Gas to allocate much of its costs onto the regulated market to show that its rate of return was low and so ensure a lax value for x. But it also wanted to load costs onto the firm market because there were suspicions abroad that excessive profits were being made. If costs were being charged against the domestic and the firm markets then fewer could be allocated to the interruptible market, and British Gas argued that the onshore costs of supplying the interruptible market were negative, i.e. they claimed that they made savings by supplying the interruptible market. The justification was that, as interruptible customers could have their supply halted when there was pressure on the network (see p. 166), this market gave British Gas flexibility in balancing the pipeline system at times of peak demand and so made it possible to enter into contracts in the firm market which otherwise it would be too risky to take on. Price rather curtly commented that while she could believe that the cost of supplying the interruptible market was low, she found it hard to accept that it was negative.

Another illustration of the tendency to maximise the reporting of costs in the accounts occurred in the case of British Gas Transco's calculation of the value of its capital assets (Vass 1996: 159). Transco wished to value its assets at current replacement cost, which would be higher than a valuation, closer to the costs that the shareholders paid for the assets, which the regulator wished to use. The advantage of a higher capital valuation was that the company's rate of return would appear lower and its costs higher and the figures could be used to justify a lower value for x. At various stages during the negotiations, between the regulator Claire Spottiswoode and British Gas, the regulator argued that British Gas had valued its assets at £17b when a figure of between £9b and £11b would have been more appropriate, that its forecasts of capital expenditure were too high and that its depreciation mechanisms were excessive (Barnett 1996a; Beavis and Barrie 1996b). British Gas countered by saying that if it had to cut its prices at the rate demanded by the regulator it would have to make up to half its workforce redundant. The two sides could not agree. The issue went to the Mergers and Monopolies Commission who found, in 1997, in favour of the regulator.

Regulation, on the evidence presented, can be seen as a cat and mouse game in which the companies being regulated seek to minimise the information they have to give the regulator and present what they are obliged to give in a way that minimises the chance of a tough price cap. This is not necessarily an ignoble perspective; simply a recognition that most people in organisations seek to arrange their job so that it minimises the pressures on them and in so doing they are probably also working towards the best interests of the organisation and its shareholders. The regulators, on the other hand, have to keep pressurising the companies with threats of referral to the MMC to prevent them from having too easy a life.

In the mutually dependent relationship between the regulator and the regulated, accusations that decisions were made according to the needs of the parties rather than to the benefit of the common good were not only levelled at the utilities. The regulators also came in for criticism. Vass reported that:

> The poor public perception of the privatised utilities has often been equally visited on the regulators.
>
> (Vass 1996: 156)

In particular he pointed out the criticisms made of the regulator of the National Lottery who had accepted hospitality and travel from one of the companies backing Camelot, the lottery franchisee. This incident increased worries that regulators would be captured by the companies they regulated. Price argued:

> Privatising the industries has removed much of this trust [which had been granted to the nationalised industries], exposed the activities of the industries to a wider public gaze, and some of the lack of confidence applies to the regulatory system itself.
>
> (Price 1996: 172)

But she also pointed out that the business of regulation had probably been lucky in having regulators of good calibre. There was worry amongst the pundits and commentators about the accountability of regulators and their role in relationship to the well being of the consumers. Under the statutes that created them, regulators have a joint responsibility for consumer protection and for ensuring that the industries they supervise can finance themselves. The regulators' task therefore is to balance the competing requirements of consumers and shareholders. Some have argued (Vass 1996: 165) that consumers should have a direct say in the workings of the utilities. The combination of a lack of public confidence, and difficulties with gaining information to base regulatory decisions on, makes regulators concerned with protecting their own backs.

Barnett (1996b) argued that the regulators, Littlechild at OFFER, Spottiswoode at OFGAS, Cruickshank at OFTEL and Byatt at OFWAT have become powerful public personalities who had to be concerned about their own careers and the need to keep their jobs, if Labour won the (1997) election, by acting as the consumers' champion. There was a suspicion amongst industry analysts that the regulators were vying amongst themselves to be the toughest on their industries. Barnett quoted one analyst as saying:

> He [Littlechild] appears to have picked a number to match Spottiswoode [when she threatened to cut Transco's prices by 20–28 per cent] and then worked backwards to justify it. This is now all about politics and who wants to keep their jobs if Labour wins the next election.
>
> (Barnett 1996b)

Terry (1994) identified the phenomenon of *regulatory momentum* which leads to regulation becoming a fixture rather than a temporary precursor to full competition. Also, as Terry notes:

> Regulators think hard about the political ramifications (even though they are above politics) before they fix the magic figure of x and no regulator presumably wants to work himself out of a job in a hurry.
>
> (Terry 1994)

There is a general agreement that the regulators have been of a high ability but that does not prevent them from thinking politically about their own offices and roles.

The point of the regulation of privatised industries is to prevent senior managers and shareholders from benefiting, either by higher pay perks and dividends or an easy life without competition, from their monopoly position. This leads to public rows about whether those who own and run the privatised utilities are putting their individual interests before those of the society at large. The biggest rows have concerned the pay of the utilities' senior managers. Inevitably public rows become matters of political concern and this makes the regulators public figures of immense importance. They do, after all, have influence over the prices of fundamental commodities and over the share prices of huge corporations. The regulators therefore have to maintain their political and public position. They have to defend themselves against politicians, whom they have the power to put in difficult positions, against consumer groups who doubt where their loyalties lie and against the utilities who see them as ravening beasts. In these circumstances they have to take their jobs, and the continuance of their offices, into account. The process of regulation can provide occasions for working out conflicts between opposing sets of individual interests.

The mechanisms and the heuristics

This chapter has been about the mechanisms used to put public services onto a market footing. The problem with bureaucratically planned and delivered services is, in the eyes of right-wing commentators, that public officials will always make decisions to suit their career development and not to maximise the benefits to the organisation. The market, on the other hand, in its classical form, is seen as a device for converting personal advantage into the common good. As Adam Smith famously put it:

> every individual necessarily labours to render the annual income of the society as great as he can ... He intends only his own gain, and he is in this, as in many other cases, led by an invisible hand to promote an end which was no part of his intention.
>
> (Smith 1993: book IV, chapter 2)

The purpose of this chapter has been to investigate how well the various devices used to marketise public services have performed this sleight of hand. The analysis has suggested a number of points of criticism. Not all would have been accepted by Smith, since his concern was only with maximising the aggregate amount of the nation's wealth and not with the equity of its distribution. Poverty was accepted as a natural and useful aspect of society in the eighteenth century. There are six mechanisms discussed in this chapter and the evaluation of them suggests that each can be criticised from the standpoint of one of the six heuristics of resource allocation presented in chapter 2 . These conclusions will now be summarised.

Creating financially and legally accountable bodies

In the discussion of this aspect of creating markets the criticisms made largely came from an ecological perspective. The ecology heuristic is the one which seeks to take into account the expectations of all the parties interested in a decision. The creation of a financially accountable body detracts from the application of this heuristic because it limits the number of factors the decision makers must consider. Organisations which face the threat of insolvency must privilege commercial interests over other factors. Typically, many public sector organisations have allowed other considerations to take precedence over commercial ones. These factors might include, in the case of a university for example, raising the academic status of the institution, maintaining best professional practice and codes of behaviour and designing courses to meet the expectations of the academic staff rather than of the paying customer. If a business school has won a contract to provide management development programmes to a major public company and there is a dispute between some academic staff and the public company's management development managers about which particular line should be taken in designing a course then, in a commercially accountable higher education corporation (which is how the new universities are legally constituted), the client's view may well carry the day.

Flynn (1993: 160–1) has analysed the tensions which can be created by such changes. He suggested that organisations can be divided into those with a profit orientation and those with public service values. Similarly, the staff of organ-isations can be categorised as either responding to a service ethic incentive or a monetary reward incentive. In a housing department where there is an obligation to meet financial targets in relation to rent arrears, for example, but where the staff see housing as a social service, there is likely to be a tension between staff and management.

An illustration of how creating responsive bodies can restrict the range of factors taken into account can be seen in those sections of the 1988 Local Government Act concerned with competitive tendering. These sections prevent local authorities from taking non-commercial issues into account when placing contracts with organisations for the delivery of public services (Bradley *et al.* 1993: 740). The consequence of this is that, all other things being equal, only those bidders who take a purely commercial view of the contract will successful. This stance contrasts with the ecological view which would require decision makers to take into account the views and preferences of a wide range of interest groups.

Creating purchaser–provider divisions

The criticisms commonly made of this mechanism are based upon the utility heuristic which is concerned with the maximisation of the outcome from any decision or system. The core of the criticism is that the transaction costs of making a purchaser–provider split work can be greater than the allocative bene-fits that are derived from it. At a political and managerial level these transaction costs are often seen as the direct costs of the staff and other resources needed to make the market work. The Labour Party's criticism of the internal market in the health service was that the cost of all the accountants and computers needed to raise and pay the internal bills was more than the system's compet-itive benefits. The Audit Commission (1996), for example, raised the question of whether the gap between the £232m cost of running the fundholding scheme and the £206m savings that fundholders made on their budgets in the period from the start of fundholding until the end of 1994/5 was offset by discernible improvements in the quality of service received by patients. Economists define transaction costs in a more extensive way and raise the question of whether the benefits of a market structure outweigh the costs caused by the imperfec-tions of the market's structure.

Quasi-markets

The equity of quasi-markets may be challenged from the perspective of the fairness heuristic. Quasi-markets have the potentiality for cream skimming and the creation of two tiers of public service. The fairness heuristic in contrast can be used to argue that people's chances of gaining access to public services should be equal; and that those services, once accessed, should be standardised.

Quasi-markets are based on diversity and choice and therefore can always be criticised as being unfair.

Vouchers

The deservingness heuristic is often used as a position from which to criticise voucher schemes. The argument is developed by defining two classes of person: the deserving who have been thrifty and built up savings with which they can buy services for themselves, and the feckless and undeserving who have acted irresponsibly and so have no resources with which to meet their own needs. A voucher scheme rewards the deserving because it makes a contribution to the purchase of a service that they would have been willing to fund themselves. But it penalises the undeserving because they only have the value of the voucher with which to buy the services they need and these are often of insufficient value to cover the cost. This argument can be played in two ways of course. Some will see it as a justification and others as a condemnation of voucher systems.

Putting funding on a market basis

This market-making mechanism contrasts with the heuristic of individual need. The central precept of those who argue from this perspective is that need should be the trigger to funding. Need is seen as a sufficient justification for the funding of a service. But when funding is placed on a market basis, need is no longer enough. Service providers also have to show that the need they wish to meet is somehow more deserving or worthwhile than the needs other providers wish to meet. In the system for funding research in universities for example, many of the bids made for funding will be judged to be needful but only a small fraction of them will be funded. In the case of BOT and PFI projects the proposers have to identify not only a need for the project but also its viability as an investment before they decide to bid for it.

Privatisation and regulation

The criticisms of this marketisation mechanism have concentrated on those privatised organisations which are near monopolies. The criticisms have been drawn from the individual gain heuristic. The argument made is that senior managers of privatised companies place their advantage, and that of their shareholders at the top of their priority list. The highest profile examples of this have been the controversy over top pay in the privatised utilities and the priority given to share buy backs and extraordinary dividends which favoured the shareholders over the customers. But, as has been seen in the earlier discussion, individual gain can be seen operating in the way that managers present costs to make the regulators' demands on them softer. Tullock (1996) argues that it is not only in public organisations that managers put their own interest first, the same phenomena can also be seen in large private organisations. He termed this behaviour internal rent seeking. His argument suggested that it is better for a manager to gather internal information about their organisation, which can be used to further the manager's career, than to obtain external information which can be used to make the organisation more efficient. He did point out, however, that eventually the shareholders may rein in managers who have benefited themselves beyond the degree that is conventionally accepted.

The creation of markets does not, as supporters of Adam Smith might anticipate, drive out of consideration the heuristics of resource allocation identified in this book. The practical imperfections of market mechanisms create gaps through which they can be insinuated back into the argument. The imperfections may be defined in a market's own terms, (for example, a market mechanism may not lead to the common good because its transaction costs are too high), or in deontological terms as when it is argued that the market is based on behaviours (the application of deservingness or personal gain) which are unacceptable as a matter of principle, or in equity terms as when it is argued that a market shows no concern for justice in the way that services and resources are distributed amongst members of society.

6

THE DIALECTIC OF RESOURCE
ALLOCATION

In previous chapters I have described in detail the two main approaches to resource allocation, markets and bureaux, each of which has its own complex mixture of mechanisms and criteria. My purpose in this chapter is to create a systematic and coherent theoretical framework which may be used to elucidate the changes that have happened in the public sector as markets have increasingly taken the place of bureaux. The method chosen to carry out this task is the Hegelian dialectic, which is now acceptable as a mode of organisational analysis. Pascale (1990: 142–3), for example, used it in his analysis of the Ford Motor Co. He described its use as 'intellectual yoga'. I will use it to essay an overview of the logical development of thinking about public sector resource allocation and priority setting. The dialectic can be seen as the rhetorical development of the contradictions inherent in public services. In plainer terms this claim means using the structure of dialectical analysis to write a 'history' of the articulation and development of arguments about public services. Argument is clearly a dialectical process of thesis, antithesis and, perhaps, synthesis: the dialectic should provide a useful guide to a review of the development of the idea of public service.

The issues argued about within the dialectic are the heuristics and mechanisms, which have been defined in earlier chapters, that may be used to decide resource and service allocations. As a dialectical approach is being used, these heuristics will be paired in a developing series of oppositions which follow the typical form of a triad. The first term in a dialectical triangle represents blank formality, whilst the second term represents sheer diversity (Mabbott 1967: 34). The formal terms always begin with a concept, expressed in ideal terms – social status, need, the common good, equal opportunity and the safety net – which have to be deductively applied, often with some difficulty, to concrete reality. The informal terms are embedded in social reality. They begin with individuals' multiple attempts at – personal gain, moral principles, choices and entrepreneurial actions – which are inductively, and not always successfully, given ideological shape and respectability. The first dialectical term represents a belief in the power of reason; a belief that things can be planned or, at the least, that the playing fields for markets can be levelled. The second

213

dialectical term, however, represents a belief in the chaotic unpredictability of things and the need to cope with the consequences of this teeming complexity. This aspect of the dialectic represents the negation of the formal and abstract term. The third term of a dialectic is synthesis which represents the negation of the negation and is an attempt to transcend the opposition between the first two terms. This does not mean that the arguments and concerns of the first two terms are abolished; it means they are brought together in a way that overcomes the contradictions that lie between them.

These rhetorical developments are played out within a developing series of institutional relationships, or structures, formed from a series of overlapping roles. Five main roles will be identified that play parts in the institutional relationships.

- *The users*: the people who directly or indirectly use or consume a service.
- *The providers*: the staff who are directly involved in providing a service to the users. This frequently, but not necessarily, involves face-to-face contact.
- *The commissioners/payers*: the people who determine in detail what services shall be provided, who pay directly for, or resource, a service. This role often involves negotiation with a resourcing body to obtain the funds to provide a service.
- *The resourcers*: the institutions that raise the public revenue to fund public services. They are mostly politically accountable to an electorate which includes some, but by no means all, users.
- *The regulators*: the statutory bodies, such as OFWAT and OFLOT that are charged with supervising private organisations who have a near monopoly position and who provide public services or utilities.

There is a range of possible relationships between payers, resourcers, users, regulators and providers of services. To give an example of the possibilities, the traditional (1974 reorganisation) structure of local authorities was one in which the roles of resourcer (in part), payer and provider were rolled up in one body, the local authority. The local authority decided how much revenue to raise through the rates. Two-thirds of their revenue actually came from central government grants, but if they were unhappy with the level of rate support they could increase their rate revenue without incurring any financial penalty. The local authorities were in any case influential in the negotiations which took place as part of the rate support grant process (Redcliffe-Maud and Wood 1974: 110–11). Building on this financial independence local authorities decided what services should be provided and in what quantity. They also employed the staff to deliver these services. The idea of the enabling authority (Local Government Management Board 1989), which was developed in the late 1980s and the early 1990s, separated the three roles. The government became the resourcer, through its control of grants to local authorities and through its capping mechanisms (Flynn 1993: 45–7), and determined the revenue that local authorities could raise and spend. The role of provider was distributed by contracting out service delivery to a range of public and private organisations; the only role that remained with local authorities was that of commissioner/payer.

To give a further illustration of relationships possible, the user of a public service may be a customer who both consumes and pays for a service, paying to use a public leisure centre would be a case in point; on other occasions they may be a client, who is someone who consumes a service but does not (directly) pay for it, a child in the care of the local authority, for example. It is an integral part of the argument, to be developed in this chapter, that these relationships change as the dialectic develops. The sequence of institutional relationships is shown in figure 6.1, its significance will become apparent as the analysis of the dialectic develops.

In summary, the dialectic represents a rhetorical development of the idea of public service through the working out of contradictions between the heuristics and mechanisms of resource allocation. These tensions resonate with the developing institutional relationships between the various roles involved with public services. The main deviation, in the way the dialectic is used here, from its canonical form is that it is seen as being recursive, folding back in on itself, rather than moving towards some final realisation of morality in the world. The dialectic will be used to create a conceptual framework that will summarise and structure the analysis presented in this book. But, to avoid making the process too arid and theoretical, the development of the dialectic will be explained through a series of, mostly recent, media controversies about public services. The overall structure of the dialectic is shown in figure 6.2.

The private client relationship: the dialectic of patron and client

The heuristics of holism and personal gain

The GP's night visits

The dialectic of public service resource allocation begins, before the notion of a public service has developed, when the provision of any service is a private matter between the provider and the client. It is, fortuitously, possible to illustrate the tensions within this private sector stage of the dialectic with examples from the current public sector because some practitioners still try to operate as if their relations with their clients were a purely private concern. Let me start with the case of the conscientious general practitioner reported in *The Times* (Fogg 1993). This doctor took his family health services authority (FHSA) to the County Court because he had not been paid for the number of out-of-hours emergency visits he had made to his patients. He paid more home visits than any other GP in the area. In 1990 he had made 487 home visits,

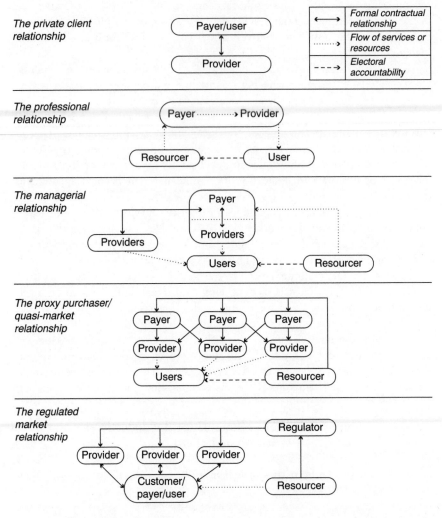

Figure 6.1 The provision of public services relationships between principals and agents

in addition to those he had made on his 6.30 p.m. round. The doctor claimed that the number of home calls reflected his dedication (he ran a single-handed practice and had been on call virtually every evening since 1957) and the high, and personalised, standard of service he wished to provide for his patients. Those of his patients who were reported in *The Times* supported this view. As one of them said:

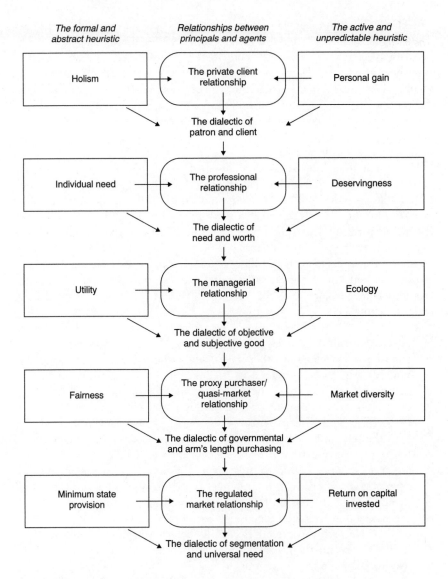

Figure 6.2 The delivery of public services: a phenomenology of the heuristics for allocating public goods

He loves his job. He is always so reassuring and jolly by day or by night ... Years ago my grandmother suffered a stroke on Christmas Eve; the doctor came to visit my father the following day, Christmas Day, to offer comfort.

(Fogg 1993)

The FHSA, however, seemed to view the doctor's activities in a different light. They appeared worried that he could claim £45 for each home visit made between 10 p.m. and 8 a.m. and about the enormous expense he was committing the authority to. They also seemed to imply that the doctor was making *routine* visits out of hours when the service should have been restricted to emergencies only. The nature of the FHSA's managers' thinking was, perhaps, revealed when the doctor said that the FHSA had required him to undergo humiliating medical investigations but that no evidence of psychiatric illness or disturbance had been found.

How might this case be conceptualised? The GP had a clear view of the nature of his responsibility to his patients that I will label as holistic. He viewed his patients as individual human beings and not as bundles of clinical indicators and conditions. His responsibility, as he saw it, seemed to extend beyond the merely medical. This approach conjures up images of what lawyers refer to as private client work. In this Victorian conception the core of the lawyer–client relationship may have been providing legal services but it stretched towards a broader stewardship of the client's general interests and well being. Actually this idea is much older than the Victorian age and it is well illustrated by a quotation from Plato's *The Laws*:

A state's invalids includes not only free men but slaves too, who are almost always treated by other slaves, who either rush about on flying visits or wait to be consulted in their surgeries. This kind of doctor never gives any account of the particular illness of the individual slave, or is prepared to listen to one; he simply prescribes what he thinks best in the light of experience, as if he had precise knowledge, and with the self confidence of a dictator. Then he dashes off on his way to the next slave-patient . . . The visits of the free doctor, by contrast, are mostly concerned with treating the illnesses of free men; *his* approach is to construct an empirical case-history by consulting the invalid and his friends; in this way he himself learns something from the sick and at the same time he gives the patient all the instruction he can. He gives no prescription until he has somehow gained the invalid's consent; then, coaxing him into continued cooperation, he tries to complete the restoration to health.

(Plato 1970: 181–2)

The second of these two types of doctor describes the holistic style of service provision. In a holistic approach the question of resource and service allocation is determined by the necessity of responding to the widest interpretation of the user's needs. Primacy in such a relationship lies with the client, and so, for example, the doctor cannot do anything until it has been discussed, negotiated and agreed with the patient. The relationship between the provider and the receiver of services is essentially personal.

But within the case of the conscientious GP there is a tension between holism and another criterion, that of personal gain. The implication of the FHSA's actions was that the trigger for the provision of services, in this GP's case, was not the holistic needs of the patient but the opportunity of financial gain for the practitioner. I do not wish to make any judgement about this particular case, nor is it necessary to know what the outcome of the legal action was. But I do wish to argue that there is a dialectical tension between holism and personal gain which exists generally within the private client, or patron–client, relationship. Such a relationship, like that between this GP and his patients, is unusual within the context of public services because its holistic focus makes it very expensive. Indeed, it was the expense that caused the FHSA to take action to change that relationship or at least to minimise its cost. But the private client relationship has to be the start of the conceptual analysis of public service.

The contradiction between holism and personal gain needs to be explained. As an ideal type this relationship is one between a patron (the dominant figure) who pays for the service and a client who provides it, and generally serves the patron's interests. But, as in Hegel's Master/Slave dialectic (Findlay 1970: 98), the patron eventually comes to depend upon the services of the client. The service provider therefore acquires a dominance over the patron which is negated by their formal relationship. In order to reinforce this *de facto* superiority over the patron, in the face of formal subordination, the client ensures that he personally gains from the relationship. Although the steward of a Renaissance magnate (by way of simile) was formally a servant, his position was often the source of great wealth. The argument is that a holistic criterion of service has its negation in the achievement of personal gain. As a consequence of this dialectic the client becomes the dominant, not the subordinate, partner.

The working out of this contradiction between patron and client can be seen in the various definitions of the word client. In the classical definition a client is dependent upon a patron. In return for specified services from the client the patron supports and protects her or him. But there is an almost equally ancient definition, of the client as one who pays for a service, as a customer. A customer is the dominant partner in a relationship with a supplier, although a frequently cheated one. As an illustrative quotation, dated 1413, from the *Oxford English Dictionary* has it, 'Ye wold putte your clyentes at the more cost in the fyllinge of youre pourses.'

These competing definitions encapsulate the tension within the private client relationship in which there is instability in the relative status of the client and the patron. The patron is formally the superior but the patron is also dependent upon, and may be exploited by, the client. In different respects therefore the user of the service can be patron (and the provider is in the role of client) or client (when in the role of customer).

The case of the conscientious GP gives us a glimpse of the meanings and values involved in such a relationship. But clearly the private client relationship is more common in private practice than in public service. The contradiction between holism and personal gain can be illustrated by recent developments in private medical practice. In 1993 the Monopolies and Mergers Commission investigated this market and concluded that, as far as the provision of consultant medical services was concerned, a complex monopoly situation existed (Nuki 1993) and that consultants were, in effect, involved in a price fixing cartel. At the time of writing the Commission still had to decide whether the situation was unfair. About 12,000 of the country's 19,000 consultants were reported to work in private practice and the proportion of hospital consultants' incomes that this work represented had increased from 13 per cent in 1975 to 31 per cent in 1990 (Laurance 1993b). This seemed to constitute, in the eyes of the regulator, a suspicion that, in this market, personal gain was an equal partner to the provision of a personalised service.

Dialectics may contain more than one contradiction. And within the dialectic of holism and personal gain there is at least one other. It is implicit in the contrast, provided by Plato, between the service received by the freeman and that provided to the slave. Good holistic service is seen as a matter of personal gain in a zero sum game; if someone receives it, it must be at the cost of someone else's loss. Eventually, therefore, the benefit of a holistic service stems not from the service itself; but from the fact that someone else has been denied it. The value of a service comes from the precedence it gives those who receive it. A similar process has been described by V. S. Naipaul. In his earliest book on India (Naipaul 1967) he commented on the role and function of the sweeper caste. Although their task was to clean buildings, he noted that, in the perception of the higher castes, the formal provision of the service was more important than its effectiveness. The sweepers, he argued, merely moved the dirt and dust around, because the real purpose of the activity was to reinforce their dependent status and the superior status of the patron. Logically, part of the negation of holism is its movement from a focus on service to a focus on status and the consequent unavailability of holistic services to all equally.

Within the personal client relationship the contradiction between the client's inferior status and their ability to exploit the patron is paralleled by the contradiction between the value of the client's work and its symbolic role in defining the dependence of the service provider. The former tends to diminish the status of the patron in relation to the client while the latter tends to elevate the patron relative to the client. These competing tendencies reinforce the conclusion that in this stage in the development of services the emphasis is on the personal relationship between the user of services and the provider.

As in all good dialectics the thesis and antithesis are transcended by a synthesis. In this case the private client relationship is superseded by the professional relationship; and it is this nexus which has been at the root of public service provision in this century. The professional relationship introduces a third, and more modern, definition, of the client as a person helped by a social worker or a social agency. In this usage the personal element, either of patronage or profiteering, is replaced by an attempt at the objective assessment of the client by the professional.

The professional relationship: the dialectic of need and worth

The heuristics of individual need and deservingness

The coronary patient with a habit

The dialectic of need and worth can be illustrated by a *cause célèbre* which exercised the media in 1993 (Mihil 1993). This involved a married man, in his forties with a family, who had been suffering from serious heart disease for a number of years. He needed heart by-pass surgery but his consultant refused to carry out the operation unless, and until, the patient gave up smoking. Smoking was seen by the doctor as contributing towards the disease and it was reckoned to seriously diminish the patient's chances of surviving the operation. Eventually the patient did give up cigarettes; but he died before the operation could be performed. The message in the press coverage, or at least in the tabloids, was that the man's death might have been prevented.

There is a conflict in this story between two heuristics of resource allocation: individual need and deservingness. The individual need heuristic rests upon an objective and expert assessment of a client's needs undertaken by a qualified expert. This assessment includes arriving at a diagnosis of the condition and deciding whether there are any treatments or services which are appropriate to the client (Daniels 1981). The rule of thumb which underpins the heuristic of individual need suggests that any treatment which has some chance of improving the client's lot should be provided. The decision to provide a service is triggered by the establishment of a need, the decision about when the service should be provided is based upon the relative priority of the need. Greater needs are met first, lower weighted needs are met later. If this principle had been applied in the case of the heart patient who smoked, he would have received the operation. Individual need is the heuristic that was implicitly supported by the press in this case, and it has been the basis of much medical and social work practice within the welfare state.

However, the patient's consultant took a different line of argument and refused treatment. I am not attempting to discover the motives of the consultant because it would be impossible and impertinent to do so; but I shall use the incident as a trigger for speculation about possible justifications of the decision not to operate. It might be argued that the patient's smoking made the operation inappropriate and that therefore the patient no longer had a need of it. Another possible reason derives from the utility heuristic. An argument from a utility perspective would point out that smoking reduced the patient's chances of surviving the operation and therefore the operation would not be cost effective, the ends might not justify the expenditure (Rogers 1993).

But at this stage, it is useful to concentrate on another possible justification for the decision, not to operate on the patient, which is based on the heuristic of deservingness. This approach looks at clients as morally self-responsible subjects and not as objective bundles of needs and symptoms. People using this approach would seek to discover whether the client's needs were the result of their own actions or behaviours. If they were not, if the client was simply suffering as a consequence of bad luck, then the client would be deserving of having their need met. If, however, the client had caused, at least in part, their condition, by persistently smoking, for example, then the patient would be undeserving. An undeserving patient may be treated less well and their case lose priority. It cannot be known how these various elements, and others, operated in the case of the consultant's views, but there was a suspicion in the press's coverage that the patient was being punished for having contributed to his own condition, and for exacerbating the offence by perversely refusing (for some time) to give up smoking.

This story illustrates a dialectic between objective need and worth (or deservingness) that develops within the framework of the professional relationship. The difference between the private client relationship and the professional one is that the roles of user and payer/commissioner, which are combined in the private client relationship become separated in the professional relationship, and the role of payer/commissioner becomes associated with that of provider in the person of the professional who assesses needs and provides the service (figure 6.1). The role of the GP prior to the introduction of new contracts and fundholding (Riggs 1996) exemplifies the professional relationship. General medical services were paid for from general taxation but the degree of budgetary and managerial accountability imposed on the GP was low. The service was not cash limited, for example, and the provider could draw financially upon the resourcer (the health authority) with little constraint. The GP consequently could assess patients' clinical needs and either meet those needs, or invite others (such as hospital consultants) to meet them, without having to worry about the financial implications. The patient received the service free at the point of delivery. Whereas in the private client relationship the link between service and payment is close, in the professional relationship it is indirect and distant.

One consequence of the separation of the roles of payer and user is that the user may become very demanding of the provider. They may want more because it is free. In the NHS the patient may become difficult, grasping of services and ungrateful. (Although there is also a contrary tendency for patients to be overly grateful for any service they receive and consequently there can be an unwillingness to complain.) In a situation in which the client is seen as adopting a demanding manner, the professional's intention of remaining emotionally distant from the patient, responding only to their objective need and avoiding the temptation to make moral judgements, can be severely strained. Howe (1985) in his study of social security offices (q.v. p. 83) argues that many staff begin to use the deservingness heuristic as a defence mechanism against difficult clients. Instead of treating such clients objectively they preserve their own self-esteem by delivering less to the undeserving clients and more to the deserving. Similar observations have been made of the ways in which school teachers react to pupils who are labelled difficult (Jasmin 1981; Ashton 1981: 184).

The professional relationship therefore creates a dialectical contradiction between the perceived need to view the client objectively and the personal pressure to respond to their worth. The training received by public sector professionals, particularly those in the caring professions, urges them not to take moral and subjective factors into account, but the pressure of face-to-face service delivery makes it tempting for them to do so. This polarity is transcended by transferring the focus of the service away from the individual to the wider ends of public service organisations, defined as either institutional survival or the common good.

The managerial relationship: the dialectic of objective and subjective good

The heuristics of utility and political ecology

The Crown Prosecution Service and the decline in prosecutions

The Jeremy Thorpe case

Compulsory competitive tendering

In late 1993 the Crown Prosecution Service (CPS), which had taken over responsibility for criminal prosecutions from the police in 1986, came under sustained criticism from the Bar Council and the London Federation of Police (Rose 1993). The core of the criticism was that, although reported crimes were increasing, the number of prosecutions was decreasing. The number of Crown Court prosecutions had fallen nearly 20 per cent between August 1992 and August 1993. The critics further argued that the CPS was too keen to drop borderline cases to save money and they often reduced the seriousness of a charge so that it would go to the cheaper Magistrates Court rather than to the more expensive Crown Court. Barbara Mills, the head of the CPS explained the same facts in a more sympathetic way. 'We do not,' she said, 'prosecute on a wing and a prayer.' She also argued that the role of the CPS was to weed out weak cases, for which there was no corroboration of police evidence, and so, perhaps, reduce the number of miscarriages of justice. There was an agreement between the protagonists that the CPS was using an utility, cost effectiveness, heuristic; the issue was whether this was right and whether, instead, the service should respond, ecologically, to the pressures from powerful lobbies to increase the rate of prosecutions.

A similar tension existed in another story, this time from 1992. Jeremy Thorpe, the former leader of the Liberal Party accused the North Devon Health

Authority of denying him brain surgery for Parkinson's disease on grounds of cost (Jones 1992). It was acknowledged by all sides that the treatment, involving the implantation of foetal cells, was experimental. Thorpe argued from an individual need perspective that, 'treatment should be available to everyone who needs it ... No one should be denied treatment on the grounds of expense.' The Director of Public Health, however, argued that:

> The success rate for this type of operation is no more than 30 per cent and we do know that people under the age of 50 are more likely to benefit than those who are older ... My own feeling is that we should not be funding any treatments which have a success rate of less than 50 per cent. No one would expect us to fund a journey to Lourdes.
>
> (Jones 1992)

Thorpe finally received the treatment following a referral by his London GP. His Devon GP could not refer outside of the area because, following the creation of the internal market for healthcare, the contracts for care were with local hospitals. On one interpretation this case involved the health authority choosing between a utility heuristic, doing what was cost effective, or an ecological approach, responding to legitimately expressed pressure.

Both the utility and the ecology heuristic are concerned with outcomes. People whose values and beliefs include the utility heuristic believe in objective facts and the validity of statistics. Their belief in instrumental rationality focuses on optimisation; they are concerned with maximising the aggregate amount of good done with a specific volume of resources. In the Benthamite perception of utilitarianism they aim at the greatest good of the greatest number. Such concern for the quantity of good done means that there can be no interest in the interpersonal distribution of benefit. If a few people have problems which can be resolved, but only expensively, whilst many others have problems that can be solved cheaply, then a strictly utilitarian heuristic might, in certain circumstances, lead to the expensive problems being left unresolved (Creese and Gentle 1974). It is this focus that can be identified, amongst a plethora of other value considerations, within the decisions of both the CPS and the health authority.

Ecology, however, is a heuristic approach that is concerned with subjective outcomes. People who think in this way assume that resources and services should be allocated so that the critical demands and expectations of the major stakeholders involved with the delivery of a service are met. Stakeholders may be organised lobbies of staff, politicians, policy communities, users and consumers and voluntary bodies. From within the ecological approach the extent to which the wishes of a particular constituency are met will depend upon the provider's assessment of the groups' abilities to impact upon the survival and activity of the providing institution. The outcome aspired to within the framework of the ecology heuristic is a political environment in which powerful groups' perceptions about the providing institution are supportive of the institution's long-term survival. Success, from an ecological viewpoint, is a matter of perception and not a matter of fact. In distinction to the utility heuristic, ecology:

> implies a surrender of an illusory hope of providing ultimate justifica-
> tions for a particular social order and for policy.
>
> (Hodge 1990: 44)

There is a postmodern aspect of ecological thinking which does not require humane and civic-minded behaviour to be based on absolute systems of value and on rational calculation of the common good. The utility heuristic is based on a metanarrative that has its roots in the Enlightenment project's intention to displace superstition and nepotism with objectivity and reason; the ecological heuristic makes no such grand claim.

The dialectical tension inherent within the managerial relationship is between competing pulls from different conceptions of organisational achievement. The two stories told at the start of this section illustrate the strain for public service providers caused by these two heuristics. The contradiction exists within the framework of a managerial relationship for the institutional provision of public services. This relationship differs from the professional one in that the easy and undemanding relationship between payer and provider of services is replaced by a tougher one. As has already been discussed, in the professional relationship, the payer and provider are often the same person. Even in those circumstances where the professional provider is hierarchically subordinate to a manager who formally holds the budget for a service, the managers come from a similar professional background and are broadly supportive of the providers' values and principles.

In the managerial relationship, however, the managerial function becomes stronger, as in the case of the introduction of general management into the NHS (McNulty 1990). Both institutionally and ideologically the gap between management (the payers and commissioners) and service providers becomes sharper. The roles of payer and provider, that were close in the professional relationship, become distanced in the managerial relationship. Ideologically managers are expected to take on new values, and indeed a new language, based on utility (Clarke 1995), which separates them from the individual need-based principles of the professional service deliverers. Structurally the creation of internal Chinese walls, between customer and provider units within single public authorities, allows compulsory competitive tendering (CCT) and service level agreements (SLAs) to establish a contractual relationship between payer and provider within a single institution. It is for this reason that within the managerial relationship element in figure 6.1 there is a dotted line separating payer and provider even though they are shown in the same box to signify that they belong to a single organisation. SLAs are formal agreements between sub-units of an organisation which specify what services the sub-unit will provide in return for an agreed budget. CCT in contrast allows outside organisations to bid for work and so it is possible within the managerial relationship for services to be provided by public or private companies which are separate from the commissioning organisations (Carnagham and Bracewell-Milnes 1993). There has been some relaxation in the interpretation of the 1970 Goods and Services Act which will allow local authorities to contract for work for other local authorities (Gosling 1996).

The entrance of private sector providers into the public service arena introduces new concepts (such as those of the enabling authority and of the commissioning authority) into the public service dialectic. Both of these ideas break the institutional link, which is unquestioningly accepted within the professional relationship, between identifying the services needed and the delivery of them. An enabling and a commissioning authority determines needs and priorities, identifies who is to receive what services and then pays another institution (such as a direct works unit or a private company) to provide the service. It also is responsible for monitoring the quality of the services provided and checking whether the provider is keeping to the contract.

Contracts, which in the professional relationship are uncommon, are funda-mental in the managerial relationship. More people spend more time negotiating and drafting contracts. In the case of service level agreements within local authorities the intensity of negotiation may not be very high; and they often concentrate on cost and resource levels to the relative exclusion of issues of service quantity and quality. The negotiation in these cases is little more than the traditional hierarchical budget planning process given a new name. Where negotiations are conducted between legally separate public sector bodies (as in the NHS internal market), or between commissioning bodies and private sector companies, the negotiations can be very serious. In negotiations between health authorities and provider units and trusts, for example, some participants have started to play the game of heavyweight negotiation by, for example, with-holding their signatures from contracts and by extending discussions into the financial year to which the contract applies, in order to put more pressure on the other side. But the focus of the negotiations can still be very narrow and the Audit Commission (1996) has suggested that many GP fundholders in the internal market are continuing to purchase the same services from the same providers as they used before the new arrangements.

After the introduction of CCT the Conservative government was keen to open up the provision of public services to private sector companies. In the initial rounds of CCT, let us take the 1983 round in the NHS as an example, the health authorities were not enthusiastic in putting their services out to competitive tender. They argued, for example, that they should be allowed to use outside tenders mainly as a means of setting a cost baseline for in-house services (Mailly 1986). A DHSS circular required the health authorities to submit a timetable for competitive tendering for laundry, catering and cleaning services. When the exercise was completed most of the contracts had been awarded to in-house bidders; this caused cries of unfair competition from private companies and the government began to work towards increasing the number of contracts awarded to the private sector (Mailly 1986: 16). A struggle ensued between those public sector organisations determined that the in-house bidder should win the contracts and the government who wished the contracts to go to the private sector. Consultancy organisations appeared who offered to tell public sector organisations how to write contract specifications in such a way that the in-house bidders would stand a greater chance of winning the tender (CIPFA and Chief Executives' Forum 1996: 158). In 1995 this process was still underway and the Department of the Environment (1995) published a consultation draft of *Guidance on the Conduct of Compulsory Competitive Tendering by Local Authorities* which was intended to 'stimulate greater efficiency and secure better value for money by requiring fair competition between local authorities' own in-house teams and private contractors'. The emphasis on fair competition between in-house teams and private contractors can be seen as an aspect of the attempt to maximise the distance between the roles of service commissioning and of service provision. The tenor of the guidelines reflected an anxiety to increase the amount of public services provided by private companies. Local authorities, for example, were prevented from referring to the implications of TUPE (cf. p. 242) in a way that might discourage potential private sector bidders. CCT was clearly seen by government as a way of minimising public sector involvement in the delivery of services and of maximising the private sector's contribution.

The history of competitive tendering indicates an aspect of the contradiction between subjective and objective conceptions of worth. If the intention of the government had been solely to improve the cost efficiency of services then they would have had no particular concerns about the balance between in-house and private contractors amongst the successful tenderers. Their concern to limit the participation of in-house teams suggests that they were responding to an ecological pressure from their supporters and right-wing think tanks to express their ideological preference, and support, for private companies and their dislike of the public sector. The history of CCT encapsulates the dialectical tension between a utility-based approach (concerned with getting the best value for money) and an ecological approach which led government to see CCT as a device for making the public sector weaker and the private sector stronger. The formal aim of CCT was utilitarian, to improve efficiency. The intention, from a government perspective, was not to change the services provided or to change the people who received them; rather, it was to increase the amount of services that could be achieved from a given level of resources. But informally the government, local authorities and NHS trusts were ecologically concerned to ensure that their preferred sector, private or public, did well in their CCT bids.

In services where there can be argument about the definition of need, such as social services, one of the consequences of the separation of the roles of payer/commissioner and provider is that the professional service deliverer loses some of their power to define the services a particular client needs. In the institutional relationships previously described, the role of assessing the services a user needed generally rested with the grass roots providers of the service. They acted as gatekeepers, deciding who would be admitted to the category of the needy, as well as deciding the nature and the level of the provision. Hospital consultants decided what their patients needed and social workers decided the provision for their clients. The strategic level of need assessment was often, despite desperate attempts at broad canvas planning, the consequence of the aggregation of all these local service level decisions. The establishment of a commissioning role is often a clear attempt to remove the gatekeeping role (if not the whole of the assessment process) from the service provider. The intention of managers, in their role as commissioner/payer is not to take over the task of detailed assessment but to set a tighter framework of strategy and policy within which service providers should determine needs. It represents therefore a standardisation of the providers' needs assessment role rather than a removal of the responsibility.

The consequence of contracting out service delivery, internally or externally, and of standardising the role of needs assessment, was that the strategic management of services became more important than the professional delivery of it. This implied a concern, not for professional standards of service delivery, but with a strategic interest in efficiency, economy and effectiveness; the three Es as they are referred to in the public sector (Butt and Palmer 1985). Effectiveness is the one which causes difficulty in this phase of the dialectic. The dilemma is whether this should be assessed objectively or subjectively. The dialectical contradiction is between viewing effectiveness as an objective or as a subjective notion. The utility heuristic is contradicted by the ecology criterion because utility proceeds on the basis of maximising achievement against an objective; but values and objectives cannot be finessed out of technical calculation, only out of ecological negotiation. The synthesis of this opposition comes through the use of market mechanisms. Markets may be interpreted variously, as a device for objective optimisation and for reconciling differing subjective preferences, and so they appear to offer a synthesis of the contradictions of the managerial phase of the phenomenology of public services.

The quasi-market relationship: the dialectic of governmental purchasing and proxy purchasing

The heuristics of market diversity and fairness

Buying a Duccio

GP fundholding and total commissioning

The principal difference between the managerial relationship and the quasi-market cum proxy purchaser relationship is that the latter attempts to change the allocation of public services and is not simply intended to improve their efficiency. The GP fundholding scheme, for example, was intended by the government to change the pattern of medical services by moving the decision making from hospital consultants to GPs. It was believed that family doctors would use different priorities than those used by hospital consultants. The arguments that occur within the quasi-market relationship concern the mechanism for determining access to proxy purchasers such as GPs and hospital consultants, and hence, to the services provided by the market. One important aspect of this debate is the extent to which users of services should be able to choose between suppliers and proxy purchasers (who negotiate services on behalf of their clients as in the case of fundholding). Choice implies that there should be a range of possible suppliers available to proxy purchasers and a range of proxy purchasers available to users. The justice of this characteristic of quasi-markets is a matter of dispute. The second major argument concerns the nature of the suppliers and proxy purchasers. The issue in this debate is, whose needs and interests are the proxy purchasers and suppliers concerned with?

The proponents of the quasi-market argue that there should be many purchasers/commissioners and that they should be seen as 'single issue' purchasers. That is to say, they should not be concerned with the overall issues of allocation and delivery of services but only with the services that are needed by, and provided to, their particular constituency. In other words, to give some illustrations, the members of a school governing body should only be concerned with the needs and services of their particular school and not with the entire local or national educational service; and fundholding GPs should be concerned with their patients only and not with those of other practices in the area. The multiplicity of commissioners is designed to produce diversity in the supply of public services to the marketplace so that, to continue with my two examples, different schools and different general practices will be offering different types of services. In policy terms this variety is seen by the supporters of quasi-markets as enabling services to be responsive to local needs and as giving some choice to service users.

The contradiction within this relationship is that the quasi-market can create two (or more levels of service) which fits ill with the public service notion of equal access to equal services. Some schools and some practices will be better than others and therefore some users will receive better services than others. The opponents of quasi-markets argue that they are unfair and do not provide equal access. They hold to the fairness heuristic which places a priority on equality of access to services and is prepared to accept a uniform standardisation of services in order to achieve this end. The education provided by a school, they would argue, should be the same irrespective of whether it is located in Shetland or Cornwall and whether its catchment area is middle class or working class. Those who prefer markets might argue that over time the hidden hand will ensure that all providers will rise to the standard of the best but their critics suggest that supply constraints in the market will prevent the system settling down at a higher equilibrium point. In the school system, for example, the practical and political difficulties of closing down the less popular schools has led to the provision of too many school places in the system as a whole (Audit Commission 1997). This in turn makes it difficult to justify additional resources for expanding the popular schools. The government responded to this situation by repealing the minimum space requirements for schools. This allows an increased movement of pupils to the popular schools but will make it difficult for the expanding schools to maintain the quality of their provision.

Even if a levelling up of services within a quasi-market were possible this would still not meet the requirements of those who argue for fairness. If a quasi-market reaches equilibrium, it means that the appropriate range of services is being provided to meet the range of diverse demands being expressed by the users and commissioners. It would not mean that all providers were delivering equal and standardised services because some people's demands and expectations are higher than others. In any case the benefits of the quasi-market actually depend upon the market not reaching a point where all providers are delivering equal services. Indeed without diversity amongst service providers there are no benefits in having an internal market. If all providers offered the same services and the same level of access, there would be no rational basis for a user to prefer one provider to another; and the choice of which GP you went to or which museum you visited would be arbitrary. From the perspective of an argument based on the heuristic of fairness this would be an acceptable situation; indeed, its supporters would insist that all potential users should have equal access to services irrespective of where they live and through which agency (GP, local authority, museum service, and so on) they obtain services. This, in summary, is the internal contradiction within the quasi-market relationship; in using such markets to improve services to all users the standardisation of services loses priority and some users have services which are not as good as those provided to other users.

The next aspect of the quasi-market relationship that needs to be discussed is the institutional framework within which the dialectic is worked out. The nature of the commissioning and purchasing institutions is central to this discussion. The main development, already flagged up, is that purchasing and commissioning institutions cease to be 'governmental' and become 'single issue'. The defining characteristic of a 'single issue' purchaser is that they are drawn from a particular interest or stakeholder group. In quasi-markets the power to commission services is taken from bodies with a nominal responsibility for the whole community and given to bodies which represent particular interests. Governmental bodies retain the right to set the general rules and strategic framework within which the proxy purchasers work, but they place themselves at arm's length from the operational and priority setting work of the proxy purchasers. The justification for empowering particular groups is that they stand as proxies for particular groups of people or for particular policy objectives, and because they are unencumbered by overarching responsibilities, they can more effectively fight for the needs of their particular interest within internal markets. To give an example, the Training and Enterprise Councils (TECs) were set up, with a majority of business people on their boards, to give a new, and local, emphasis to the allocation of training services and to ensure that training services meet the requirements of the local business community.

In contrast to proxy purchasers, people within the characteristic institutions of the managerial relationship believe themselves to have an overall governmental responsibility, that is to say, they have a regard for the common good within their area of competence. Derek Senior expressed this point in the 1970s when he argued, in relation to local government, that:

> Local government has a general responsibility for the well-being of the communities it represents: its concern is not confined to the discharge of the duties imposed upon it by Parliament. It must seek to promote community well-being in all its aspects.
>
> (quoted in Eddison 1973: 3)

The role of this type of institution differs from that of proxy purchasers who are concerned with a specified range of services or policy objectives and not with general well being, and who are charged with seeing things from a sectional point of view.

The difficulty with holding a belief in an overarching concern for the well being of a community is how, in practical terms, the content of well being is to be determined. Senior managers in governmental institutions within the managerial relationship tend to apply the ecology heuristic in an attempt to balance out the many competing demands upon them. In the quasi-market relationship people recognise the difficulties of planning priorities in a pluralist world in which competing values are incommensurable. They begin to believe that there can be no rational mechanism for judging between conflicting claims based on beliefs and values. In the quasi-market therefore, given the difficulty of grounding such choices, it is sensible to go for diversity, flexibility and choice. It is part of this stage of the dialectic that those who choose the groups who will be proxy purchasers increasingly do so on the basis of personal or group advantage and find it difficult to articulate a rational basis for their choice. During the Conservative administration the extension of quasi-markets was a mechanism for stuffing public bodies with people thought to be sympathetic to Tory philosophy.

One of the contradictions inherent within the quasi-market stems from the dissatisfaction the mechanism causes to those who lose out by not becoming proxy purchasers. The changes in the governance of schools brought about by the 1989 Education Act provide an illustration. The combination of budgetary and managerial accountability borne by governors within the local management

231

of schools (LMS) scheme, and the change in the composition of governing bodies in favour of parent governors, has changed the role of parents (or at least of organised parents) from that of a pressure group to a managerial role. The parents on the schools' governing bodies have in effect become proxy purchasers negotiating educational services from the head of their schools on behalf of all the parents and their children. The teaching staff of schools, who in many ways were the *de facto* controllers of what happened in schools under the old system, have become largely dispossessed of power by the rise of parents.

Providers who have lost their role in assessing needs, however, are not necessarily doomed to powerlessness. They may, however, have to learn to express their views in different ways, and the ability of service providers to market their services to the proxy purchasers becomes a major source of influence on the range and type of services available in the market. This was seen as a key issue by many providers in quasi-markets and the Welsh NHS, for example, invested in a large-scale training programme to teach community nurse managers and their field staff to market their services to fundholding GPs and commissioning health authorities (Jackson 1993).

The dominant heuristic in the quasi-market relationship belongs to the diverse term of the dialectic. Its contradiction comes from the formal term of the dialectic. The negation of the empowerment of some groups in the quasi-market is the disempowerment of others. More particularly, this means that the people who are represented by those who have failed to become purchasers will lose out. The formal aspect of the dialectic is represented by a preference for the fairness heuristic. People who argue from this perspective would overcome the problems of defining the common good in a world of incommensurable claims, not by privileging some, but by treating everyone the same. The impossibility of making a rational choice is avoided, from the perspective of fairness, by making no choice at all. Fairness is the formal term of the dialectic because it pays no heed to individual preferences or particularities (which are the whole point of quasi-markets) but gives to everyone the formal right to equal access and treatment. Arbitrariness, the use of such devices as queues which are indifferent to clients' particularities, provides the mechanism to do this. The heuristic of fairness only requires that all people have an equal chance of receiving a service. The concern of fairness is that, however uncomfortable the situation, it is the same for everybody. The heuristic of fairness therefore is a form of arbitrariness, all are equal under a dice-throwing regime.

In summary, the essence of the quasi-market relationship is that a particular group of stakeholders in a service are formally empowered to define the needs for that service and to contract with providers in a market for service delivery, on behalf of particular groups of users. This formal objective is negated by the impossibility of making a rational case for privileging some proxy purchasers and users over others which leads to a preference for the arbitrary nature of the fairness heuristic.

The next step in the discussion is to illustrate how the dialectic between fairness and market diversity might develop within the quasi-market relationship. Interesting articles were published in *The Listener* in 1985 by Roy Strong (1985), who was then Director of the Victoria and Albert Museum, and Timothy Clifford (1985), then Director of the National Galleries of Scotland. Although this example does not, strictly speaking, relate to a quasi-market relationship it does involve proxy purchasers and it does illustrate some of the contradictions. The starting point of the polemical exchange was Timothy Clifford's decision, the previous year when he had been head of Manchester's art galleries, to buy a crucifixion, attributed to Duccio, for £1.8m. Strong was critical of this purchase. He argued that the curators of museums had become obsessed with a doctrine of comprehensiveness which led them to acquire objects compulsively to fill gaps in their collection. So if a museum had a collection of British teaspoons the curators would seek to acquire an example of every kind that was ever produced, even if examples of the missing forms were plentifully available in other museums. According to Strong this caused museums to accumulate objects that they would never have enough space to display. He pointed out that an unwritten ambition of the National Portrait Gallery, of which he was once the director, was to own a likeness of every person listed in the *Dictionary of National Biography*, a gargantuan task given that this meant 30,000 persons up to 1900 alone.

Clifford's response to the criticism was based on the principle of fairness. He pointed out that access to art objects differed tremendously from one part of the country to another. His perception of this problem is illustrated by the analysis shown in table 6.1 of the location of works of art in public collections, of which only a part is given.

His justification for the purchase of the Duccio was based on a governmental concern for the well being of his community and their right to have access to great art: 'Children outside the home counties do not get the same opportunities for regular infusions of fine art.' To remedy this situation he stated that 'in Manchester we are interested in providing a good cross-section of masterpieces from all eras'. He also argued that museum curators, by virtue of their knowledge of their subject, should act as proxy purchasers of art on behalf of those who visit their museums.

Strong countered this governmental concern with the fairness of access to good art by developing a proto proxy purchasing theme.

Table 6.1 The geographical location of works by major artists

Artist	Home Counties	North West
Fra Angelico	3	0
Canaletto	33	3
Duccio	5	0

Source: Clifford 1985.

The obsession of museums and the Arts Council since 1945 has been to ensure the exhibition of work to the public, not to encourage the public actually to want to acquire and live with such things. What we need now is not more art in museums and galleries but more art in public hands, the broadening of collecting into new classes of society ... even with over three million unemployed there are vast sections of society which can now afford to own art.

(Strong 1985: 18)

He argued that the fairness heuristic made curators, as proxy purchasers of art, obsessive collectors and that, if this was allowed to continue, museum cellars would be full of mouldering objects. A clear alternative to this situation would be to empower other groups to be purchasers of art, perhaps even allowing the public to become their own proxy purchasers. We could imagine, in line with Strong's iconoclastic theme, an art voucher scheme in which every household received a sum which could be used towards the purchase of an art or craft object. In the 1980s the Welsh Arts Council came near to this idea by providing a financial credit scheme for people who wanted to buy art from Welsh artists. Such a scheme was close to being a proxy purchasing system in which an arts body, as a vicarious purchaser, nominated a group of artists whose work it is keen to help the public buy. In the 1970s some public libraries purchased original paintings and prints which were loaned out to the public through local libraries. As these libraries were often located in relatively deprived areas, the service could be construed as a case of librarians acting as proxy purchasers for those deprived of the consolations of art. This of course broadens the question and causes us to ask who the proxy purchasers of art should be. Should it be museum curators, local librarians, art council officials or members of the public? It is interesting to speculate what different forms of art would be purchased by these different groups.

The contradiction in this stage of the dialectic exists between the creation of market diversity by quasi-markets, on the one hand, and the inevitability of unfairness, on the other. The decision to empower some groups as proxy purchasers in a quasi-market disempowers other groups. Any decision to make a particular group a proxy purchaser of services, whether it is Arts Councils or fundholding GPs will have its contradiction in a consequentially unfair access to services. Fundholding can again act as an example. The rules of the NHS internal market discourage providers and units from offering better services to patients from fundholding practices by worsening the services to patients of non-fundholding practices. But this does not prevent providers giving better services to fundholders' patients, through such devices as additional outpatient clinics on Saturdays and Sundays, at no detriment to other patients, who, as they had never had these services, cannot be made worse off if others do receive them. As has been seen in chapter 5, Glennerster et al. (1994) argued that, in the first three waves of fundholding practices, fundholding could, but did not necessarily, produce a two-tier service, with patients funded in this way receiving better quality services. Empowering particular groups as proxy purchasers logically creates unfairness in access to services.

It was this perception of inequality which seems to have been behind the development of a 'total commissioning scheme' in Nottinghamshire. This was an area in which the GPs, unlike their colleagues in neighbouring Derbyshire, had proved unenthusiastic about becoming fundholders. In its place the local health authority, Nottingham Health, developed a new commissioning system which was based on a non-fundholders purchasing group. Eighty per cent of Nottingham general practitioners were, at the time of writing, involved in the commissioning scheme. The purchasing group was a representative one and each of its members liaised with a small number of practices and spent time collating opinions about local medical needs and priorities and disseminating information about plans and budgets. The role of the purchasing group was to advise Nottingham Health on the purchasing of secondary care and it was directly involved in making purchasing decisions and in the contract negoti-ations with hospitals. There is also a medical advisory committee which includes in its membership representatives from the purchasing group and from the fund-holding practices as well as members from the local provider units. Nottingham Health was trying to develop the scheme as an alternative to fundholding by creating IT links between it and the non-fundholding GPs and by developing a new weighted capitation system to allocate budgets to fundholders and non-fundholders on an equitable basis. The perceived lack of fairness caused by fundholding was the driving force behind this scheme, as Nottingham Health argued in a pamphlet on the commissioning scheme:

> [the commissioning scheme] gives all general practitioners the oppor-tunity to be fully involved in purchasing strategy and negotiations . . . As a powerful and efficient purchaser, Nottingham Health aims to improve service provision whilst *maintaining equal access to all health care services for the whole community* . . . Allocating resources according to an agreed capitation based formula will create a 'level playing field' for fundholders and non-fundholders. The purchasing power of the Health Commission will be used to *ensure that all patients can obtain equal access to health care.*
>
> (Nottingham Health Commission, n.d., my italics)

The argument about fundholding within the Nottingham area is an example of the contest between the imperatives of market diversity and fairness which characterises the quasi-market stage of the dialectic of resource allocation.

In a quasi-market services will differ from area to area, indeed this respons-iveness to local conditions is one of the justifications of the quasi-market, but this is also its negation, its inability to meet the criterion of fairness. Although in this relationship the market mechanism is dominant, it is not a *laissez-faire* market. Certain groups are enabled to act paternalistically towards the service users and define their best interests for them. The paternalistic market is not a fair market, granting equal access to all, and it is challenged by those who believe that their interests and aspirations are equally entitled to be privileged.

The dialectical transcendence of this contradiction comes by changing the definition of fairness, from equality of access, to the provision of a safety net to catch those who fall from the first tier of service to the second tier, or below.

The regulated market relationship: the dialectic of segmentation and universality

The heuristics of return on capital invested and minimum state provision

Access to gas and schools

School dinners; fertility services

Conditions of service

Critical illness insurance

In this phase of the development of the idea of public services the relationship between provider and user again becomes a private and contractual one. Individuals decide which services they wish to receive and they contract directly with a private sector body to provide them. The provision of services becomes a matter for the private market, but with three limitations affecting its operation. First, there is the provision of a public, statutory body whose purpose is the regulation of the market to ensure that powerful or monopolistic providers do not exploit the consumers. In following the trend set by the privatisations of the public utilities this will be called an OFFREG body such as OFWAT, the watchdog body for the water industry. Second, government may use public revenues to provide a public safety net service for those who cannot, or will not, buy in the marketplace. The nature of the safety net will become a major issue, for example, if people are encouraged to make personal and private provision for the residential care they may need in old age. The third constraint is that the government may choose to fund or subsidise consumers so that they can participate in the market, even if only at a minimum level.

Education will provide a useful illustration from which the institutional relationships in this stage of the dialectic can be explained. Four major changes in the provision of education have brought this about. The first is the financial principle that funding follows the pupil or student. As schools and colleges are funded on a per capita basis, students, in effect, possess an educational voucher which they or their parents can spend in the school or college of their choice. The notion of the voucher has a long history, dating from at least the early 1970s, when the idea of educational vouchers first came into prominence (MacBeath 1976: 58, 68). There are some limitations on this financial portability. In the case of school sixth forms, for example, only about four-fifths of the funding follows the pupil and small sixth forms have a degree of financial protection. The second change was the introduction of parental choice of schools; this had always been available in higher and further education but was only introduced in primary and secondary education by the 1980 and 1988 Education Acts. Under these Acts parents can express a preference about the school they wish their children to go to and can appeal if their preference is not granted. This change had the effect of creating a competitive market between schools. The third change was the devolution of budgets and financial responsibility to the institutional level which gave schools and colleges much individual responsibility for their resource allocation decisions and for the school's performance. The final change was the creation of institutional diversity through the policy of encouraging schools to opt out of local education authority control, the setting up of City Technology Colleges and the freeing of FE colleges from local authority control. The intention, and perhaps the impact, of these changes was to create a marketplace of diverse institutions between whom the customer could choose. One difference between the situation in education at the time of writing and the voucher ideal is that the quantum of finance provided to each student and pupil cannot be used to buy a private sector education. One other important distinction, in relation to primary and secondary schools, is that they have a responsibility to offer an education to children who live in their catchment area (if space is available). In a full market relationship an institution would be able to choose to whom it wished to provide a service. The regulatory bodies in this area include OFSTED who quality assure schools and HEQC and HEFC who monitor quality in higher education.

Within a regulated market relationship a tension exists between the pressure on companies to segment their markets and to concentrate their effort on those segments which will deliver the best returns and the concern of the government, and of any regulatory bodies, to ensure that basic services which every citizen requires – utilities, education, health and social care and so on – are universally available to all citizens. Herein lies the dialectical contradiction between companies' wish to react to diversity amongst their customers and government's concerns to provide for the common needs of the population.

The colloquial expression for segmentation is cherry picking. This means that providers seek customers who will consume in large amounts and who can afford to pay whilst seeking to discourage small consumers who will have to be badgered to pay up. In May 1994 OFGAS and the Department of Trade and Industry published a joint consultation document which seemed 'not just to condone but to encourage cherry picking' (Spring 1995: 37). The report stated:

> It is natural for new entrants into a monopolistic market to target its most profitable, or cross-subsidising areas first. Such a strategy is often known as cherry picking. To the extent the strategy is successful, the previous monopolist risks being left increasingly with the less profitable, or cross-subsidised, areas of the market. In the absence of countervailing action, there would be pressure for relative prices to rise in these previously cross-subsidised areas of the market, where prices may have been below cost.
>
> (ibid.: 37)

It was reported that in the south west region of the UK, where a pilot scheme was run in 1996 which allowed customers to buy their gas from any of a number of competing suppliers, that customers who agreed to pay their bills by direct debit were being offered much cheaper tariffs than those customers who would not. In February 1997, when the competitive market for domestic gas supply was extended from Cornwall, Devon and Somerset into Avon and Dorset, Centrica, the supply arm of British Gas, announced that it wanted to end the universal tariff under which everyone paid the same price for their gas irrespective of their location. They were also seeking permission from the regulator to discriminate between big and small household consumers of gas. As the Chief Executive of Centrica said:

> We are going to offer a whole range of payment options which will give customers better choice to suit their needs: there will be new tariffs to suit particular circumstances.
>
> (Barnett 1997b)

The Gas Consumers' Council reported that the trend in the newly opened market would be to offer attractive deals to large users and to those who would pay by direct debit. Customers who paid by meter would be paying more for their gas than those paying by direct debit.

Despite these moves towards discretionary pricing the obligation for universal service remained. This meant that gas suppliers could not refuse to provide gas to customers on commercial grounds. But, according to Spring's gloss on the OFGAS and DTI consultation document discussed above, there was an inherent distaste in the document for regulated standards of service, even to protect the most vulnerable:

> It may be that the development of attractively priced competitive services in the market designed for older and disabled customers makes it unnecessary to retain prescribed levels of service.
>
> (Spring 1995: 37)

The effect of these trends, if they were to become standard practice, would be to undermine, within the gas industry, the universal service obligation, backed by statute, which required any consumer within a certain distance of a gas main to be supplied at a uniform price and service level regardless of the level of offtake (ibid.: 44).

In dialectical terms the government and the regulators represent the formal term of the dialectic, the right of all citizens to have access to the services they need for civilized existence, whilst the providing companies represent the term of teeming diversity, the antithesis that negates the thesis. For the providing companies customers are not formal entities to whom rights attach, but flesh and blood individuals who have very real credit histories and patterns of consumption. A formal entitlement to a service may exist but if the provider decides that a consumer is too poor a credit risk, or that they consume too little to make it economic to provide them with a service, then the providers may seek to impose such demanding terms and prices that the consumer is effectively denied access to the service.

As I write this, I have to one side of my desk an offer from an insurance company to sell me critical illness insurance cover which will serve as an example of market segmentation as a contrast to a governmental responsibility for health-care. Government agencies, by definition, have an all inclusive responsibility (subject to statutory limitation) to the people within the community or location they are responsible for. They cannot pick and choose their customers or the services they provide. GPs, for example, carry a general, 24-hour, responsibility for the primary healthcare of their patients. And although they can refuse to take patients onto their list, the FHSA or health authority has the responsibility of finding everyone a GP. This right is specified and detailed in a Citizens' Charter. Insurance companies, however, can respond to the imperative of segmentation; they can choose which customers to take on and which diseases they will insure against. When I apply for insurance cover the forms I fill in and the medical examination I might be required to undergo will serve to identify for the insurance company the degree of risk they would be taking on. If the risk is a little above the average I may only have to pay an increased premium, but if the risk is significant I may be refused cover. Their sales blurb specifies a list of medical conditions that the insurance covers, which includes the most common illnesses, but clearly not all of them (Fieldman 1997). The imperatives of return on capital mean that companies cannot take the risk of providing universal services, and people who fail to fit companies' market niches, or who fall ill with complaints not included in the policy schedule, will have to look to government to provide a safety net.

Each of these competing forces, universalism and segmentation, has its characteristic criterion for making decisions about resource allocation and priorities. For the companies in the marketplace it is return on capital. Shareholders demand a sufficient return on their investment to justify retaining their shares and this, together with the need to fund future investment, inclines the managers of companies to allocate resources in a way that will maximise the return on investment at least in the short term. But government and the regulatory bodies are minded to require that resources are allocated, at least in some degree, to the provision of a safety net for consumers. Their concern is that people in a weak market position in relation to the providing companies, and this may include staff as well as customers, obtain at least a minimum standard of service or treatment. In the case of the public utilities of course, the fact that many are natural monopolies reinforces the need for regulation.

The manifestation of these contradictions can be seen historically in the struggle between regulatory forces and private companies over the degree to which the market should be regulated and on the extent, and the mesh size, of the safety net provision. The supporters of the free market argue that regulation and the cost of safety net services prevent companies from competing effectively in an aggressive and globalised market. Many companies use overseas acquisitions and developments as a way of removing, at least a part of, their business, from the constraints imposed upon them in the domestic market. British Gas, for example, had a clear strategy of developing its overseas businesses to avoid domestic regulation. In 1993 British Gas agreed deals in Malaysia, Trinidad and Thailand and was involved in forty-five countries (*Economist* 1993). The intensity of the struggle will wax and wane with the ideological persuasion of the government in power; some governments will be more anxious to extend the safety net than others.

An illustration of the conflict between the needs of providers, who have to respond to market disciplines, and the concerns of others to provide services as a social safety net can be seen in the history of school meals (Hodgkinson 1996). School dinners were first provided in schools set up by the 1870 Education Act, by voluntary and charitable effort, because many people thought that the distraction of hunger was preventing pupils from benefiting from their education. In 1906 local authorities were allowed to spend ratepayers' money on school meals. But education catering remained an undeveloped service until World War II, when the need for a population fit to fight and withstand the pressures of war led to the service acquiring priority in the eyes of policy makers. The 1944 Education Act required local authorities to provide pupils with a 'decently cooked main meal of the day'. In 1955 the nature of this social policy safety net was closely defined by a government circular which laid down minimum nutritional standards for school meals. These stated that the meals should have a calorific value of between 650 and 1,000 calories and should include 20 g of milk and 30 g of animal protein.

In the 1980s the safety net was diminished because of a need to cut public expenditure. The first change came in the 1980 Education Act which gave local authorities the right to withdraw from the provision of school meals (except for those children eligible for a free school meal) and which also abolished the minimum nutritional standards. This Act signalled a change in the nature of school catering which ceased to be a social service and became a commercial undertaking. Canteens became cash cafeterias catering for children's preferences for junk food. In 1988 local authorities were required to put education catering out to competitive tendering. But by 1994, 86 per cent of the contracts had been won by in-house local authority bids. Private caterers saw school meals as a high risk proposition: prices were fixed, margins were low, schools were closed for many weeks a year and, if a LEA decided to close down the service, the contractor would be left with the redundancy bill. Another factor was the reduction in the subsidy that local authorities were able, or willing, to provide for school meals. By the mid-1990s the subsidy had effectively disappeared. The consequence of the changes of the 1980s was, not to transfer school meals to the private sector, but to make the local authority providers more responsive to market pressures and less concerned with the paternalistic role of providing for the nutritional needs of pupils. The safety net lost priority, in the minds of the caterers, to the need to retain market share and to earn enough to keep the operation going. The nature of the service changed. The formal civility (heavily policed by teachers contractually bound to lunch time supervision) of 'family service' at which everyone ate the same balanced meal was dialectically contradicted by the teeming diversity of individual kids queuing in the school cafeteria to buy their junk food snacks.

In response to these developments a national school meals campaign began in 1992 to lobby for the reintroduction of nutritional standards for school meals. There were several research reports published which suggested that poor nutrition was beginning to have an effect on some children's development and health. One study (Mills and Bright 1996) suggested that the most socially deprived 11-year-old school children had lower educational attainments, and were 13 cm shorter, than their peers. The Department for Education issued new nutritional guidelines in February 1997 (Judd 1997), which, among other things, suggested that chips should be straight cut rather than crinkled because they absorb less fat. But the guidelines were voluntary, the DfEE thought it improper to dictate the contents of school meals to schools (who were by this time responsible for meals). The notion of a safety net, in this case in the form of prescribed nutritional standards, could not survive within a service which has to make a financial return, despite the loss of local authority subsidy and the expectations of children and their parents that school meals will be cheap, in order to survive.

When services are available from private providers in the market pressures emerge to limit the size of, or abolish, the safety net. This can also be illustrated by the public debate which has taken place since 1993 about fertility services, and particularly about in vitro fertilisation (IVF) treatments (Klein et al. 1996: 75–7) within the NHS. The debate had been prefigured by a growth in the availability of private sector fertility services. The extent to which such services should be provided within the health service was at the core of the argument. Some argued that fertility services were not an essential medical service and should not be publicly funded. Others argued that having children was a fundamental human right and that therefore infertile couples should be treated at the public's cost. The judgement is made more difficult by the estimated cost of £11,000 per live birth, which is higher than for other forms of fertility treatment (Klein *et al.* 1996: 75). In one particular case the debate focused on whether a woman of over fifty years should be allowed to have publicly funded fertility treatment. By 1996 at least ten health authorities had excluded in vitro fertility services from the list of clinical procedures they would fund. Even those authorities that were willing in principle to fund the treatment would normally only do so if the doctor had made an overwhelming clinical case (NAHAT 1996). Fertility treatment is an example of a service for which a case can be made for public provision but which can also survive as a business within a private market. In cases such as these, and chiropody, dentistry and alternative therapies are other examples, it is tempting for public authorities to withdraw the service, or only retain a minimal safety net to meet the needs of very particular client groups such as children and pregnant women. Within the regulated market relationship the return on capital heuristic leads to commercially viable segments of public services being withdrawn from the scope of public provision and being made a private matter between patients and providers. The dialectical tension comes from the demand, of those who do not want or cannot afford to use the private market, that these services should be part of the minimal public provision funded by government.

A further aspect of the dialectic can be seen in the legal proceedings concerning the transfer of staff's conditions of service when a public service is tendered out or a public organisation is privatised. The European Community's Acquired Rights Directive of 1977 laid down that employees whose jobs were transferred from one employer to another took with them their existing rates of pay and conditions of service. These rights were incorporated in a set of statutory instruments in 1981 known as the Transfer of Undertakings (Protection of Employment) regulations (TUPE). An issue concerning TUPE arose in the implementation of compulsory competitive tendering (CCT). In many cases a tendering company achieved a low bid by worsening staff's pay rates and conditions of service. The European Commission petitioned the European Court to rule that the British government was wrong to exclude the public sector from the TUPE regulations (Gosling 1992). In 1993 the government accepted that TUPE covered privatisations (Harper *et al.* 1994).

The application of TUPE to privatisations and potentially to competitive tendering (Department of the Environment 1995: §35–8) represented a clash between the safety net heuristic and the return on capital heuristic. The return on capital heuristic demanded that staff costs were brought down to their minimum within a competitive market. This requirement implied, among other things, that conditions of service should be different in different companies and in different parts of the country. But such changes contradicted the universalistic argument, which has traditionally dominated the public sector, that public sector conditions and pay rates should apply across the country. In the building industry, to take a particular example, one of the original justifica-tions for local authority direct building works was that they would act as exemplary employers, who would be a counterweight to the injustices of the private sector building industry, by treating all employees equally and well (Langford 1982). The TUPE regulations can be seen as an aspect of the safety net heuristic in that they are used to argue for a decent and standardised minimum in pay and conditions of service against employers' demands for a more flexible and cost efficient workforce.

Market providers seek to segment the market to avoid moral hazards and non-profitable services and clients. They also seek to minimise the public provi-sion in order to make their own services attractive and, by keeping the level of tax down, maximise the amount of money people can spend on their services. People following the universalistic rhetoric try to extend and deepen the public safety net for those who cannot afford to pay in the market. The contradiction is transcended by a return to the private client relationship. Society is declared not to exist; and public choice is seen to be best achieved through a strong methodological individualism (Lane 1993: 150–63). At this stage therefore it is denied that the concept of a public service can have any validity: there are only services. If there is no public aspect to the delivery of services, then the notions of universal provision and of the safety net are unnecessary. Any culture based on the idea of a public service ethos must of course also disappear with this dialectical shift, and employment in government service will come to be seen as a personal rather than an official function. As such, the purpose of government employment will be seen as providing personal financial benefits. The dialectic will have returned to the point at which it began.

A summary

The rhetorical progression in the idea of public services just described is summarised in table 6.2. The nature of the analysis perhaps needs clarification. It is intended as a logical, rhetorical sequence that may be useful for dissecting and analysing public and organisational debates about the allocation of public resources and services. To illustrate this process I have a Sunday newspaper article in front of me that follows up the issue of the smoker with coronary heart disease discussed earlier (Jones 1993). The British Medical Association had asked its ethics committee to develop new guidelines for such situations. Dr Horner, the chair of the committee, was reported as saying that the committee may recommend that surgery may be withheld from people who persistently indulge in behaviour that might reduce the chances of a successful outcome; he argued:

> This is not taking a moral stand, or punishing patients who take risks ... Doctors have an ethical duty not to waste resources.
>
> (Jones 1993)

Table 6.2 The phenomenology and dialectics of public services: a summary

The dialectic	The institutional context	The abstract and formal term of the dialectic	The active and unpredictable term of the dialectic	The contradictions within the dialectic	The synthesis – the third term of the dialectic
The dialectic of patron and client	The private client relationship	The heuristic of holistic service – non-self-interested service to the patron	The heuristic of personal gain – the provider seeks to maximise their personal advantage	The formal idea of service is negated by its role in enforcing the superior status of the patron, relative to the client, and by the providers' attempts to diminish their formal dependence by exploiting the patron	The synthesis means depersonalising the relationship between user and provider and introducing government into the nexus
The dialectic of need and worth	The professional relationship	The heuristic of individual need – responding to clients' objective needs	The heuristic of deservingness – responding to people according to their moral worth	The providers' formally objective relationship with the user is contradicted by the providers' moralising reactions to users' untidy problems, their occasional moral culpability and their dependence on the provider	The synthesis comes from focusing on populations rather than individuals
The dialectic of objective and subjective good	The managerial relationship	The heuristic of utility – rational planning and optimisation	The heuristic of ecology – balancing pressures and demands	The formal clarity of utility maximisation is contradicted by the paradox of consequences, by the need to do what is seen to be right according to stakeholding groups and by the intrusion of politics into policy analysis	The synthesis involves giving up goal seeking and allowing the hidden hand of the market to take its place

Table 6.2 Continued

The dialectic	The institutional context	The abstract and formal term of the dialectic	The active and unpredictable term of the dialectic	The contradictions within the dialectic	The synthesis – the third term of the dialectic
The dialectic of governmental and arm's length purchasing	The quasi-market relationship	The heuristic of fairness – everyone has a formal right to equal access to standardised services. This is achieved by arbitrary means (e.g. waiting lists)	The heuristic of market diversity – the mechanism for public service delivery should maximise variety, difference and choice	The use of a market mechanism produces choices for service users. But creating choices means that some users will receive better services than others. This is because quasi-markets disenfranchise those not granted proxy purchasing power and limits the choice of users who cannot obtain access to proxy purchasers. The quasi-market also has difficulties in overcoming rigidities in the system of supply (closing poor schools and expanding good ones for example), and so it provides some users with a second-class service	The synthesis comes from making the users purchasers and defining fairness in terms of access to the market and not in terms of providing equal services to those with equal needs
The dialectic of segmentation and universal need	The regulated market relationship	The heuristic of the safety net – the provision of universal basic services, especially for those worst off who cannot afford market prices	The heuristic of return on capital – the supplier segments the market and concentrates on the most profitable segments	The formal ability of the market to maximise the benefits available to all is negated by eccentric individuals who do not fit the market niches. The greater the degree of market segmentation, the larger the number who do not fit and the greater the need for a safety net. As governments tax and regulate companies to provide the net, the companies' returns are diminished and they need to segment further to improve their return on investment	The synthesis is the denial of the existence of notions of society and of public service. This means a return to the client-patron relationship and the use of charity as the means for helping the needy

He told another reporter that:

> Some doctors are alleged to have played God and denied patients treatment because they did not like their lifestyle: but they are very few.
>
> (Laurance 1993a)

The concepts presented in this chapter provide a framework for the theoretical deconstruction of such statements. A degree of rhetorical accumulation is also illustrated by this example. Debates involve not only the dialectical contradictions discussed within each institutional relationship, but also contradictions between the other possible combinations of heuristics. Dr Horner's remarks were presented by him as a conflict between utility and individual need. But there was within his remarks a hint of arguments derived from the deservingness and segmentation heuristics. Viewed from Dr Horner's own position it is clear that he was having to balance the imperative to obtain cost effectiveness against the ecological pressure from the press not to deny patients the healthcare they needed. The conceptual framework of this chapter therefore has to be seen as an ideal type; the arguments amongst organisations and stakeholder groups are much more complicated.

There are many things the framework and concepts described in this chapter are not. They are not a historical or chronological description of the development of public services. I am not arguing that institutions will go through, or have been through, these stages in this order. At any one time it is clear that different parts of the public services will be at different stages in the dialectic. At present, for example, the utilities are largely in the stage of the regulated market, healthcare is provided through a quasi-market but library services are still mainly delivered through the professional relationship, and dentistry, for many, is provided through the private client relationship. In many public organisations the whole range of the dialectic will be represented by the activities and arguments of different groups and individuals. To caricature the possibilities, some professional staff will believe themselves to be working within the professional relationship, senior managers may think themselves to be working within the managerial relationship whilst other professionals and managers could be negotiating contracts within a quasi-market relationship. Politicians within the organisation will argue for and against the market, whilst some staff may be practising in the private market in addition to their public sector work.

The framework is a phenomenological one, and its nature needs to be explained. A phenomenology, as Hegel uses the term, represents a series of stages in which our experience of an object or process and our subjective understanding of it develop as a consequence of their mutual interaction. Each new stage of this interdependent process does not replace the previous understanding but incorporates, or transcends, it. In the managerial stage therefore concern for individual need, which characterised the previous professional stage, is not obliterated. It can still affect people's thinking and arguments but it is seen as one set of issues within a broader understanding of the problems of public sector resource allocation. Whereas, in the professional stage, the individual need heuristic represented the boundary of thinking on the subject, within the managerial stage, it is one component in more complex debates. This framework is similar to Kohlberg's model of ethical reasoning as adapted by Snell (1993), who described the way in which people become more sophisticated as they learn new ways of thinking about ethical controversies. The fact that someone can use higher, in Kohlberg's terms, methods of reasoning does not mean that on many occasions they will not use the simpler and lesser forms of argument. A phenomenology therefore is not a historical and chronological description of an unfolding social process. It is the history of our understanding of things. But this understanding does not develop purely in intellectual terms; rather, intellectual understanding changes as people cope with the contradictions they experience in their sensual perception of the world.

Hegel believed that the phenomenological process was one which led to a fixed conclusion and transcendence. The dialectics would work themselves to a point in which the contradiction between the objective world and the subjective self was resolved or left behind. The model described in this chapter, being altogether less sophisticated and being particular rather than universal, is circular rather than linear. The assumption I have made is that people and communities are destined to continuously re-invent the contradictions and resolutions outlined in the model. The pull of counter-argument on argument and response to challenge will always, eventually, bring debates about resource allocation and public services back to where they had already been. The universe of argument is infinite but bounded. I have used Hegel's dialectic to provide the engine needed to drive the dynamics of the model but, because I have not granted to reason the power of final resolution, the model is not a Hegelian one. The model is like a myth which has the power to clarify our understanding through the telling of a story. Such tales resonate with our experience but they do not give a narratively accurate description of it. The quality of a myth lies in its ability to palliate contradiction without resolving it: 'Failure is admitted in our myths, and there precisely lies their function' (Lévi-Strauss quoted in Leach 1970: 58).

Phenomenological understanding can only develop in retrospect. Only after the experience of managerial and organisational reality can we understand what has happened. I was once working with a group of middle-ranking social services managers. At that time they were receiving formal instructions from the social services committee to prepare for the forthcoming internal market and competitive tendering in the services they provided. They had not made any preparations however; no business plans were finalised, no specifications had been drawn up. When they were asked why not, they said that these proposals were to be seen as part of the political manoeuvrings that were preceding the local elections that were due shortly. Once the elections were over they believed the committee would lose its interest in imposing market systems on them. Yet they had already made many small changes in their values, their arguments and their practices which would make the introduction of market thinking inevitable. They talked about how cheap it would be for private sector companies to compete for the services they provided. They thought of the charges they levied on clients as prices, decided in a marketplace, and not as *subs* within the context of the mutuality of community support. When one of their areas was overstaffed they were not thinking how they might find work to keep the surplus staff busy but how they might employ staff more flexibly so that their workforce could be kept in balance with the demand. The fact that they had recognised the market as an alternative to the present arrangements, even though they objected to it, had begun to change and redirect their thinking. The possibility of the market acted as a lurking other, hidden, self that shadowed their thinking and activities. Just as Dr Jekyll was unaware of the growing power of Mr Hyde so did the market insinuate itself into their thinking. They were not aware of this; and when they became so it would be too late to change it. They would have made too many pragmatic compromises with it. Hegel argues that the phenomenological development of a theme will go on 'behind the back of consciousness' and the process will only be apparent to the phenomenological observer or in phenomenological retrospect. As Findlay, an interpreter of Hegel (1970: 89) remarked, the scientist, as someone who is seeking to understand, will be led from the things of sense perception, the appearance of complexity of everyday life, to the non-sensuous things of the scientific understanding: 'It is we, the phenomenological observers, practising our external reflection, who can understand the whole transition.'

The owl of Minerva spreads its wings only with the falling of the dusk
(Hegel 1952: 13)

7

A POLEMIC

Conclusions about resource allocation
and public services

People are not balanced in their thinking about priorities. Take the following example from Kahneman and Tversky's (1982) article on the psychology of preferences. Imagine you are on the way to a theatre with a couple of tickets which cost you fifty pounds. When you arrive you discover you have lost the tickets. Would you buy new tickets for the performance? Now imagine you are going to the same play without having bought tickets in advance but with every intention of buying some at the box office. When you prepare to pay you realise you have lost the cash you were going to buy the tickets with. Would you still buy the tickets, presumably using the credit card which you have not lost?

In both cases you are in exactly the same situation. You have lost fifty pounds and you are faced with the decision of whether to spend another fifty pounds. However, most people, when asked this question in psychological surveys, say that they would be more likely to buy new tickets if they had lost the money than if they had lost the tickets. One interpretation of these findings advanced by Kahneman and Tversky is that mentally the two losses are accounted for separately. The loss of the cash is thought about as though it was disassociated from the theatre trip, it is posted to a different account, and is therefore not taken into consideration when deciding whether to buy tickets. But the loss of the tickets cannot be thought about except within the context of the theatre visit and so people consider that if they do buy new tickets the cost of watching the play will have been doubled.

A similar process can be seen in resource allocation. The use of heuristics in resource allocation decisions about public services leads to a restricted range of considerations being taken into account. This can result in people making decisions which, on more careful consideration, look unbalanced. Such disequilibrium in thought processes explains why the statements about resource allocation listed in chapter 1 (p. 3) look either very odd or very persuasive, depending upon whether the reader's preferred heuristics fit with, or jolt against, those applied by the people making the statement. The characteristic lack of balance, attributable to each heuristic and mechanism, as discussed earlier in the book, can be briefly summarised.

- The lack of balance characteristic of the heuristic of holistic service is that the customer continues to pay for a service even past the point at which it ceases to be competent, or provide a valued outcome, because the service provider is necessary to reinforce their higher relative status.
- The characteristic lack of balance of the personal gain heuristic is that the effort given over to seeking private gain, and the level of risk, becomes disproportionate to the benefits achieved. The service providers' self-esteem comes from ripping off the punters.
- The characteristic lack of balance of the individual need heuristic is caused by a restricted breadth of vision. Service providers focus on the need presented to them and they are less aware of hidden need. In the area of social services for children, for example, the high profile of child protection work has led to the problems of children in need (as defined by the Children Act) being relatively neglected.
- The lack of balance characteristic of deservingness is also caused by proximity. This causes *Daily Mail* readers, for instance, to confuse their local prejudices with universal ethical principles. Small-scale, but local, anti-social behaviour, such as minor benefit cheating, is castigated much more heavily than large-scale, but distant, bad behaviour, for example large-scale tax evasion.
- The lack of balance characteristic of utility is its concern with the quantifiable and the tendency of its proponents to dismiss any subjective evidence as 'merely anecdotal'. The detailed discussion of methods of measuring relative rates of morbidity in Mays and Bevan's (1987) analysis of RAWP (the system that was used for distributing budgets between regional health authorities) is a good example of the genre.
- The characteristic lack of balance of the ecology heuristic is disdain for numbers and numeracy. Their interest is in political networks, not in network analysis.
- The characteristic lack of balance of the market diversity mechanism, which focuses on the provision of choice to consumers, is its blind spot on the question of the costs of creating and providing diversity. In the NHS, for example, the supporters of fundholding and the internal market remain quiet about the transaction costs involved.
- The heuristic of fairness requires equal access to services which do not differ according to post code. The heuristic's characteristic lack of balance is to ignore the inflexibility, and unresponsiveness to the particular needs of individual users, that standardised access to standardised services can cause.
- The characteristic lack of balance of the return on capital employed heuristic is rent seeking because its followers believe it to be an easier way of maximising returns than trying to meet the changing demands of purchasers (Stretton and Orchard 1994: 38–40). For example, the management of public utilities try to improve their return on investment by doing

all they can to secure a soft regime from the regulator. They attempt this by controlling the flow of information to the regulator, by political lobbying and by trying to get the media and the public on their side.

- The characteristic lack of balance of the safety net heuristic is to focus exclusively on the claims of the needy. Its supporters fix upon a Rawlsian criterion of redistributive justice which states that one state of society is better than another if it results in a gain in welfare for those members of society who are worst off (Rawls 1972).

The changing pattern of preferences for the heuristics

A major conclusion of this book is that resource allocation and market creation are examples of heuristic thinking, and that these cognitive processes are, by definition, unbalanced. It must follow from this conclusion that the matter of resource allocation is not optimisation, but acceptability. If each heuristic and mechanism has within itself the elements of its own limitations, then none of them can be optimal. The question confronting people interested in public services is not 'what is the best way of allocating and delivering public services?' but 'what, in any particular time and place, is the most broadly acceptable way of allocating and delivering public services?' It also follows that there must have been changes in the historical pattern of acceptance. Some heuristics and mechanisms will have increased in favour whilst others will have lost public acceptability. The conclusion drawn from the material in this book is that the heuristics of holistic service, individual need, fairness and utility have become less popular and the heuristics of personal gain, deservingness, ecology, market diversity and return on capital have become more common. In summary, those heuristics that belong to the dialectical term of diversity have gained ascendancy over those heuristics belonging to the formal term of the dialectic (as described in chapter 6, and particularly in table 6.2). This claim needs substantiation.

Those heuristics and values that have become less popular in discussions about public services will be discussed first. The idea of a holistic approach to public services has largely disappeared in a trend that has been developing since the early 1980s but which has accelerated in the last few years. This can be illustrated by changes in the way that a university education is delivered (cf. p. 154). In the early 1980s higher education was not delivered as a standardised package. Lecturers knew their students because numbers were small and what was taught and how it was taught depended upon the responses of the students and the interests (or eccentricities) of the lecturers. At its best the system allowed an education to be adapted and shaped to the needs of students. In the 1980s the delivery of higher education became standardised. The product is now the same for all students, so that a group of a hundred students studying a particular module will be put in separate seminar groups but they will be all working on the same topics and doing the same exercises.

There is less scope for the lecturers to respond to the differences between students and seminar groups.

The loss of variety in services can lead to them being branded as well as standardised. It will not be long, perhaps, until, in the new market for the provision of home social care, clients will be offered the 'Domestic Bliss Home Care Support Plan' rather than individualised care delivered to meet their needs at a particular time. The managerial advantage of branding and packaging services is that, as they can be delivered by any available member of staff, it is unnecessary to ensure that a client always receives their services from the same person. The personal relationship between providers and customers, which is at the heart of holistic service, is severed.

The individual need heuristic has had diminished impact on debates about service delivery in the 1990s. This is largely because the application of individual need has become too expensive. The development can be seen most clearly in the National Health Service. The growth of clinical science and medical technology means that there are more services that can be provided. At the same time, people's expectations about the level of health and well being that are seen as the norm have increased. The combined effect of these changes is to increase the demands placed upon the health service. As Enoch Powell argued long ago (1966), in one of the few areas in which his forecasts turned out to be correct, the NHS generates need for healthcare rather than diminishes it, as the founders of the NHS anticipated. The ambition to meet all need becomes Quixotic and there is an acceptance amongst politicians, civil servants and managers that there has to be rationing (or prioritisation) in the NHS. In the early 1970s individual need was the predominant occupational ideology of professional staff in the caring professions and, whilst it is still their fundamental belief, it plays a diminished role in their day-to-day work and discussions because the application of individual need blinds the speaker to the question of where the money to pay for services is coming from.

Fairness is an emotive word for many people. But as a guiding value in public services it has lost its power. This is because, in a time of tight constraint on funding and resources, the application of fairness implies the spreading of misery equally amongst many people. From a political perspective this is a deeply unattractive option. It is for this reason that politicians are unwilling to remove or reduce universal (and fair) benefits such as child allowance. The widespread pain of such a change would produce a strong political reaction. In times of resource constraint politicians and policy makers are unlikely to allocate services universally and fairly because, once established, they would be politically difficult to close down or cut.

The last of the heuristics to have its role in debates about public services diminished is utility but it only began to lose significance in recent times. This value was an important aspect of public debate in the 1970s when, through such devices as management by objectives, corporate management and programme planning, budgeting systems (PPBS), a serious attempt was made to instil management values into public organisations. The trend became more pronounced in the early 1980s when competitive tendering was introduced. In the wake of CCT came market testing, cost cutting, downsizing, objective setting and performance measurement, a combination which became known as the new public management (NPM). NPM was widely seen as an attempt to import management (and utilitarian values) into the public domain. In 1988 the tide began to turn against the utility heuristic when the government began to seek its aims for the public service by the use of markets, quasi-markets and competition rather than by the encouragement of managerial values (Rhodes 1995: 5). Utility is still an important aspect of debate about public services but this does not disguise its relative decline as markets became more important than planning.

The heuristics and values that have gained prominence in public discussion are from the diverse and active term of the dialectic of public services. Perhaps one of the most surprising developments, given the predominance of the professional individual need ideology during most of the postwar years, has been the re-emergence of the idea of deservingness. A new consensus has developed across the party political spectrum which states that a life supported by welfare payments creates a sense of dependency which saps people's motivation to find a job and take responsibility for themselves. The policy consequences of this view can be seen in changes to invalidity and unemployment benefits under the Conservative government (*Economist* 1997: 37) and in the new Labour government's proposals for encouraging people off welfare and back into work, a process the Labour Party has referred to as the re-moralisation of welfare. A recognition of the likely future costs of welfare has also caused policy makers to stress self-responsibility in a wide range of areas including pension provision, student grants and loans, taking exercise and eating healthily to minimise the risk of disease and infirmity in later life and following the rules of safe sex to diminish the incidence of AIDS. All these attempts to make people more responsible, to make them more deserving in the eyes of policy makers carry, as a concomitant of their up-beat message, an unwillingness to be generous and responsive to those who are undeserving because they will not take any action to improve or protect themselves.

Personal competence and gain have also become acceptable themes in public discussions about public services. This is not a claim that people in the public sector have become corrupt, simply it is a recognition that the old idea of disinterested public service has been replaced. It has become acceptable for a public official to consider their own interests in the way they make decisions and carry out their jobs. This public acceptance of private interest is normally dated to Mrs Thatcher's famous announcement that there is no such thing as society only an aggregation of individual interests.

A logical development from the increased acceptance of deservingness and individual gain is an emphasis on choice and diversity in the provision of public services. This change, as has been seen in earlier chapters, has led to the increased use of quasi and free market mechanisms to deliver public services. In these systems the best of services will go to those who understand the quasi-market and who are motivated, for instance, to find the best GP or the best school for themselves and their families. Stephen Dorrell, then Secretary of State for Health, accepted this situation when, in a radio phone-in programme during the 1997 election, he told a caller, complaining about the service she received from the health service, to find herself a good fundholding practice and change doctors. In short, the heuristic value of diversity and choice has developed because it rewards the deserving and those who have the skill and energy to advance their private interests.

A consequence of choice and diversity in the provision of public services has been greater variety in the range and type of public or near-public bodies used to provide public services. The diversity of bodies has given importance to the ecology heuristic in decision making about public services. The ecology heuristic is used more when there is a constellation of stakeholders associated with a service. Like Pascal's sphere the new and diverse public sector has its circumference everywhere and its centre nowhere (Borges 1970: 224–7). Rhodes (1995) argued that the public sector is increasingly constituted from networks, as well as from hierarchies and markets, as government moves from a system of government into a system of governance:

> This use sees governance as a broader term than government with services provided by any permutation of government and the private and voluntary sectors. Inter-organisational linkages are a defining char-acteristic of service delivery and I use the term network to describe the several interdependent actors involved in delivering services. These networks are made up of organisations that need to exchange resources (for example money, information, expertise) to achieve their object-ives, to maximise their influence over outcomes and to avoid becoming dependent on other players in the game.
>
> (Rhodes 1995: 9; see also Rhodes 1988: 42–3)

Networks are self-organising. This is because government, in a diffuse network, is not at the centre, controlling all the activities of all of the bodies on the circumference, even though it is the main source of funds. The constituent organisations have a high degree of autonomy balanced by their interdepend-ency. In such a situation decision making about priorities and resource allocations will be based on the ecology heuristic as organisations attempt to balance out the various demands made upon them by other organisations in the network. It has been argued earlier that senior management in public sector hierarchies have always used the ecology heuristic, the movement from hier-archies to networks has increased the need for this heuristic.

Finally, the heuristic of return on capital employed, the heuristic of the bottom line, has become stronger in discussions about public services. This is partly a consequence of privatisation which means that more services are delivered by public companies that have to make a decent return to keep their shareholders and the City happy. But it is also a result of re-structuring within the public sector. The departments of central government which provide services (as opposed to develop policies) have increasingly been re-created as independent bodies under the Next Steps agency programme. It is an easy move from this position to require an agency to maximise its earnings from its customers so as to reduce its dependency upon central government funding. In bodies as different as the Meteorological Office, the Geological Survey and the Fire Services' College their managements have to make decisions between projects and developments on the basis of their cost and revenue effectiveness rather than on academic or professional criteria. Services such as the Customs and Excise have set up units to sell their expertise to overseas countries, especially the new states that have emerged from the collapse of the Soviet Union, and universities work hard at identifying commercially viable projects to minimise their dependence on government grants. Consequently much talk within public sector organisations is about revenue streams, cost effectiveness and the bottom line.

In summary, during the 1980s and 1990s there was a loss of faith in the ability of public officials to decide, by the use of professional judgement, computer models, cost–benefit analysis and work-measured input standards, what public services should be provided and to whom. The formal and rational methods of policy and decision making were judged inadequate for the task. The belief in the heuristics of the formal term of the dialectic became less fashionable, although it never entirely disappeared. Its place was taken by the view that government should merely create a set of rules and a structure within which the people and organisations should be free to seek their own best interest by exercising choice. In other words, the heuristics of the dialectical term which represents activity, individualism and diversity have become dominant.

The polemic

This is the stage in the chapter at which the polemic against the unfettered application of the active and diverse heuristics begins. A polemic is a controversial refutation of the opinions of others. Although I am uncertain of the extent to which I am going against the tide, given the result of the 1997 general election. On a personal level I declare myself a closet rationalist. I would like to think that the formal mechanisms of utility, individual need, fairness and of the safety net could be made to work. But they could not. Under the old system of public service that held sway in the 1960s and the 1970s the actual distribution of services was not correlated to the distribution of need; services were not delivered in a way that maximised utility; and there was not equal access to services irrespective of where people lived. Criticism of the formal heuristics does not imply that the mechanisms of the active and diverse term of the dialectic are without fault. It is arguable that whereas the values of deservingness, individual gain, diversity and choice and return on investment have become dominant in the debates, about and within the public sector, there has been a groundswell of public discontent with them.

What is the cause of this discontent with the heuristics of diversity and choice? The answer lies in the tendency of the formal heuristics to fail through incompetence whereas the heuristics of the active term fail through malice or indifference. It is often thought that to be damaged as a result of incompetence is less hurtful than to be harmed by malice or indifference. A bureaucrat whose computer algorithm was inadequate, or the professional service deliverer whose judgement turns out to be flawed, will be viewed as honest failures. At worst they will be seen as wimps. Seedhouse (1994: 132, 134), by way of illustration, seemed to show only pity for the NHS managers who are condemned, by the inadequacy of their philosophies of healthcare, to make disconnected, *ad hoc* and irrational decisions about health services forever. But a free market provider who shows bland indifference to someone's complaint will be regarded with bitterness. Similarly, a bidder to a National Lottery fund whose application has been beaten by a slickly presented and powerfully lobbied bid will feel as if they have been treated maliciously. Such appeared to be the case in the example of the failed bid for the proposed Cardiff opera house and in the way the architect of the first scheme was removed from the project (Frean and Binney 1995; Tait 1996). Mistakes caused by incompetence can be forgiven (or compensated by suing for negligence); being treated maliciously or indifferently cannot.

My claim in this polemic is not that the heuristics of personal gain, deservingness, ecology, choice and return on capital invested, always result in resource allocations that are based on indifference or malice. The problems only begin when the tensions within the heuristics allow malice or indifference to seep out. Most decisions are unaffected by these considerations or, if they are, the impact is only small. In any situation that can be defined by a probability distribution, most events will cluster around the mean. In the case of the public services the dangers emerge with the uncommon events which fall to either end of the distribution.

Some illustration of the argument is necessary. Malice can emerge from the application of the heuristics of personal gain, deservingness and ecology. Under the personal gain heuristic an individual's chance of receiving a service will depend on whether providing it would suit the provider. For example, in a system dominated by personal gain, in the form of customary gifts and payments, the system may be effective as long as the going rate for bribes is known and accepted by all and the officials receiving the pay-off are non-discriminatory in choosing from whom they will take bribes. But if such a system mutates into an unpredictable one of protection rackets and arbitrary largesse to favoured individuals, then the situation becomes intolerable. This sort of transition seems to have happened in some of the countries of the former Soviet Union where a degree of institutionalised corruption has been replaced by the criminal unpredictability and maliciousness of Mafia groups.

When the heuristic of deservingness is being applied, the service someone receives depends upon whether the potential recipients are classed as deserving or undeserving. Whether, in turn, a group is labelled as undeserving will greatly depend upon malice. This claim can be verified by considering those syndromes which are, or have been seen as, moral panics, or as manifestations of hysteria. The category includes ME (myalgic encephalomyelitis, also known as chronic fatigue syndrome or CFS), anorexia nervosa, Gulf War syndrome and recovered memory syndrome. The classification of people as undeserving is not always done according to high moral principles; it can be the result of malice against difficult people. When syndromes are not recognised as part of the medical canon of disease, the people who claim to suffer them are criticised, as inventing their own illness, and for being troublesome in their constant clamouring for attention. They exhibit all the necessary criteria for being maliciously dubbed undeserving. People pressing CFS's claim for recognition, being aware of the dangers of being labelled undeserving, seek to classify sufferers as deserving by rejecting the idea of a psychological basis of the disease. They argue that CFS is a viral infection (and its sufferers, consequently, the deserving victims of ill chance) and attack those who, they claim, maliciously fail to understand the nature of the disease (Showalter 1997: 128–9). There is a dynamic in these cases which increases the chances that those with the disease will be seen as undeserving. When their claims are initially rejected, the syndrome's propagandists respond maliciously against their critics; this causes irritation amongst the medical establishment who strengthen their criticisms, which, in turn, makes the voices of the syndrome's lobby shriller. Malice, mutually expressed, by both sides in the controversy becomes the motivating emotion behind the application of the deservingness heuristic. Some, but not of course all, of these conditions do achieve the status of a medically recognised disease; and, when they do, the claims for resourcing their treatment simply face the normal hurdles confronting any bids for funding within the NHS and the malice towards them disappears.

The example of recovered memory syndrome, and the public argument about whether it should be seen as part of a moral panic or as a genuine psychological phenomenon, can illustrate the potential for malice within the ecology heuristic. If the argument were settled, according to precepts of the ecology heuristic, the chances of the acceptance of the syndrome by doctors would depend upon influence that could be brought to bear on the gatekeepers of the medical canon. The operation of the ecology heuristic is based on the assumption that the merit of a group depends upon it taking the trouble to become well informed and to organise itself as a coherent and collaborative group. But in practice the ecological clout of groups, such as recovered memory syndrome therapists, patients and supporters, is not based on Augustan principles. The proponents and detractors are involved in emotive arguments about the incidence of child abuse and the rights of parents and others facing accusations of child abuse. Those who see recovered memory syndrome as false memory syndrome accuse recovered memory therapists of unprofessional practice. They are, in response, accused of being, or supporting, abusers (Showalter 1997: 155–6). In the memory wars, as they have been termed, the criterion of ecological merit diminishes into malice. In these struggles the ecological victory goes to the group that can muster the greatest venom in its attacks on their opponents.

Service providers who work in quasi or free markets exhibit indifference rather than malice, although its impact can be equally invidious. Market providers are, at the worst, indifferent to whom their customers are, as long as the customers buy the service; they are indifferent to what services are bought, as long as some are bought; and they are indifferent to those who cannot afford to buy a service. Market-based providers are not obliged to work for the common good. They can refuse to accept someone as a customer and they can choose which services they want to contract to supply; and they are not accountable to anyone, other than their shareholders, for these decisions. Indifference can affect how public services are delivered. In the market for nursery education, briefly created by the Conservative government's voucher scheme in 1996–7, one unanticipated consequence was a reduction in the choice of providers available to parents as schools rapidly became a dominant force in the market and threatened to drive out voluntary play groups (cf. p. 200). Other oddities can occur. For example the impact of the deregulation of bus services was often to worsen services by increasing the number of ancient and beat-up buses working the routes. Sometimes markets increase the differentials in the quality of services provided to different groups. Some people, for example, hoped that the privatisation of the rail system would lead to the creation of premier services for the business traveller with the provision of a cattle truck type of service for everyone else. In other cases, such as that of British Gas, the exploitation of a monopoly position led organisations to downsize their workforces to such a degree that they could no longer provide a reliable service to their customers. All of these instances are occasions when market-based providers showed indifference towards their customers.

The heuristics of the active and diverse term of the dialectic of public services have become dominant. This was a consequence of the formal heuristics' failure to live up to their ambition. The relative decline of holism, individual need, utility and the principle of the safety net is an aspect of the more general move in management thinking from analytical to intuitive and emergent approaches to decision making and strategic thinking (cf. chapter 2). But, as can be seen from the preceding discussion, the heuristics of diversity are not without their own problems. They can be distorted by their tendency to incorporate malice and indifference. These two stances share a common characteristic. They are both consequences of cynicism. As Nirad Chaudhuri (1987: 128) put it, 'cynicism tries to compensate for the absence of moral courage by airing malice'.

But a lack of moral courage can also be exhibited as indifference; a drawing back from responsibility to work for justice in society. The indifferent person is one who ignores questions of social justice and prefers to tend their own garden. Such cynical quietism can only be overcome by putting mechanisms in place which minimise the chances of distortion when the heuristics of diversity are being applied.

There are three areas in which changes need to be made to deal with the consequences of the, occasional, distortions within systems for allocating public resources dominated by the heuristics of diversity. They are:

- the development of *collaboration* in the networks of public service deliverers;
- the development of appropriate *controls* on the services provided;
- the development of the managerial *competencies* necessary to cope with the complexities and ambiguities of public service diversity.

Collaboration

The heuristics of the active side of the dialectic of public service provision favour diversity in the provision of public services. Allocation decisions are made by diverse individuals in different ways. Collaboration is therefore necessary in a distributed system. The NHS can once again provide an example. It is widely accepted by politicians and officials that rationing of medical treatments is inevitable (Scrivens 1979) but in the quasi-market for health services there is an issue about how rationing decisions should be made. The logic of the market would imply that local purchasers of healthcare, the GP fundholders and the health authorities, should be left to set their own priorities in the light of their local circumstances. Some might decide that they will fund particular treatments which others might not. But the health service is proclaimed as a national health service and there is a case for saying that health priorities should be decided nationally through a process of strategic planning. The argument is that local priority setting makes the range of healthcare available to any person dependent upon the lottery of geographical location and that this is an unacceptable state of affairs. In a market-based system the planning required to overcome this problem can only be based on collaboration, especially when the planning needs to be done jointly between the private sector (GPs and other private sector health providers) and public bodies such as the Department of Health and the health authorities. As Gray has concluded:

> As the nature of public–private sector relationships continues to change, it behoves public and private sector managers alike to develop the requisite skills for diagnosing when cross sectoral alliances are appropriate and advantageous mechanisms for addressing problems.
>
> (Gray 1996: 77)

Another example of the need for collaboration in distributed systems is the provision of information about train travel in the new, and highly distributed, privatised railway system. Passengers require information about their intended journeys and they are not concerned with the boundaries drawn between the responsibilities of the various organisations running the rail network. The passenger information system must be run on a collaborative basis.

There is no inherent reason why markets should not be collaborative. Brian Mawhinney, the former Conservative health minister, has said:

> market relationships in the private sector . . . are built upon partnership and long-term agreements. I believe we can learn a lot from private sector experiences in this area.
>
> (quoted in Wistow *et al.* 1996: 170)

This point of view echoes development in management theory, such as relationship marketing and partnership sourcing, which try to persuade managers that collaborative relationships in the marketplace are better than adversarial ones. But collaboration is not easy to achieve. It was reported to me by many practice managers, during a management course, that when their GPs received a copy of a glossy consultative document, describing their health authority's strategic plan, which invited them to engage in the planning process, they binned the report. Similarly, the rail regulator has had to issue threats to the rail companies to improve the performance of the passenger information service. One of the struggles of operating under the heuristics of diversity is the fight to achieve collaborative effort. Cropper (1996: 90–7) points out that collaboration can only be sustained where it creates value for those involved by:

- creating opportunities to identify and express the common purposes of distributed groups;
- institutionalising and developing channels and links between collaborating partners, for example, a partnership founded to share professional best practice (such as the M1/M69 Staff Development Network for Universities) may extend its role by jointly bidding for research and development projects;
- creating opportunities for synergy such that the partnership can achieve things that the members individually could not;
- by providing models of collaborative working that help people avoid pessimistic squabbling between sectional interests.

Control

The tendency for systems of public service delivery to distort, based on the active and expansive term of the dialectic, requires that they are held in check by some countervailing forces of control. Control may be applied by the use of standards, charters and performance league tables, by the setting up of inspection bodies, by creating rules for the regulations of markets (as in the case of GP fundholding) and service provision (e.g. the Human Fertilisation and Embryology Authority) or in the setting up of statutory regulators who check the behaviour of monopoly providers. All of these controls are concerned with the quality of public services or with the rectitude of the service providers' behaviour. But what if the problem is not the quality of service or administration but whether the resources available are being used to provide the right services to the right people? What, in other words, if the question is one of the appropriateness of a resource allocation decision?

Users of public services have only limited rights of redress if they think that a body providing public services has made a mistake in its resource allocation decisions. There are means of complaint against inadequate process and maladministration; people can appeal to ombudsmen or seek judicial review, but there is no means of having the ethical heart of a resource allocation decision reviewed. Seedhouse (1994: 4) in his book *Fortress NHS* invented a dialogue in a health authority which had appointed an organisational ethicist. Of course, few of the board members in this fictional authority understood what he said or agreed with it when they did understand it. The ethicist preferred to be called a philosopher, meaning someone who could create a rational theory within which proper decision making could take place. The title of ethicist, he felt, implied that the job holder was a moral hack, with a special expertise, that enabled him or her to give clear answers to the particular *ad hoc* ethical conundrums that appeared on management meeting agendas. But the dialogue raises the issue of whether there should be a regulatory authority which could review complaints and challenges to the resource allocation decisions made by public authorities.

How could such a regulatory body be structured and how would it work? It should not be a body with the power to overrule the decisions of other public bodies. It would be closer in role to a research organisation or think tank that publishes reports on current and difficult ethical and resource allocation questions such as: balancing the demands of road users with those of the environmental movement, the allocation of National Lottery money to good causes, or the funding of cosmetic surgery in the NHS. The questions investigated would best be identified from complaints made by the public.

There is already a public body that is close to this specification. The Audit Commission was set up by the Local Government and Housing Act of 1982 and it took on an additional responsibility for the NHS in 1990 (Jones 1996: 88). In addition to being responsible for the verification of the accounts of local authorities, health authorities and NHS trusts, it is also required to encourage the search for value for money (VFM) by these bodies. This it does in part by carrying out and publishing VFM studies. The remit of the Commission could be extended so that its concern with VFM was broadened to include the wider ethical and value considerations of resource allocation.

Competency

In a world of public service dominated by the heuristics of the active and diverse term of the dialectic, rather than those of the ordered and formal term, public officials and managers need different skills and competencies from those required of them by a bureaucratic setting. When the formal heuristics are being applied, managers and officials have a limited ethical task. They have to work out which set of values should be applied in the practice of public management. Rohr (1976) referred to this set of values as the regime values of a country and, in the case of the USA, he argued that it can be determined by studying Supreme Court decisions. Others argued that the appropriate set of values can be drawn from the application of scientific method to the study of policy options. Others again (McCreadie 1976; Reidy 1984) considered Rawls' principles of distributive justice as a basis for ethical decision making in the public services. All agreed that the ethical task is to identify a set of values that can hold sway.

When the heuristics of personal gain, deservingness, ecology, choice and return on investment are dominant, however, the nature of the public official's ethical task is different. It is to act as an ethical adjudicator between competing principles and values. It is to hold the arena within which ethical dilemmas are rehearsed. The important ethical competencies in this context are a tolerance of ambiguity and a wide range, as identified by Snell (1993), of ethical reasoning skills. The quality of managers' ethical reasoning skills is not judged by their rootedness in some overarching ethical theory but in their ability to think through tricky ethical dilemmas that arise from the malice or indifference embedded in the informal heuristics and mechanisms. I have suggested elsewhere (Fisher 1996) that the appropriate stance for a manager working in a diverse and pluralistic context is soft postmodernism. The competencies needed by a soft postmodernist manager are not the functional ones defined by the occupational lead body (which are concerned with the implementation of a clear mission and agreed core values) but the capacity for humour, irony, tolerance, and for constantly rethinking tricky issues.

In a review of public policy analysis Dryzek (1983) suggested some of the new ways of thought that public managers and officials, working in a postmodern context, need to learn. To set the scene, he pointed out that people are either gods or beasts in the ways they respond to complexity and uncertainty. Those who react in a godlike manner assume that analytical, synoptic and self-conscious thought will eventually win through, and they wait in millennial expectation for the outbreak of rationality. Those of a beastly cast of mind decide it is best to leave policy making to the irrational and unpredictable processes of organisational politics. Dryzek believed there is a middle way between that of the gods and of the beasts. The presence of plurality and conflict, he suggested, requires more cogitation rather than less; but thought of a different kind to that implied by the rationality which is fixated on the evaluation of options. He argued for:

a shift in the content of policy analysis, away from methods emphasising the assessment of pre-ordained and well-defined alternatives, and
towards policy design.

(Dryzek 1983: 345)

Policy design focuses on creativity and the contemplation of futures. In the
paper Dryzek sketched out some of the methods that policy design might use.
He defined a range of tools for thinking about policy issues, some suitable for
low degrees of uncertainty and complexity and some for those policy debates
which are mired in confusion. For topics with a relatively high degree of difficulty he suggested *design writ large*. In this approach to policy analysis the
criterion of optimisation is replaced by the yardstick of robustness.

> A robust policy alternative is one expected to perform tolerably well
> across the whole range of scenarios *given* any one of the pertinent
> theoretical perspectives. An alternative that is robust is likely to be
> sub-optimal under any given paradigm ... Its main virtue is its invul-
> nerability to the weaknesses in our understanding and to unexpected
> changes in the environment of policy.

(ibid.: 361)

Strategic thinking is the approach suggested for the issues of the highest order
of complexity, by which he meant a type of policy proposal which expands the
options open to future policy makers rather than doing things in the present
that will limit the choices open to those in the future.

To cope with the plurality of the active and informal heuristics, managers and
officials need, in summary, to develop a non-cynical postmodern stance and be
trained in ethical reasoning and policy design. This is a new agenda and challenge for management developers concerned with the public service domain.

The ending

Public services remain central to the lives of most people, especially those
living in Western and developed economies. But the people who deliver and
manage these services, professional staff, managers and politicians have never
been popular. In the 1970s when I started my first job in local government
you took care not to mention the nature of your employment in polite company.
The public's esteem of public employment has not greatly improved since then.
This contrast might be a paradox were it not in people's nature to resent that
upon which they depend. No one likes other people when they claim to know
what is best for them.

What this book has shown is that the mask of omniscience never looked
well on the faces of public officials and managers. Their claims to know what
services others needed were based on value preferences, and a flawed process

of heuristic thinking, and not upon objective, cold and rational analysis. If therefore politicians and public officials were not to be trusted to define the common good then it was necessary that the decision making gap should be filled by, either the self-organising mechanisms of the market, or by the arbitrary preferences of public professional staff. But when the forces of diversity and choice were let loose, we collectively recognised that there were some things that offended our sensibilities, and that we did share some notions of the common good. It is then we realised that the formal heuristics used by public officials and politicians (such as individual need, holism, utility, fairness and the safety net), insecure and ungrounded as they are, are necessary to prevent the grosser distortions in service provision of which markets and the heuristics of diversity are capable. The error-prone rigour of the formal heuristics, and the expansive but inequitable, nature of the heuristics and mechanisms of diversity need to be mediated by the common sense of collaboration, control and competence. This conclusion is shown diagrammatically in figure 7.1 in which it is suggested that collaboration is necessary to make quasi-markets and purchaser–provider divisions work; control is necessary to hold the ring between unfettered profit seeking and the safety net needs of the population; and, finally, a postmodern competence is required to work in the complexities of the modern world of public services.

APPENDIX
Cave rescue

Purposes

- To study 'values' in group decision making

- To practise consensus-seeking behaviour

Method

1 Any number of groups comprising 4–7 participants may be directed simultaneously

2 The facilitator distributes a copy of the cave rescue briefing sheet to each participant together with the volunteer personal details sheet

3 Five minutes are allowed to assimilate the data and then 45 minutes for discussion

4 At the end of the period one ranking sheet per group is completed and handed to the facilitator. The facilitator leads a discussion reviewing the exercise

Reproduced from 50 *Activities for Teambuilding*, Mike Woodcock, Gower, Aldershot, 1989.

Cave rescue briefing sheet

Your group is asked to take the role of a research management committee who are funding a project into human behaviour in confined spaces.

You have been called to an emergency meeting as one of the experiments has gone badly wrong.

Six volunteers have been taken into a cave system in a remote part of the country, connected only by a radio link to the research hut by the cave entrance. It was intended that the volunteers would spend four days underground but they have been trapped by falling rocks and rising water.

The only rescue team available tell you that rescue will be extremely difficult and only one person can be brought out each hour with the equipment at their disposal. It is likely that rapidly rising water will drown some of the volunteers before rescue can be effected.

The volunteers are aware of the dangers of their plight. They have contacted the research hut using the radio link and said that they are unwilling to take a decision as to the sequence by which they will be rescued. By the terms of the Research Project, the responsibility for making the decision now rests with your committee.

Life-saving equipment will arrive in 50 minutes at the cave entrance and you will need to advise the team of the order of rescue by completing the ranking sheet.

The only information you have available is drawn from the project files and is reproduced on the volunteer personal details sheet. You may use any criteria you think fit to help you make a decision.

Reproduced from 50 *Activities for Teambuilding*, Mike Woodcock, Gower, Aldershot, 1989.

Volunteer personal details sheet

Volunteer 1: Helen

Helen is 34 years old and a housewife. She has four children aged between 7 months and 8 years. Her hobbies are ice skating and cooking. She lives in a pleasant house in Gloucester, and was born in England. Helen is known to have developed a covert romantic and sexual relationship with another volunteer (Owen).

Volunteer 2: Tozo

Tozo is 19 years old and a sociology student at Keele University. She is the daughter of wealthy Japanese parents who live in Tokyo. Her father is an industrialist who is also a national authority on traditional Japanese mime theatre. Tozo is unmarried but has several high-born suitors as she is outstandingly attractive. She has recently been the subject of a TV documentary on Japanese womanhood and flower arranging.

Volunteer 3: Jobe

Jobe is a man of 41 years and was born in Central Africa. He is a minister of religion whose life work has been devoted to the social and political evolution of African peoples. Jobe is a member of the Communist Party and has had several visits to the former Soviet Union. He is married with 11 children whose ages range from 6 years to 19 years. His hobby is playing in a jazz band.

Volunteer 4: Owen

Owen is an unmarried man of 27 years. As a short-commission officer he spent part of his service in Northern Ireland where, as an undercover agent, he broke up an IRA cell and received a special commendation in dispatches. Since returning to civilian life he has been unsettled and drinking has become a persistent problem. At present he is a youth adventure leader, devoting much energy to helping young people and leading caving groups. His recreation is preparing and driving stock cars. He lives in Brecon, South Wales.

Volunteer 5: Paul

Paul is a man of 42 who has been divorced for 6 years. His ex-wife is now happily re-married. He was born in Scotland, but now lives at Richmond,

Reproduced from 50 Activities for Teambuilding, Mike Woodcock, Gower, Aldershot, 1989.

Surrey. Paul works as a medical research scientist at the Hammersmith Hospital and he is recognised as a world authority on the treatment of rabies. He has recently developed a low-cost treatment which could be self-administered. Much of the research data is still in his working note books. Unfortunately, Paul has experienced some emotional difficulties in recent years and has twice been convicted of indecent exposure. The last occasion was 11 months ago. His hobbies are classical music, opera and sailing.

Volunteer 6: Edward

Edward is a man of 59 years who has lived and worked in Barnsley for most of his life. He is general manager of a factory producing rubber belts for machines. The factory employs 71 persons. He is prominent in local society, and is a freemason and a Conservative councillor. He is married with two children who have their own families and have moved away from Barnsley. Edward has recently returned from Poland where he was personally responsible for promoting a contract to supply large numbers of industrial belts over a 5-year period. The contract, if signed, would mean work for another 25 people. Edward's hobbies include collecting antique guns and he intends to write a book about Civil War Armaments on his retirement. He is also a keen cricket supporter.

Reproduced from 50 *Activities for Teambuilding*, Mike Woodcock, Gower, Aldershot, 1989.

Ranking sheet

Order of rescue	Name
1	
2	
3	
4	
5	
6	

Reproduced from *50 Activities for Teambuilding*, Mike Woodcock, Gower, Aldershot, 1989.

BIBLIOGRAPHY

Aaronovitch, D. (1994) 'The babies in a benefit battleground', *The Guardian*, 13 September, 19.

Abercrombie, M. L. J. (1960) *The Anatomy of Judgement: An Investigation into the Processes of Perception and Reasoning*, Harmondsworth: Penguin.

Abrams, M. (1978) *Beyond Three Score Years and Ten*, London: Age Concern.

Adams, J. (1995) 'Environment: money talks', *The Guardian*, 26 April, 28.

Anthony, A. N. and Herzlinger, R. (1975) *Management Control in Non-profit Organisations*, Homewood, Illinois: Richard D. Irwin Inc.

Aristotle (1969) *The Ethics of Aristotle*, trans. J. A. K. Thompson, Harmondsworth: Penguin.

Ascher, K. (1987) *The Politics of Privatisation: Contracting out Public Services*, Basingstoke: Macmillan Educational.

Ashton, P. (1981) 'Primary teachers' approaches to personal and social behaviour', in Simon, P, and Willcocks, J. (eds) *Research and Practice in the Primary Classroom*, London: Routledge & Kegan Paul.

Aslett, C. and Powers, A. (1986) *The National Trust Book of the English House*, Harmondsworth: Penguin.

Audit Commission for Local Authorities in England and Wales (1985) *Managing Social Services for the Elderly More Effectively*, London: HMSO.

Audit Commission for Local Authorities in England and Wales and the National Health Service (1995) *Making Markets: A Review of the Audits of the Client Role for Contracted Services*, London: HMSO.

—— (1996) *What the Doctor Ordered. A Study of GP Fundholders in England and Wales*, London: HMSO.

—— (1997) *Trading Places: The Supply and Allocation of School Places*, London: Audit Commission Publications.

Bailey, S. J. (1995) *Public Sector Economics: Theory, Policy and Practice*, Basingstoke: Macmillan Press.

Baines, D. L. and Whymes, D. K. (1996) 'Selection bias in GP fundholding', *Health Economics*, 5, 2, March–April, 129–40.

Baldick, C. (1990) *The Concise Oxford Dictionary of Literary Terms*, Oxford: Oxford University Press.

Baldwin, S., Godfrey, C. and Propper, C. (eds) (1990) *Quality of Life: Perspectives and Policies*, London: Routledge.

Bale, J. (1996) 'Parents sue over failure to identify learning problem', *The Times*, 7 May, 4.

Barnett, A. (1996a) 'Gas regulator cools cuts', *The Observer*, 11 August, Business section, 3.

—— (1996b) 'Out of obscurity into the spotlight', *The Observer*, 18 August, Business section, 6.

—— (1996c) 'Bid to save private finance disaster', *The Observer*, 7 July, Business section, 6.

—— (1997a) 'So, farewell to British Gas', *The Observer*, 16 February, Business section, 8.

—— (1997b) 'British Gas to end one price for all', *The Observer*, 9 February, Business section, 1.

Barr, N. (1985) 'Economic welfare and social justice', *Journal of Society and Politics*, 14, 2, 175–87.

Barrie, C. (1995) 'Electricity takeover turmoil intensifies', *The Guardian*, 18 November, 38.

—— (1996a) 'Legal threat to keep gas flowing', *The Guardian*, 28 November, 20.

—— (1996b) 'Grid teetered as viewers switched on 10 p.m. cuppa', *The Guardian*, 2 May, 7.

Barrie, C. and Beavis, S. (1995) 'Electricity supply crisis triggers grid investigation', *The Guardian*, 5 October, City 1.

—— (1996) 'Shepherd urged to rescue TECs from a legal morass', *The Guardian*, 12 April, 18.

Barrie, C., Beavis, S. and Weston, C. (1996) 'Second front: the day they'll pull the plug', *The Guardian*, 31 December, Guardian 2, 2.

Barrie, C. and Donovan, P. (1996) 'OFT chief slates Lang over merger', *The Guardian*, 31 January, 15.

Bartlett, W. (1993) 'Quasi-markets and educational reforms', in LeGrand, J. and Bartlett, W. (eds) *Quasi-markets and Social Policy*, Basingstoke: Macmillan Press.

Bawden, F. (1996) 'Vouchers "could cut pre-schools"', *The Observer*, 16 June, 15.

Beavis, S. (1995) 'Merger of electricity and water firms "could lead to consumer ransom risk"', *The Guardian*, 8 September.

—— (1996) 'Mineowners seek end of "bias" towards gas', *The Guardian*, 26 February, 14.

Beavis, S. and Barrie, C. (1996a) 'Cabinet blocks power takeover', *The Guardian*, 25 April, 1, 2.

—— (1996b) 'Problems lurk in the gas pipeline', *The Guardian*, 2 August, 10.

Bell, A. (1995) ' The telecommunications industry 1994/5', in Vass, P. *Regulatory Review 1995*, London: Centre for the Study of Regulated Industries (CRI) and the Chartered Institute of Public Finance and Accountancy (CIPFA).

Berg, S. V. (1995) 'Regulatory developments in the USA: an overview', in Vass, P., *Regulatory Review 1995*, London: Centre for the Study of Regulated Industries (CRI) and the Chartered Institute of Public Finance and Accountancy (CIPFA).

Bernstein, R. J. (ed.) (1985) *Habermas and Modernity*, Cambridge: Polity Press in association with Oxford: Blackwell.

Betts, C. (1996) 'Contract now, pay later', *Public Finance Foundation Review*, 11, August, 6.

Billig, M. (1991) *Ideology and Opinion: Studies in Rhetorical Psychology*, London: Sage.

—— (1996) *Arguing and Thinking: A Rhetorical Approach to Social Psychology*, 2nd edn, Cambridge: Cambridge University Press.

Bjorkman, J. W. (1985) 'Equity and social policy: conceptual ambiguity in welfare criteria', *The International Journal of Sociology and Social Policy*, 5, 2, 16–32.

Blythin, P. (1983) 'Would you like to wait over there?', *Nursing Mirror*, 157, 23, December, 36–7.

Borges, J. L. (1970) *Labyrinths*, Harmondsworth: Penguin Books.

Bottery, M. (1992) *The Ethics of Educational Management: Personal, Social and Political Perspectives on School Organisation*, London: Cassell Educational.

Bourn, M. and Ezzamel, M. (1986) 'Organisational culture in the National Health Service', *Financial Accountability and Management*, 2, 3, Autumn, 203–25.

Boyd, K. M. (1979) *The Ethics of Resource Allocation in Health Care*, Edinburgh Medical Ethics Group, Moral Issues in Health Care, 2, Edinburgh: Edinburgh University Press.

Boyfield, K. (1992) 'Private sector funding of private sector infrastructure', *Public Money and Management*, 12, 2, April–June.

Bradley, A. W. Ewing, K. D. and Wade, E. C. S. (1993) *Constitutional and Administrative Law*, 11th edn, London: Longman.

Braid, M. (1994) '"Explosive ruling" on water companies', *The Independent*, 26 August, 3.

Brayne, F. L. (1945) *Better Villages*, 4th edn, Bombay: Oxford University Press.

Bright, M. (1997) 'Nurseries failing to vouch for standards', *The Observer*, 19 January, 12.

Brighton Healthcare Trust (1995) *Patient Waiting Times – Quarterly Report*, World Wide Web: http://www.pavilion.co.uk/Health services/BrightonHealthCare/perform2.htm

Brindle, D. (1993) 'Hospital "fast track" for own-budget GPs', *The Guardian*, 26 January, 7.

—— (1995) 'MPs call for firmer NHS treatment rules', *The Guardian*, 13 March, 5.

—— (1997) 'Council poised to privatise care services', *The Guardian*, 20 January, 1.

Briscoe, M. E. (1982) 'Subjective measures of well being: differences in the perception of health and social problems', *British Journal of Social Work*, 12, 137–47.

British Medical Association (BMA) (1995) *Core Values for the Medical Profession in the Twentieth Century*, London: BMA.

Brown, A. (1995) *Organisational Culture*, London: Pitman Publishing.

Brown, C. (1996) 'Civil servants spaced out by northern promise', *The Independent*, 19 April, 8.

Brown, R. G. S. (1975) *The Management of Welfare*, Glasgow: Collins.

Bruce, M. (1968) *The Coming of the Welfare State*, 4th edn, London: B. T. Batsford.

Burns, P. (1995) 'Yardstick competition in UK regulatory processes', in Vass, P. *Regulatory Review 1995*, London: Centre for the Study of Regulated Industries (CRI) and the Chartered Institute of Public Finance and Accountancy (CIPFA).

Butt, H. and Palmer, B. (1985) *Value for Money in the Public Sector*, Oxford: Basil Blackwell.

Butterworth, E. and Holman, R. (1975) *Social Welfare in Modern Britain*, Glasgow: Collins.

Carley, M. (1988) *Performance Monitoring in a Professional Public Service: The Case of the Careers Service*, PSI Research report No. 685, London: Policy Studies Institute.

Carnagham, R. and Bracewell-Milnes, B. (1993) *Testing the Market: Competitive Tendering for Government Services in Britain and Abroad*, London: Institute of Economic Affairs.

Cassell, C. (1996) 'A fatal attraction? Strategic HRM and the business case for women's progression at work', *Personnel Review*, 25, 5, 51–66.

Charter, D. (1996) 'Bill soars for voucher publicity', *The Times*, 7 May, 4.

Chartered Institute of Public Finance and Accounting (CIPFA) and the Chief Executives' Forum (1996) *27 Case Studies of CCT/Market Testing in Great Britain*, London: CIPFA.

Chaudhuri, N. C. (1987) *Thy Hand, Great Anarch! India 1921–1952*, London: Chatto and Windus.

Clarke, J. (1995) *Doing the Right Thing? Managerialism and Social Welfare*, seminar paper in the series Professionals in Late Modernity, Seminar No. 5, Power and values in public sector markets: the experience of professionals, sponsored by Cardiff Business School and the ESRC, London: Imperial College, 26 June 1995.

Clifford, T. (1985) 'There is no substitute for the real thing', *The Listener*, 114, 2919, 25 July, 19–23.

Clifton, S. (1984) 'Manipulating physiotherapy', *Health and Social Services Journal*, 19 April, 467.

Cohen, P. and Illman, J. (1995) 'Case history: no pain, no gain', *The Guardian*, 15 February, Guardian 2, 14.

Colling, T. (1993) 'Contracting public services: the management of compulsory competitive tendering in two county councils', *Human Resource Management Journal*, 3, 4, Summer, 1–15.

Collison, P. and Kennedy, J. (1985) 'Preferences for work location among social workers', *Social Policy and Administration*, 19, 1, Spring, 24–31.

Committee on Standards in Public Life (Nolan Committee) (1995a) *Summary of the Nolan Committee's First Report on Standards in Public Life*, CCTA Government Information Service, World Wide Web: http://www.hmsoinfo.gov.uk/hmso/document/nolan/nolan.htm

—— (1995b) *Issues and Questions Paper – Local Spending Bodies*, CCTA Government Information Service; World Wide Web: http://www.open.gov.uk/hmsoinfo/document/nolan/nolan.htm.

—— (1996) *Summary of the Nolan Committee's Second Report*, CCTA Government Information Service, World Wide Web: http:// www.hmsoinfo.gov.uk/hmso/document/nolan2/nolan2.htm.

Comptroller and Auditor General (1996) *Construction of Quarry House*, London: HMSO.

Creese, A. L. and Gentle, P. (1974) 'Planning in district management: use of a teaching game', *The Lancet*, 10 August, 338–40.

Cropper, S. (1996) 'Collaborative working and the issue of sustainability', in Huxham, C. (ed.) *Creating Collaborative Advantage*, London: Sage.

Culyer, A. J. (1976) *Need and the National Health Service: Economics and Social Choice*, London: Martin Robertson.

Culyer, A. J. and Wright, K. G. (eds) (1978) *Economic Aspects of Health Services*, York Studies in Economics, London: Martin Robertson.

Dallas, M. (1996) 'Accountability for performance – does audit have a role?', in *Adding Value? Audit and Accountability in the Public Services*, London: Public Finance Foundation and Chartered Institute of Public Finance and Accountancy (CIPFA).

Daniels, N. (1981) 'Health care needs and distributive justice', *Philosophy and Public Affairs*, 10, 2, 146–79.

Dasgupta, A. K. (1974) *Economic Theory and the Developing Countries*, London: Macmillan.

Dearlove, J. (1973) *The Politics of Policy in Local Government*, Cambridge: Cambridge University Press.

Deem, R. and Behony, K. J. (1993) 'Governing bodies and local education authorities: who shall inherit the earth?', *Local Government Studies*, 19, 1, Spring, 56–76.

Department for Education and Employment (1996) *Nursery Education Vouchers*, CCTA Government Information Service, World Wide Web: http://www.open.gov.uk/dfee/nursery/require/require.htm

Department of Education and Science (1983) *Curriculum 11–16: Towards a Statement of the Entitlement Curriculum. Curricular Re-appraisal in Action (The Red Book III)*, London: HMSO.

Department of the Environment (1972) *The New Local Authorities: Management and Structure (The Bains Report)*, London: HMSO.

—— (1995) *Guidance on the Conduct of Compulsory Competitive Tendering by Local Authorities*, London: Department of the Environment.

Department of Health (1989) *Working for Patients*, London: HMSO.

—— (1995) *Responsibilities and Objectives of the Department of Health*, London: Department of Health, CCTA Government Information Service, World Wide Web: http://www.open.gov.uk/

Department of Health and Social Security (1983) *The NHS Management Enquiry (The Griffiths Report)*, London: DHSS.

Department of Social Security (1989a) *Caring for People: Community Care in the Next Decade and Beyond*, London: HMSO, Cmnd 849.

—— (1989b) *Community Care: An Agenda for Action (Griffiths Report II)*, London: HMSO.

Derrida, J. with Bennington, G. (1989) 'On colleges and philosophy', in Appignanesi, L. (ed.) *Postmodernism: ICA Documents*, London: Free Association Books.

Dewey, C. (1993) *Anglo-Indian Attitudes: The Mind of the Indian Civil Service*, London: Hambledon Press.

Dillner, L. (1995) 'Doctor at large', *The Guardian*, 20 June, Guardian 2, 10.

Downes, P. (ed.) (1988) *Local Financial Management in Schools*, Oxford: Basil Blackwell.

Dryzek, J. S. (1983) 'Don't toss coins into the garbage can', *Journal of Public Policy*, 3, 4, 345–68.

DuGay, P. (1994) 'Colossal immodesties and hopeful monsters', *Organisation*, 1, 2, 125–48.

Dworkin, R. (1977) *Taking Rights Seriously*, London: Duckworth.

—— (1985) *A Matter of Principle*, London and Cambridge, Mass.: Harvard University Press.

Eastwood, A. and Maynard, A. (1990) 'Treating Aids. Is it ethical to be efficient?', in Baldwin, S., Godfrey, C. and Propper, C. (eds) *Quality of Life: Perspectives and Policies*, London: Routledge.

Eco, U. (1983) *The Name of the Rose*, trans. W. Weaver, London: Secker and Warburg.

—— (1985) *Reflections on the Name of the Rose*, trans. W. Weaver, London: Secker and Warburg.

Eco, U. with Rorty, R., Culler, J., Brooke-Rose, C. and Collini, S. (eds) (1992) *Interpretation and Overinterpretation*, Cambridge: Cambridge University Press.

The Economist (1993) 'Don't you just love being out of control?', 23 October, 69.

—— (1997) *The Economist Election Briefing*, London: *The Economist*.

Eddison, T. (1973) *Local Government: Management and Corporate Planning*, Aylesbury: Leonard Hill Books.

Eden, C., Jones, S. and Sims, D. (1979) *Thinking in Organisations*, London: Macmillan Press.

Edmonstone, J. (1982) 'Why management development hasn't worked (so far) in the NHS', *Hospital and Health Services Review*, 78, 10, November–December, 293–6.

Edmonstone, J. and Havergal, M. (1995) 'The death (and re-birth) of OD', *Health Manpower Management*, 21, 1, 28–33.

Edwards, J. T., Nalbandian, J. and Wedel, K. (1981) 'Individual values and professional education: implications for practice and education', *Administration and Society*, 13, 2, 123–43.

Eisner, E. W. (1979) 'The use of qualitative forms of evaluation for improving educational practice', *Educational Evaluation and Policy Analysis*, 1, 6, November–December, 11–19.

Elliott, J. (1991) *Action Research for Educational Change*, Milton Keynes: Open University Press.

Elliott, P. (1973) 'Professional ideology and social situation', *Sociological Review*, 21, 211–28.

Ellwood, S. (1991) 'Costing and pricing in health care', *Management Accounting*, 69, 10, November, 26–8.

Etzioni, A. (1993) *The Spirit of Community: Rights, Responsibilities and the Communitarian Agenda*, New York: Crown.

Ferlie, E. and Judge, K. (1981) 'Retrenchment and rationality in the personal social services', *Policy and Politics*, 9, 3, 311–30.

Ferlie, E., Ashburner, L., Fitzgerald, L. and Pettigrew, A. M. (1996) *The New Public Management in Action*, Oxford: Oxford University Press.

Festinger, L. (1957) *A Theory of Cognitive Dissonance*, New York: Row Peterson.

Fieldman, S. (1997) 'Insuring against illness can be a sick joke', *The Observer*, 23 March, Money Matters, 17.

Filley, A. C., House, R. J. and Kerr, S. (1976) *Managerial Process and Organisational Behaviour*, 2nd edn, Brighton: Scott Foresman and Company.

Findlay, J. N. (1970) *Hegel: A Re-examination*, London: George Allen & Unwin.

Fischer, F. (1983) 'Ethical discourse in public administration', *Administration and Society*, 15, 1, 5–42.

Fisher, C. M. (1996) 'Managerial stances: perspectives on manager development', in McGoldrick, J. and Stewart, J. (eds) *Human Resource Development: Perspectives, Strategies and Developments*, London: Pitman.

Flynn, N. (1993) *Public Sector Management*, 2nd edn, Hemel Hempstead: Harvester Wheatsheaf.

Fogg, E. (1993) 'Doctor who always calls fights for night fees: Dr. Sandy Jordan', *The Times*, 29 March, 5.

Francis, D. and Young, D. (1979) *Improving Work Groups: A Practical Manual for Team Building*, La Jolla, California: University Associates.

Frean, A. and Binney, M. (1995) 'Storm over a refusal of a lottery grant', *The Times*, 23 December, 1.

Frykenberg, R. E. (1965) *Guntur District 1788–1846: A History of Local Influence and Central Authority in South India*, Oxford: Clarendon Press.

Galton, M. and Delafield, A. (1981) 'Expectancy effects in primary classrooms', in Simons, B. and Willcocks, J. (eds) *Research and Practice in the Primary Classroom*, London: Routledge & Kegan Paul.

Gardner, M. (ed.) (1970) *The Annotated Alice: 'Alice's Adventures in Wonderland' and 'Through the Looking Glass' by Lewis Carroll*, Harmondsworth: Penguin.

Garrett, J. (1972) *The Management of Government*, Harmondsworth: Penguin.

George, P. (1985) 'Towards a two-dimensional analysis of welfare ideologies', *Social Policy and Administration*, 19, 1, Spring, 33–45.

Gibb, F. (1994) 'High Court ruling "blows hole in privatisation plan"', *The Times*, 26 August, 15.

Gibbs, G. (1996) 'Utility watchdogs "are failing public"', *The Guardian*, 29 April, 15.

Giddens, A. (1985) 'Reason without revolution? Habermas's *Theorie des kommunikativen Handelns*', in Bernstein, R. J. (ed.) *Habermas and Modernity*, Cambridge: Polity Press in association with Oxford: Blackwell.

Glennerster, H., Matsaganis, M., Owens, P. and Hancock, S. (1994) *Implementing GP Fundholding: Wild Card or Winning Hand?*, Buckingham: Open University Press

Glennerster, H., Owens, P., and Matsaganis, M. (1992) *A Foothold for Fundholding: Research Report 12*, London: King's Fund Institute.

Gosling, P. (1992) 'Contracting out in trouble', *The Independent*, 12 November, 26.

—— (1996) 'No need to axe the specialists', *The Independent*, 17 January, 18.

Gray, B. (1996) 'Cross-sectoral partners: collaborative alliances among business, government and communities', in Huxham, C. (ed.) *Creating Collaborative Advantage*, London: Sage.

Gray, J. A. M. (1997) *Evidence-based Healthcare*, Edinburgh: Churchill Livingstone.

Gregory, R. (1987) *The Oxford Companion to the Mind*, Oxford: Oxford University Press.

The Guardian (1996) 'The rich will vouch for vouchers', *The Guardian* 23 January, leading article.

Gudex, C. (1986) *QALYs and their Use by the Health Service*, Discussion paper No. 20, York: Centre for Health Economics, University of York.

Handy, C. *Understanding Organisations*, 3rd edn, Harmondsworth: Penguin.

Harper, K., Wolf, J. and Milne, S. (1994) 'Euro-court extends UK workers' rights', *The Guardian*, 9 June, 2.

Harrison, B., Smith, C. and Davies, B. (1992) *Introductory Economics*, London: Macmillan.

Harrison, M. (1997) 'Inquiry into how public lost £300. on gravy train', *The Independent*, 6 January, 1.

Harrison, R. (1972) 'How to describe your organisation', *Harvard Business Review*, 50, 3, May–June, 119–28.

Harrison, S. (1986) 'Management culture and management budgets', *Hospital and Health Services Review*, 82, 1, January, 43–6.

Hart, D. (1974) 'Social equity: justice and the equitable administrator', *Public Administration Review*, 34, 1, January–February, 3–10.

—— (1983) 'The honorable bureaucrat among the Philistines', *Administration and Society*, 15, 1, 43–8.

Hart, D. and Scott, W. (1973) 'Administrative crisis: the neglect of metaphysical speculation', *Public Administration Review*, 33, 5, September–October, 415–27.

Harvey, D. (1989) *The Condition of Postmodernity: An Enquiry into the Origins of Cultural Change*, Oxford: Basil Blackwell.

Heclo, H. and Wildavsky, A. (1981) *The Private Government of Public Money: Community and Policy inside British Politics*, 2nd edn, London: Macmillan.

Hegel, G. W. F. (1952) *Philosophy of Right*, trans. T. M. Knox, Oxford: Clarendon Press.

Hepworth, N. (1995) 'Fraud and corruption', *Public Money and Management*, 15, 1, January–March, 4–6.

Hetherington, P. (1996) 'EU may ask for return of funds in rail sell-off', *The Guardian*, 29 April, 5.

Hickson, D., Hinings, C., Lee, C., Schneck, R. and Pennings, J. (1971) 'A strategic contingency theory of intra-organisational power', *The Administrative Science Quarterly*, 16, 216–29.

Hodge, J. (1990) 'The quality of life: a contrast between utilitarian and existentialist approaches', in Baldwin, S., Godfrey, C. and Propper, C. (eds) *Quality of Life: Perspectives and Policies*, London: Routledge.

Hodgkinson, M. (1996) 'An historical and strategic analysis of education catering in England and Wales', unpublished PhD thesis, The Nottingham Trent University.

Hogarth, R. (1980) *Judgement and Choice*, New York: John Wiley and Sons.

Hood, C. and Jackson, M. (1991) *Administrative Argument*, Aldershot: Dartmouth.

Houlihan, B. (1983) 'The professionalisation of housing policy making: the impact of housing investment programmes and professionals', *Public Administration Bulletin*, 41, April, 14–31.

Howe, L. E. A. (1985) 'The deserving and the undeserving: practice in an urban local social security office', *Journal of Social Policy*, 14, 1, 49–72.

Hugill, B. (1995) 'Poor students warned to forget about Oxford', *The Observer*, 11 June, 1.

Hulme, G. (1996) 'Public expenditure bulletin: financial rectitude just around the corner?', *Public Finance Foundation Review*, 11, August, 7–9.

Hunter, D. J. (1979) 'Coping with uncertainty: decisions and resources within health authorities', *Sociology of Health and Illness*, 1, 1, 40–68.

—— (1984) 'Consensus management or chief executives? Lessons from the NHS', *Local Government Studies*, 10, 3, May–June, 39–50.

Huxham, C. (ed.) (1996) *Creating Collaborative Advantage*, London: Sage.

Institute of Municipal Treasurers and Accountants (IMTA) (1969) *Cost Benefit Analysis in Local Government*, London: IMTA.

—— (1972) *Output Measurement Discussion Papers: 1. Housing, 2. Personal Social Services, 3. Public Protection, 4. Environment, 5. Leisure, 6. Transportation*, London: IMTA.

Jackson, C. (1993) 'Lessons in talking business', *Health Visitor*, 66, 10, October, 352.

Jackson, W. E. (1969) *Local Government in England and Wales*, Harmondsworth: Penguin Books.

Jacques, D. (1992) 'Self-appraisal: problems and insights', conference presentation at *Appraisal: Implications for Academic Staff Development in Higher Education*, organised by the Standing Conference on Educational Development (SCED) and Derbyshire College of Higher Education.

Jasmin, A. (1981) 'Teachers' assessments in classroom research', in Simon, B. and Willcocks, J. *Research and Practice in the Primary Classroom*, London: Routledge & Kegan Paul.

Jenkinson, V. (1981) 'Measuring the quality of nursing care – can it ever be assured?', conference paper, London: Kings' Fund Centre.

Jick, T. D. and Murray, V.V. (1982) 'The management of hard times: budget cutbacks in public sector organisations', *Organisation Studies*, 3, 2, 141–69.

Johnson, G. and Scholes, K. (1993) *Exploring Corporate Strategy*, 3rd edn, London: Prentice-Hall.

Jones, B. (1996) *Financial Management in the Public Sector*, London: McGraw-Hill.

Jones, J. (1992) 'Health chiefs reject Thorpe's claims over veto on treatment', *The Independent*, 25 January, 4.

—— (1993) 'NHS set to abandon drinkers and smokers', *The Observer*, 7 November, 1.

Jones, J. E. and Pfeiffer, J. W. (eds) (1974) *The 1974 Handbook for Group Facilitators*, Iowa City: University Associates.

Joseph, K. (1975) 'The cycle of deprivation', in Butterworth, E. and Holmes, R. (eds) *Social Welfare in Modern Britain*, Glasgow: Collins.

Joss, R. and Kogan, M. (1995) *Advancing Quality: Total Quality Management in the National Health Service*, Buckingham: Open University Press.

Judd, J. (1997) 'Healthy school dinners – chips with everything as long as they're not crinkle cut', *The Independent*, 26 February, 4.

Kahneman, D., Slovic, P. and Tversky, A. (eds) (1982) *Judgement under Uncertainty: Heuristics and Biases*, Cambridge: Cambridge University Press.

Kahneman, D. and Tversky, A. (1982) 'The psychology of preferences', *Scientific American*, January, 136–50.

Kakabadse, A. (1982) *Culture of the Social Services*, Aldershot: Gower.

Kemm, J. R. (1985) 'Ethics of food policy', *Community Medicine*, 7, 289–94.

Kerblay, B. (1971) 'Chayanov and the theory of peasantry as a specific type of economy', in Shanin, T. (ed.) *Peasants and Peasant Societies*, Harmondsworth: Penguin.

Kerr, J. H. (1962) 'Selected paras. concerning survey and settlement operations in Darbhanga District (1896–1903)', *The Journal of the Bihar Research Society*, Vol. 48, parts I–IV.

Kingston, P. (1996) 'Education: schools still saddled with those bits of paper', *The Guardian*, 5 November, Education Guardian, 3.

Kirchenbaum, H. (1977) *Advanced Value Clarification*, La Jolla, California: University Associates.

Kirk, G. S. (1976) *The Nature of the Greek Myths*, Harmondsworth: Penguin.

Klein, R. (1982) 'Reflections of an ex-AHA Member', *British Medical Journal*, 27 March.

Klein, R., Day, P. and Redmayne, S. (1996) *Managing Scarcity: Priority Setting and Rationing in the National Health Service*, Buckingham: Open University Press.

Knight, B. (1973) *Managing School Finances*, London: Heinemann.

Kochen, M. and Deutsch, K. W. (1980) *Decentralisation: Sketches towards a Rational Theory*, Cambridge, Mass.: Oelgesachlager, Gunn and Hain.

Kouzes, J. M. and Mico, P. R. (1979) 'Domain theory: an introduction to organisational behaviour in human service organisations', *Journal of Applied Behavioural Science*, 15, 4, October/November/December, 449–69.

Kuhn, T. (1970) *The Structure of Scientific Revolutions*, 2nd edn, London: The University of Chicago Press.

Laffin, M. (1986) *Professionalism and Policy: The Role of Professions in the Central–Local Government Relationship*, Aldershot: Gower.

Laffin, M. and Young, K. (1985) 'The changing role and responsibilities of local authority chief officers', *Public Administration*, 63, 1, Spring, 41–60.

Lambert, J., Paris, C. and Blackaby, R. (1978) *Housing Policy and the State: Allocation, Access and Control*, London: Macmillan.

Lane, J.-E., (1993) *The Public Sector: Concepts, Models and Approaches*, London: Sage.

—— (1995) *The Public Sector: Concepts, Models and Approaches*, 2nd edn, London: Sage.

Langford, D. A. (1982) *Direct Labour Organisations in the Construction Industry*, Aldershot: Gower Publishing.

Lascelles, D. (1995) 'The electricity industry 1994/5', in Vass, P. *Regulatory Review 1995*, London: Centre for the Study of Regulated Industries (CRI) and the Chartered Institute of Public Finance and Accountancy (CIPFA).

Laurance, J. (1993a) 'Doctors must not play God', *The Times*, 8 November, 5.

—— (1993b) 'Hospital surgeons accused of running a private fees cartel', *The Times*, 14 July, 5.

Lawson Dick, O. (ed.) (1972) *Aubrey's Brief Lives*, Harmondsworth: Penguin Books.

Leach, E. (1970) *Lévi-Strauss*, London: Collins.

Leach, S. (1982) 'In defence of the rational model', in Leach. S. and Stewart, J. (eds) *Approaches in Public Policy*, Institute of Local Government Studies, London: George Allen and Unwin.

Leach. S. and Stewart, J. (eds) (1982) *Approaches in Public Policy*, Institute of Local Government Studies, London: George Allen and Unwin.

Legge, K. (1995) *Human Resource Management: Rhetoric and Realities*, Basingstoke: Macmillan Business.

LeGrand, J. (1984) 'Equity as an economic objective', *Journal of Applied Philosophy*, 1, 1, 39–54.

—— (1987) 'Equity, health and health care', in *Three Essays on Equity*, London: The SunTory Toyota International Centre for Economics and Related Disciplines, Welfare State Project, Discussion paper No. 23, London School of Economics.

—— (1991) *Equity and Choice: An Essay in Economics and Applied Philosophy*, London: HarperCollins Academic.

LeGrand, J. and Bartlett, W. (1993) (eds) *Quasi-markets and Social Policy*, Basingstoke: Macmillan Press.

Levacic, R. (1991) 'Markets and government: an overview', in Thompson, G., Frances, J., Levacic, R. and Mitchell, J., *Markets, Hierarchies and Networks: The Coordination of Social Life*, London: Sage.

Levin, H. (1960) *James Joyce: A Critical Introduction*, 2nd edn, London: Faber and Faber.

Lewin, L. C. (1968) *Report from Iron Mountain on the Possibility and Desirability of Peace*, London: Macdonald.

Lewis, J. (1975) 'Variations in service provision: politics at the lay–professional interface', in Young, K. (ed.) *Essays on the Study of Urban Politics*, London: Macmillan.

Library Association (1996) *Mission Statement*, Library Association home page, World Wide Web: http://www.fdggroup.co.uk/la.htm

Lindblom, C. (1959) 'The science of muddling through', *Public Administration Review*, 7, 2, 70–88.

—— (1979) 'Still muddling, not through yet', *Public Administration Review*, 9, Spring, 517–26.

Local Authorities Management Services and Computers Committee (LAMSAC) (1977) *Quantitative Methods for Use in Local Government: A Report of the O and M and Productivity Panels*, London: LAMSAC.

Local Government Management Board (1989) *Managing the Enabling Authority*, Luton: Local Government Management Board.

Luckham, B. (1971) *The Library in Society*, London: Library Association.

Mabbott, J. D. (1967) *The State and the Citizen*, 2nd edn, London: Hutchinson and Co.

Madhok, R. (1995) 'Equitable service provision: a feasibility study of the common waiting lists model', *International Journal of Healthcare Quality Assurance*, 7, 1.

Maine, H. (1881) *Village-Communities in the East and West*, 4th edn, London: John Murray.

MacBeath, J. E. C. (ed.) (1976) *A Question of Schooling*, London: Hodder and Stoughton.

McCarthy, U. (1995) *The Private Finance Initiative: Policy and Practice*, London: Chartered Institute of Public Finance and Accountancy (CIPFA).

McClean, A. and Marshall, J. (1991) *Cultures at Work: How to Identify and Understand Them*, Luton: Local Government Management Board.

McCreadie, C. (1976) 'Rawlsian justice and the financing of the National Health Service', *Journal of Social Policy*, 5, 2, 113–31.

McIntosh, I. and Young, M. (1990) *Over-75s Assessment Checklist*, Orpington: Geriatric Medicine.

Mackenzie, W. J. M. (1967) *Politics and Social Science*, Harmondsworth: Penguin.

Mackie, J. L. (1977) *Ethics: Inventing Right and Wrong*, London: Penguin Books.

MacLeod, D. (1996a) 'Poor are victors in voucher battle', *The Guardian*, 9 July, 6.

—— (1996b) 'Voucher schemes for 3 year olds', *The Guardian*, 17 April, 9.

McNulty, T. (1990) 'Organisation, cultures and organisational change in the NHS: case studies in one district health authority', unpublished PhD thesis, Nottingham: Nottingham Polytechnic.

Mailly, R. (1986) 'The impact of contracting out in the NHS', *Employment Review*, 8, 1, 10–16.

March, J. G., Cohen, M. D. and Olsen, J. P. (1972) 'A garbage can model of organisational decision making', *Administrative Science Quarterly*, 17, 1–25.

Mayo, K. (1927) *Mother India*, London: Jonathan Cape.

Mays, N. and Bevan, G. (1987) *Resource Allocation in the Health Service: A Review of the Methods of the Resource Allocation Working Party (RAWP)*, Occasional Papers on Social Administration No. 81, London: Bedford Square Press.

Meadows, J. (1986) 'Local health service resource allocation and planning', *Public Finance and Accountancy*, 7 November, 17–19.

Midgeley, C., Ashworth, J. and Newton, P. (1997) 'Outrage at "fat cat" lottery pay rises', *The Times* 29 May, 1.

Mihil, C. (1990) 'Thatcher shuns out of court deal for haemophiliacs with HIV', *The Guardian*, 9 November, 2.

—— (1993) 'No treatment ban on smokers', *The Guardian* 18 August, 2.

Miller, N. and Munn-Giddings, C. (1993) *Whose Need is it Anyway?*, ESSRG Working Paper, West Bergholt: Social Services Research Group (Eastern Region).

Mills, H. and Bright, M. (1996) 'Poverty "making children shorter"', *The Observer*, 11 August, 1.

Mintzberg, H. (1979) ' An emerging strategy of "direct research"', *Administrative Science Quarterly*, 24, December, 582–9.

—— (1987) 'Crafting strategy', *Harvard Business Review*, 87, 4, July–August, 66–75.

—— (1994) *The Rise and Fall of Strategic Planning*, Hemel Hempstead: Prentice Hall International.

Moore, P. G. (1980) *Reason by Numbers*, Harmondsworth: Penguin.

Mortished, C. (1996) 'Take or pay day', *The Times*, 13 September, 26.

Muchnick, D. (1971) *The Politics of Urban Redevelopment*, London: Bell.

Myres, J. N. L. (1986) *The English Settlements*, Oxford: Oxford University Press.

Naipaul, V. S. (1967) *An Area of Darkness*, Harmondsworth: Penguin Books.

National Association of Health Authorities and Trusts (NAHAT) (1996) *Small Steps, Big Goals*, Birmingham: NAHAT.

NHS Training Authority (NHSTA) (1986) *Better Management, Better Health*, Wootton-under-Edge: NHSTA.

Nivola, P. S. (1978) 'Distributing a municipal service: a case study of housing inspection', *Journal of Politics*, 40, 39–81.

Nottingham Health Commission (n.d.) *The Nottingham Total Commissioning Project*, Nottingham: Nottingham Health.

Nuki, P. (1993) 'Inquiry finds evidence of price "fixing" in health care', *The Sunday Times*, 29 August, 4/1.

Office for National Statistics (n.d.) *The UK in Figures*, CCTA Government Information Service, World Wide Web: http://www.open.gov.uk/

O'Leary, J. (1997) 'Union tells teachers to inform on parents using vouchers', *The Guardian*, 13 January, 4.

Oppenheim, A. N. (1966) *Questionnaire Design and Attitude Measurement*, London: Heinemann.

Oppenheimer, J. A. (1985) 'Public choice and three ethical properties of politics', *Public Choice*, 45, 241–55.

Ouchi, W. G. (1980) 'Markets, bureaucracies and clans', *Administrative Science Quarterly*, 25, 129–41.

Padley, G. A. (1985) *Grammatical Theory in Western Europe*, Cambridge: Cambridge University Press.

Parker, D. (1988) *The 1988 Local Government Act and CCT*, Cranfield School of Management Working Paper, Cranfield: Cranfield School of Management.

Parmar, M. and Hewitt, E. (1985) 'Triage on trial', *Senior Nurse*, 2, 5, February, 21–2.

Pascale, R. (1990) *Managing on the Edge*, London: Penguin Books.

Pereira, J. (1989) *What Does Equity in Health Mean?*, Centre for Health Economics, discussion paper No. 61, York: Centre for Health Economics.

Peters, T. J. and Waterman Jr, R. (1982) *In Search of Excellence*, New York: Harper & Row.

Pettigrew, A. M. (1973) *The Politics of Organisational Decision Making*, London: Tavistock.

Pilkington, E. (1994) 'GPs are told to explain list cuts', *The Guardian*, 18 November, 10.

—— (1995) 'Health "rationing" dilemma worsens', *The Guardian*, 27 October, 6.

Pinkus, C. E. and Dixson, A. (1981) *Solving Local Government Problems: Practical Approaches to Operational Research in Cities and Regions*, London: George Allen and Unwin.

Plato (1970) *The Laws*, trans. H. Saunders, Harmondsworth: Penguin Books.

Pollitt, C. (1985) 'Measuring performance: a new system for the National Health Service', *Policy and Politics*, 13, 1–15.

—— (1993) *Managerialism and the Public Services*, Oxford: Blackwell.

Porphyrios, D. (1989) 'Architecture and the postmodern condition', in Appignanesi, L. (ed.) *Postmodernism: ICA Documents*, London: Free Association Books.

Powell, J. E. (1966) *Medicine and Politics*, London: Pitman.

Price, C. (1994) 'Gas regulation and competition: substitutes or complements', in Bishop, M., Kay, J. and Mayer, C. (eds) *Privatisation and Economic Performance*, Oxford: Oxford University Press.

Price, C. W. (1996) 'The future of regulation', in Jackson, P. and Lavender, M. (eds) *Public Services Yearbook 1996–7*, London: Pitman Publishing.

Quintilian (1986) *The Institutes of Oratory*, Vol. 3, trans. H. E. Butler, Cambridge, Mass. and London: Harvard University Press and William Heinemann.

Ranade, W. (1985) 'Motives and behaviour in district health authorities', *Public Administration*, 63, Summer, 183–200.

Rawls, J. (1972) *A Theory of Justice*, Oxford: Clarendon Press.

Redcliffe-Maud, J. and Wood, B. (1974) *English Local Government Reformed*, London: Oxford University Press.

Reed, M. I. (1992) *The Sociology of Organisations: Themes, Perspectives and Prospects*, London: Harvester Wheatsheaf.

Reeves, M. (1988) *The Crisis in Higher Education: Competence, Delight and the Common Good*, Milton Keynes: Open University Press and the Society for Research into Higher Education (SRHE).

Reidy, A. (1984) 'Social justice and social policy', *Social Policy and Administration*, 18, 1, Spring, 27–40.

Rhodes, R. A. W. (1988) *Beyond Westminster and Whitehall*, London: Unwin-Hyman.

—— (1995) *The New Governance: Governing without Government*, seminar paper presented 10 January in the 'The State of Britain' seminar series sponsored by the Economic and Social Research Council (ESRC), Royal Society for the Encouragement of Arts, Manufactures & Commerce (RSA) and Touche Ross.

Ridley, F. F. (1995) 'Competition for quality: performance indicators and reinventing government', in Jackson, P. M. (ed.) *Measures for Success in the Public Sector: A Public Finance Foundation Reader*, London: Chartered Institute of Public Finance and Accountancy.

Riggs, S. A. (1996) 'Managing to practice: managing to change? An exploration of general medical practitioners' orientations to work', unpublished PhD thesis, the Nottingham Trent University.

Roach, P. J. M., Flemming, C., Hagen, M. D. and Parker, S. G. (1988) 'Prostatic cancer in a patient with a symptomatic HIV infection', *Medical Decision Making*, 8, 2, B2–4.

Rogers, L. (1993) 'Hospitals refuse to operate on heart patients who smoke', *Sunday Times*, 23 May, 1.

Rohr, J. (1976) 'The study of ethics in the public administration curriculum', *Public Administration Review*, 36, 4, July–August, 398–406.

Rokeach, M. (1973) *The Nature of Human Values*, New York: Free Press.

Rorty, R. (1985) 'Habermas and Lyotard on postmodernity', in Bernstein, R. J. (ed.) *Habermas and Modernity*, Cambridge: Polity Press in association with Oxford: Blackwell.

—— (1992) 'Richard Rorty interviewed by Marc Uzan', *The Guardian*, 13 March.

Rose, D. (1993) 'Bar Council in attack on Mills', *The Observer*, 31 October, 1 and 3.

Royal College of Nursing (RCN) (1986) *Feeling Better: Getting Better*, London: RCN.

Runciman, S. (1966) *Relative Deprivation and Social Justice: A Study of Attitudes to Social Inequality in Twentieth Century England*, London: Routledge & Kegan Paul.

Rushcliffe Borough Council (1996) *Rushcliffe Reports*, West Bridgford, Nottingham: Rushcliffe Borough Council.

Rushton, A. and Briscoe, M. E. (1981) 'Social work as an aspect of primary health care', *British Journal of Social Work*, 11, 61–76.

Russell, J. B. (1985) *The Devil in the Middle Ages*, Cornell: Cornell University Press.

Samuel, R. (1981) *East End Underworld: Chapters in the Life of Arthur Harding*, Routledge & Kegan Paul.

Schama, S. (1995) *Landscape and Memory*, London: HarperCollins.

Scrivens, E. (1979) 'Towards a theory of rationing', *Social Policy and Administration*, 13, 1, Spring, 53–64.

Seedhouse, D. (1994) *Fortress NHS: A Philosophical Review of the National Health Service*, Chichester: John Wiley and Sons.

Sekuler, R. and Blake, R. (1994) *Perception*, 3rd edn, London: McGraw-Hill.

Settlements (Energy Settlements and Information Services Ltd) (n.d.) *Right on Time*, Nottingham: Settlements.

Showalter, E. (1997) *Hystories: Hysteria: Hysterical Epidemics and Modern Culture*, London: Picador.

Silverman, D. (1993) *Interpreting Qualitative Data: Methods for Analysing Talk, Text and Interaction*, London: Sage.

Simon, H. (1983) *Reason in Human Affairs*, Oxford: Basil Blackwell.

Simons, B. and Willcocks J. (eds) (1981) *Research and Practice in the Primary Classroom*, London: Routledge & Kegan Paul.

Smircich, L. (1983) 'Concepts of culture and organisational analysis', *Administrative Science Quarterly*, 28, 339–58.

Smith, A. and Cannan, E. (eds) (1993) *An Inquiry into the Nature and Causes of the Wealth of Nations*, New York: Modern Library.

Smith, G. and Cantley, C. (1985) *Assessing Health Care: A Study in Organisational Evaluation*, Milton Keynes: Open University Press.

Smith, J. (1995) 'Water services 1994/95 – a watershed year', in Vass, P., *Regulatory Review 1995,* London: Centre for the Study of Regulated Industries (CRI) and the Chartered Institute of Public Finance and Accountancy (CIPFA).

Smith, L. F. P. and Morrissy, J. R. (1994) 'Ethical dilemmas for general practitioners under the UK new contract', *Journal of Medical Ethics*, 20, 175–80.

Smith, M. (1977) *A Practical Guide to Value Clarification*, La Jolla, California: University Associates.

Smith, R. (1993) 'Purchasing in practice', *Health Services Journal*, 103, 5346, 1 April, 28–9.

Smithers, R. (1996) 'Nursery voucher scheme "a failure" ', *The Guardian*, 8 November, 12.

Snell, R. (1993) *Developing Skills for Ethical Management*, London: Chapman and Hall.

Spring, P. (1995) 'The restructured gas industry', in Vass, P. *Regulatory Review 1995*, London: Centre for the Study of Regulated Industries (CRI) and the Chartered Institute of Public Finance and Accountancy (CIPFA).

Stewart, D. W. (1984) 'Managing competing claims: an ethical framework for human resource decision making', *Public Administration Review*, 44, 1, January–February, 14–22.

Stewart, J. (1971) *Management in Local Government: A Viewpoint*, London: Charles Knight.

—— (1983) *Local Government: The Conditions of Choice*, London: George Allen and Unwin and the Institute of Local Government Studies (INLOGOV).

Stewart, J., Spencer, K. M. and Webster, B. A. (1976) *Local Government: Approaches to Urban Deprivation*, Home Office Urban Deprivation Unit, London: HMSO.

Stewart, M. (1996) 'Competition and competitiveness in urban policy', *Public Money and Management*, 16, 3, July–September, 21–6.

Stewart, M. and Taylor, M. (1995) *Empowerment and Estate Regeneration: A Critical Review*, Bristol: Policy Press.

Stewart, R., Smith, P., Blake, J. and Wingate, P. (1980) *The District Administrator in the NHS*, London: King Edward's Hospital Fund for London.

Stokes, E. (1959) *The English Utilitarians and India*, Oxford: Clarendon Press.

Stoten, B. (1982) 'Planning health care services', in Leach, S. and Stewart, J. (eds) *Approaches in Public Policy*, Institute of Local Government Studies, London: George Allen and Unwin.

Stretton, H. and Orchard, L. (1994) *Public Goods, Public Enterprise, Public Choice*, Basingstoke: Macmillan.

Strong, R. (1985) 'Let's put a stop to museum imperialism', *The Listener*, 114, 2919, 25 July, 17–18.

Swales, J. and Rogers, P. S. (1995) 'Discourse and the projection of corporate culture: the mission statement', *Discourse and Society*, 6, 2, April, 223–42.

Tait, M. (1996) '. . . and fresh hopes in Wales', *The Times*, 11 September, 35.

Teeling-Smith, G. (1985) *Measurement of Health*, Studies of Current Health Problems No. 77, London: Office of Health Economics.

Terry, F. (1994) 'Who needs regulation in business?', unpublished inaugural professorial lecture, Nottingham Business School, the Nottingham Trent University.

—— (1996) 'Private finance initiative: before and after', *Public Finance Foundation Review*, 11, August, 2–4.

Thain, C. and Wright, M. (1988) 'Public expenditure in the UK since 1976: still "private government of public money"?', *Public Policy and Administration*, 3, 1, 1–18.

The Rough Guide (1996) *Britain*, London: The Rough Guide Ltd.

Thomas, R. (1996) 'Dorrell plans personal insurance route for elderly care', *The Guardian*, 8 May, 1.

Thompson, D. (1983) 'Perception, power and responsibility in management development: a study of the implications for change in the NHS', *Management Education and Development*, 14, 3.

—— (1986) 'Coalitions in the National Health Service: handling conflicting needs and pressures', paper presented to the Annual Conference of the European Association of Programmes in Health Services Studies, Bregenz, Austria, 10–13 June.

Thompson, D. J. (1967) *Organisations in Action*, New York: McGraw-Hill.

Thompson, G., Frances, J., Lavacic, R. and Mitchell, J. (1991) *Markets, Hierarchies and Networks: The Coordination of Social Life*, London: Sage.

Tickell, O. (1995) 'Accelerating on the road to a fiasco', *The Times*, 29 July, 8.

Tieman, R. (1996) 'Suppliers say Transco are overcharging them', *The Times*, 5 April, 23.

Times Literary Supplement (1986) *Correspondence on Disease and the Novel*, letters pages, 4322, 31 January, 4324, 14 February, 4326, 28 February, 4329, 21 March.

Titmus, R. (1963) *Essays on the Welfare State*, 2nd edn, London: George Allen and Unwin.

Trinder, C. (1995) 'Pay and employment trends in UK regulated industries', in Vass, P. *Regulatory Review 1995*, London: Centre for the Study of Regulated Industries (CRI) and the Chartered Institute of Public Finance and Accountancy (CIPFA).

Tuckman, B. W. (1965) 'Developmental sequences in small groups', *Psychological Bulletin*, 63, 6.

Tullock, G. (1996) 'Rent seeking in the interior', in Muscatelli, V. A. (ed.) *Economic and Political Institutions in Economic Policy*, Manchester: Manchester University Press.

Tversky, A. and Kahneman, D. (1982) 'Evidential impact of base rates', in Kahneman, D., Slovic, P. and Tversky, A. (eds) *Judgement under Uncertainty: Heuristics and Biases*, Cambridge: Cambridge University Press.

Vass, P. (1992) 'Regulated public services industries', in Terry, F. and Jackson, P. (eds) *Public Domain: The Public Services' Yearbook*, London: Public Finance Foundation.

—— (1996) 'Regulated industries', in Jackson, P. and Lavender, M. (eds) *Public Services Yearbook 1996–7*, London: Pitman Publishing.

—— (1997) 'Regulated industries', in Jackson, P. and Lavender, M. (eds) *Public Services Yearbook 1997–8*, London: Pitman Publishing.

Vickers, G. (1981) 'The poverty of problem solving', *Journal of Applied Systems Analysis*, 8, 15–21.

Victor, P. and Penman, D. (1995) 'New NHS-speak has no word for compassion', *The Independent on Sunday*, 12 March, 3.

Waddington, C. H. (1977) *Tools for Thought*, St Albans: Paladin Granada Publishing.

Wainwright, M. (1997) 'Ayckbourn wins Scarborough's "luvvies versus the lavvies" battle', *The Guardian*, 7 January, 8.

Waldron, J. (1985) 'Rights and trade-offs', *Times Literary Supplement*, 4310, 8 November, 1269–70.

Walker, C. and Smith, A. J. (1995) *Privatised Infrastructure: The Build-Operate-Transfer Approach*, London: Thomas Telford Publications.

Walker, M. (1995) 'Profile: a community spirit', *The Guardian*, 13 March, 10.

Washbrook, D. A. and Baker, C. J. (1975) *South India: Political Institutions and Political Change 1880–1940*, Bombay: The Macmillan Co. of India.

Watson, T. J. (1977) *The Personnel Managers: A Study in the Sociology of Work*, London: Routledge & Kegan Paul.

—— (1993) *Rhetoric, Strategic Exchange and Organisational Change*, paper to the 11th EGOS Colloquium, The Production and Diffusion of Managerial Knowledge, Paris: July 1993.

—— (1994a) *In Search of Management: Culture Chaos and Control in Management*, London: Routledge.

—— (1994b) 'Professing postmodernism: soft postmodernist thoughts on education and management', unpublished inaugural professorial lecture, Nottingham Business School, the Nottingham Trent University.

—— (1995) *Sociology, Work and Industry*, 3rd edn, London: Routledge.

Webb, B. and Stimson, G. (1976) 'People's accounts of medical encounters', in Wadsworth, M. (ed.) *Everyday Medical Life*, London: Martin Robertson.

Webster, B. (1982) 'The distributional effects of local government services', in Leach, S. and Stewart, J. (eds) *Approaches in Public Policy*, Institute of Local Government Studies, London: George Allen and Unwin.

Weiner, J. P. and Ferriss, D. M. (1990) *GP Budget Holding in the UK: Lessons from America*, King Edward's Hospital Fund for London, Research report No. 7, London: King's Fund Institute.

Weiner, M. (1962) *The Politics of Scarcity: Public Pressure and Political Response in India*, Chicago and London: University of Chicago Press.

Westlake, B. and Beckett, R. (1995) 'A REC's view of the OFFER distribution review', *Public Money and Management*, 15, 3, July–September, 45–52.

Weston, C. and Beavis, S. (1996) 'Gas pay out plan to avoid power cuts', *The Guardian*, 18 November, 17.

White, P. (1987) 'Self respect and self esteem and the management of educational institutions: a question of values', *Educational Management and Administration*, 15, 85–91.

White, P. (1996) 'Road passenger transport and deregulation', in Terry, F. (ed.) *Transport in Transition: A Public Finance Foundation Reader*, London: Chartered Institute of Public Finance and Accountancy.

Whitmore, R. and Fuller, R. (1980) 'Priority planning in an area social services team', *British Journal of Social Work*, 10, 3, 277–92.

Williams, A. (1972) ' Cost benefit analysis: bastard science? And/or insidious poison in the body politic?', *Journal of Public Economics*, 1, 2, August.

—— (1985) *Performance Management in the Public Sector: Paving the Road to Hell*, the Seventh Arthur Young Lecture, Department of Accountancy, University of Glasgow.

Willis, L. D. and Linwood, M. E. (1984) *Measuring the Quality of Care*, Edinburgh: Churchill Livingstone.

Winstanley, D., Sorabji, D. and Dawson, S. (1995) 'When the pieces don't fit: a stakeholder power matrix to analyse public sector restructuring', *Public Money and Management*, 15, 2, April–June, 19–26.

Wintour, P. (1991) 'Minister rejects AIDS payout', *The Guardian*, 30 November, 3, 19–26.

—— (1995) 'Division of responsibility that puts politicians in the dock', *The Guardian*, 19 October, 6.

—— (1996) 'Major's nursery plan set to fail', *The Observer*, 18 August, 1.

Wintour, P. and Schwarz, W. (1993) 'Cabinet ire as Carey backs lone mothers', *The Guardian*, 12 October, 2.

Wistow, G., Knapp, M., Hardy, B., Forder, J., Kendall, J. and Manning, R. (1996) *Social Care Markets: Progress and Prospects*, Buckingham: Open University Press.

Wolfensburger, W. and Glynn, L. (1975) *Program Analysis of Service Systems*, Toronto: NIMR.

Woodcock, M. (1979) *The Team Development Manual*, Aldershot: Gower.

—— (1989) *50 Activities for Teambuilding*, Aldershot: Gower.

Woolf, M. (1996) 'Builders deal a further blow to PFI', *The Observer*, 16 June, Business section, 5.

Wright, G. (1984) *Behavioural Decision Theory: An Introduction*, Harmondsworth: Penguin.

Wyver, J. (1989) 'Television and postmodernism', in Appignanesi, L. (ed.) *Postmodernism: ICA Documents*, London: Free Association Books.

Yates, F. A. (1969) *The Art of Memory*, Harmondsworth: Penguin.

Young, K. (1977) 'Values in the policy process', *Policy and Politics* 5, 1–22.

INDEX